Y0-DHQ-237

Ministry of Education & Training
MET Library
13th Floor, Mowat Block, Queen's Park
Toronto   M7A 1L2

Crosswords

Language, Education and Ethnicity
in French Ontario

by
Monica Heller

Mouton de Gruyter
Berlin · New York   1994

Mouton de Gruyter (formerly Mouton, The Hague)
is a Division of Walter de Gruyter & Co., Berlin.

Printed on acid-free paper which falls within the guidelines of the
ANSI to ensure permanence and durability.

Library of Congress Cataloging-in-Publication Data

> Heller, Monica.
> Crosswords : language, education and ethnicity in French
> Ontario / by Monica Heller.
> p. cm. — (Contributions to the sociology of language ; 66.)
> Includes bibliographical references (p.   ) and index.
> ISBN 3-11-014111-6 (acid-free)
> 1. French language—Social aspects—Ontario. 2. French-Canadians—Ontario—Language. 3. Language and education—Ontario.
> 4. Language and culture—Ontario. 5. Ontario—Ethnic relations.
> I. Title. II. Series.
> PC3645.O6H45   1994
> 306.4′4′09713—dc20   94-15992
>   CIP

Die Deutsche Bibliothek — Cataloging-in-Publication Data

> **Heller, Monica:**
> Crosswords : language, education and ethnicity in French
> Ontario / by Monica Heller. — Berlin ; New York : Mouton de
> Gruyter, 1994
>   (Contributions to the sociology of language ; 66)
>   ISBN 3-11-014111-6
> NE: GT

© Copyright 1994 by Walter de Gruyter & Co., D-10785 Berlin.
All rights reserved, including those of translation into foreign languages. No part of this book may be reproduced or transmitted in any form or by any means, electronic or mechanical, including photocopy, recording, or any information storage and retrieval system, without permission in writing from the publisher.
Disk conversion: Köhler OHG, Würzburg. — Printing: Gerike GmbH, Berlin. — Binding: Lüderitz & Bauer, Berlin.
Printed in Germany.

Preface

The title of this book, *Crosswords*, was chosen with a number of things in mind. First, it connotes the complex interweaving of language forms which characterizes the relationship among English and several varieties of French in francophone Toronto. It further connotes the ways in which that interweaving is both interdependent and (at least potentially) conflictual. In addition, and with hindsight I would argue not coincidentally, crossword puzzles were a central element of the ethnography- and cooperative-learning based teaching materials which I, with colleagues, introduced into Toronto French-language schools in order to foster increased awareness of language use and a greater range of proficiency in varieties of French. We used them to introduce the approach, and in particular to help students develop a sense of cooperative problem-solving. In much the same way, crosswords evoke the cooperative problem-solving and interweaving of forms which are part of doing ethnographic research, and of writing it in the forms of texts such as the one offered here.

Things that fit together but simultaneously go off in different directions; something in one corner which turns out to be related to something completely different in the opposite corner, albeit by a highly circuitous route; areas which can be discovered alongside zones of obscurity; all these convey the nature of the story I wish to tell, of how I came to learn it and the way I have found in which to tell it.

Acknowledgements

I would like to acknowledge here all those who have helped in the production of this book. Staff at Statistics Canada offices in Toronto and Ottawa were extraordinarily helpful in finding census data. Tara Goldstein and Elizabeth Yeoman helped organize data, checked facts and tracked down relevant documents. The Englisches Seminar at the University of Bern (Switzerland) not only provided me with a home for several months of my sabbatical while I worked on parts of the manuscript, but also helped in innumerable ways; I am especially indebted to Richard Watts, Daniel Stotz and Franz Andres. Pierre Fortier of the *Société d'histoire de Toronto* graciously took the time to show me relevant archival materials, and also provided access to the photographs reproduced here. Timothy Kaiser produced the maps, figures and tables with the help of Henry Knight and Paul Kaiser. Other acknowledgements are to be found in the text.

Finally, I would like to acknowledge the multiple forms of logistical, intellectual and emotional support provided by Timothy Kaiser, to whom this is dedicated.

Contents

Chapter 1: Difference and dominance: Language, ethnicity and education
1.0. Introduction: Language, ethnicity and power in Canada 1
1.1. Franco-Ontarian education and problems of difference
     and dominance 8
1.2. Minority language education 13
1.3. Outline of the book 19
1.4. Sources of data 30

Chapter 2: The French in Canada: A historical overview
2.0. French ethnicity: Stratification, assimilation and mobilization . . . 32
2.1. Colonization and *la Nouvelle France* (1534–1763) 37
2.2. Conquest to Confederation (1763–1867) 42
2.3. Internal migration (1867–1960) 46
2.4. Ethnic stratification and patterns of bilingualism 53
2.5. The ethnic mobilization of the 1960s 57
2.5.1. *La Révolution tranquille* and its aftermath in Quebec 59
2.5.2. The impact of Quebec nationalism on francophones outside
       Quebec 65
2.6. The French-language minority in Ontario 68
2.7. Franco-Ontarians in the 1990s 76

Chapter 3: Language in the ideology and politics of ethnic mobilization
3.0. The contested terrain of language 79
3.1. French and English as linguistic capital 94
3.2. French and English as ethnic emblems 98
3.3. Consequences of mobilization: Blurred boundaries
     and new hierarchies 103

Chapter 4: The school system as border patrol
4.0. The school as ethnic institution 106
4.1. *La gestion:* Who sets the rules of the game? 112
4.2. *Les non parlants* and *le multiculturalisme:*
     Who is allowed to play? 122
4.3. Power and subordination: The limits of current strategies 133

Chapter 5: Brokers and boundaries: French-language minority schools in Toronto
5.0. The Franco-Ontarian population and the French-language schools of Toronto 136
5.1. The schools: Ideology and practice of French-language education 142
5.2. The parents: Competing interests in the struggle for bilingualism 150
5.3. The students: Language choice and social boundaries 163
5.4. Brokers and boundaries 175

Chapter 6: Projet *"Coopération et découverte"*
6.0. From ethnography to action-research 182
6.1. The development of a teaching approach 184
6.2. *Projet "Coopération et découverte"* in the classroom 194
6.3. The limits of pedagogical interventions 206

Chapter 7: Franco-Ontarian education and the possibilities for pluralism
7.0. Power, boundaries and the distribution of resources 210
7.1. Language practices and the contradictions of Franco-Ontarian education 217
7.2. Conclusion 221

Notes 224

References 231

List of Abbreviations 242

Subject Index 245

Author Index 250

Chapter 1
Difference and dominance:
Language, ethnicity and education

1.0. Introduction: Language, ethnicity and power in Canada

When I arrived in Toronto in the fall of 1982, I entered into the world of the "invisible French". Walking Toronto's streets, I couldn't help but hear and see many languages: Greek on the Danforth, Chinese around Dundas and Spadina, Ukrainian and Polish in High Park, Italian on St. Clair West, to name only those I encountered first. This in itself came as a surprise, since only ten or fifteen years before Toronto had still been a bastion of English and of English-Canadian life.

French was not one of the languages figuring in Toronto's new image of itself. Yet I knew French was there. It was my language of work. My friends and colleagues spoke it at home. Their children went to French schools. The parishes of Sacré-Coeur and St-Louis-de-France provided anchors for the Catholic. How did this world manage to vanish in public life? It vanished because my friends and colleagues, for the most part, were able to put on a new mask when they left the domains of francophone life: they spoke English in public, so well as to be unidentifiable as francophones.

The term "invisible French" was coined by Thomas Maxwell in a sociological study of Toronto's francophone community conducted in the mid 1960s (Maxwell 1977). Already, Maxwell was pointing to the high assimilation rate of francophones, and the ability of those who still retained some ethnic affiliation to act like anglophones with outsiders. But that was 1966, before francophone nationalism had brought French out of the closet, before the Canadian federal government had adopted a policy of bilingualism and biculturalism from coast to coast. In 1982, coming from the linguistic barricades of Quebec, where I had learned to use language choice as a street-fighting weapon, I found it difficult to adjust to the seemingly silent acceptance of the hegemony of English in public life.

At the same time, I found my entry into the francophone community remarkably easy. In Quebec, initial encounters generally began with elaborate rituals of language choice. These were necessary to unambiguously identify one's ethnic affiliation; if they failed, they were usually followed by explicit interrogations (where were you born? where did you go to school? where do your parents live?).

In my case, such negotiations were all the more complicated when people knew my name (which is clearly not French, but the origin of which most people found hard to pin down) and when responses to other questions also indicated that I was not easily classifiable in the ethnic category system in general use. Although this is less and less frequently the case in Quebec, at the time it was still true that people found it surprising, and often difficult to comprehend, that someone who did not explicitly identify themselves as French might nonetheless be able to speak the language. In Quebec, my marginality, which I had learned to turn to my advantage, made people uncomfortable.

In Ontario, conventions of language choice were not so tied up with locating one's interlocutors in ethnic space: just as things had been in Montreal in the fifties and sixties, in Toronto of the early eighties the dominant language of public communication was English. And in Ontario, due to the prevalence of intermarriage and bilingualism among francophones, having a non-French name and being fluently bilingual required no explanation.

Just the same, in Ontario as in Quebec, the one piece of information that people find hardest to process is the fact that I am Jewish: their mouths drop open, they stutter, they fall silent. A francophone colleague of mine in Quebec has the reverse problem: a specialist in francophone-Jewish relations, he took up Yiddish and Hebrew. His Jewish interlocutors often tell him that they find it hard to believe that a Catholic could learn Yiddish (Anctil, personal communication). Religion, or more precisely, religious background, is still clearly linked to language in the definition of ethnic categories, but some ethnic categories are considered more permeable than others. It surprises no one that Jews, Catholics or any one else should speak English, but minority groups rarely speak each other's language. This has been a source of problems as the changing nature of French-English relations blurs such formerly clear boundaries, and changes in particular the ways in which language and religion form bases of criteria of ethnic inclusion and exclusion.

Having grown up in Quebec during the Quiet Revolution and its rather noisier wake, I can scarcely help but be sensitive to the problems associated with some of the basic dynamics of Canadian society, notably the relationship between language, ethnicity and power. It has always struck me as unfortunate (although entirely understandable) that so few Canadian academics have looked seriously at what this means for the everyday experience of Canadians. While historical studies have had to confront French-English relations, these have been principally confined to the political arena. We have many demographic studies (e.g., Joy 1972; Lachapelle – Henripin 1980; Castonguay 1979; Cartwright 1987), and some in the area of economics (e.g., Lacroix – Vaillancourt 1981; Vaillancourt 1985). We are probably best known for the experimental social psychological studies of bilingualism conducted by Wallace Lambert and his colleagues, and which focus on ethnic attitudes and language values (e.g., Lambert et al. 1960; Lambert 1967; Clément – Beauregard 1986; Genesee – Bourhis 1982; Bourhis 1984), and for linguistic and sociolinguistic studies of language contact (e.g. Sankoff 1980; Mougeon – Beniak 1989; Poplack 1988).

Sociologists and anthropologists (as well as many historians and sociolinguists) have frequently focussed more on social and linguistic processes within groups than on intergroup interaction, especially as academics have gotten caught up in processes of ethnic mobilization. In any case, the focus is rarely at the level of everyday life. A few studies do explore processes at the level of families or communities, such as Carisse's questionnaire-based studies of family dynamics in French-English mixed marriages in Quebec (Carisse 1966, 1969), as well as the community studies of Jackson (1988), which focus on French/English and Protestant/Catholic relations in a small town in southwestern Ontario in the mid 1960s, and of Hughes (1943) which explores the effect of the introduction of anglophone-owned industry into a small francophone town in southern Quebec in the late 1930s.

Literary treatments of the issue are also remarkably scarce. The most famous is undoubtedly MacLennan's 1945 novel about small-town Quebec; his title, *Two Solitudes*, has become a metaphor for French-English relations ever since.[1] More recent explorations have come from the marginal perspectives of the Irish Catholic or Jewish working class in Montreal (Richler 1959; Fennario 1980), or from the West: in 1989, the "Shakespeare on the Saskatchewan" festival ran a tremendously successful production of *Romeo and Juliet* in which the Capulets were francophones and the Montagues were anglophones (Nightcap Productions 1989). Within the "mainstream" of English- and French-language literary and other artistic production, the focus has been, instead, either on broader international themes, or on life on one side of the border. French-language theatre and music has played an especially important role in francophone ethnic mobilization.

Yet all of us who live on the linguistic frontier feel the impact keenly. There are countless untold stories about jobs and promotions lost or won because the candidate did or did not speak English or French, about problematic romances across ethnic lines, about people lost in the wrong part of town. We need to know more about how, in Canada, language and ethnicity make a difference to people's lives and to their life chances. How are they related to access to jobs, to education, to political representation or to religious institutions? What difference do they make to people's abilities to make friends, work with colleagues, get along with or form a family? How do they figure in a person's ability to control his or her own life, or to develop different ways of making sense of their world? More particularly, we need to know more about how the answers to these questions emerge from the ways in which people act in everyday life, about what it means to individuals as well as to groups to be caught up in social processes in which language and ethnicity are central to the way people organize their lives (cf. Gal 1989; Heller 1988; Woolard 1989; Irvine 1989).

At the broadest level, these are the questions I am trying to address. In the late 1970s, I was able to do some work in Quebec (Heller 1982a, b, 1985, 1989a; Heller et al. 1982) focussing on the way language choice in face-to-face interaction was bound up with the redefinition of ethnic boundaries and ethnic stratification. That particular moment was a turning point for ethnic relations in Quebec. The economic and political foundations of what it meant to be French and English had shifted so radically that the usual ways of carrying out everyday life were no longer possible. The dominance of English was being eroded. I was able to see the way in which people drew on their knowledge of what was going on in their world and of their position in it in order to realize (or resist) the possibilities they began to glimpse for themselves. Everyday life was a process of using language to reconstruct ethnic relations, and hence what individual members of ethnic groups could and could not do or be. Otherwise banal encounters (a trip to the doctor's or to the corner store, boarding a city bus, ordering a cup of coffee) held within them the possibility of highly charged emotional skirmishes in the war of the French and the English. I had gotten used to the public negotiation of ethnic relations; I didn't know how to interpret what looked, initially, to be the dead calm of French-English relations in Toronto. Eventually I was able to see that here was a different part of the same story, one perhaps less showy, less attention-grabbing, but no less important for the possibilities of ethnic equality in the Canadian state.

Of course, even in 1982 the French were already more visible than they had been, and things have changed even more in the ten or so years that I have been living and working in Toronto. One hears French much more often in the streets, and because of recent provincial legislation one also sees and hears it in public institutions. The switchboard operator at the institute where I work now answers the telephone with "OISE, *bonjour*".

French-speakers are involved in these changes in a variety of different ways (cf. Breton 1985). There are activists: some adopt the interactional tactics which were so successful in Quebec in the 1970s, or lobby in other ways for what has come to be known as *la cause*. Many still accept the dominance of English, although they may also quietly push for their rights in specific circumstances. Still others continue to assimilate. But unlike Québécois, mobilized Franco-Ontarians rarely assume that it is possible or desirable for an individual to be completely monolingual. Instead, they argue, bilingualism can only exist on the basis of the existence of a strong francophone community.

English-speakers in Quebec reacted to the changes there in a variety of ways. Some embraced the Québécois cause; others simply learned French, or made sure that their children did, and, while they did not assimilate, they learned to live their lives in new ways. They acknowledged the new value of the French language, and chose to make an effort to participate in those activities and networks where speaking French could make a difference to their lives. Still others resisted these changes, some by forming enclaves within Quebec and others by leaving, usually for Ontario (where there are greater economic opportunities in any case, for anyone, and especially for anglophones).

On the whole, the same is true in Ontario, that is, some people are adapting to the new power of Quebec and the new value of French, while others resist. Of course, English-speakers retain a great deal of political and economic power in Ontario, and no one feels it necessary to leave. Nonetheless, in early 1990 amidst heated debate, a number of municipalities saw fit to declare themselves unilingual English, a clearly defensive reaction to the perceived threat posed by newly-acquired francophone rights (the basis and consequences of these events will be taken up in some detail in Chapter 3).

Still, it is evident that, while there are differing positions among both francophones and anglophones, both groups contain large and vocal sections who are interested in bilingualism, and prepared to fight hard to achieve it. In Canada, this is often held up as a model of harmony, and taken as proof of the success of the federal government's policies of bilingualism and biculturalism. However, underneath that veneer of harmony there are tensions and conflicts. Now that bilingualism is valuable, it is necessary to explore who has privileged access to it, and what the consequences of regulating access to bilingualism in certain ways may be for relations of power between francophones and non-francophones.

Many francophones feel threatened by bilingual anglophones. First, they feel that bilingualism was historically their terrain, and now that it is valuable, it seems unfair that the privileged anglophones should be able to so easily take over what had been for bilingual francophones a significant path to power (Arnopoulos 1982). Second, bilingual anglophones can gain access to the formerly secret world of francophone life; the French are no longer invisible. If bilingual anglophones can successfully negotiate that access, they break apart the zones where francophones are able to constitute themselves as a distinctive group.

But it is precisely these changes and the complex and often contradictory feelings which surround them that I wish to explore here, in order to shed some light on some fundamental ethnic processes in Canadian society. At the same time, these changes also illuminate some of the general ways in which language can be embedded in simultaneous processes of ethnic boundary formation, social mobility and the construction of relations of power. In particular, I want to explore how the study of the role of language in these processes elucidates what is congruent and what is contradictory in them, that is, the ways in which the maintenance and change in the nature of ethnic boundary processes in Canada can simultaneously facilitate and hinder the construction of more equal ethnic relations (Jackson 1988). I do so in the hope that this will inform a specific political goal: the construction of a pluralist society in which it is possible to achieve equality without having to obliterate social and cultural difference.

I will explore these issues by looking in particular at the area of Franco-Ontarian education. There are several reasons for this focus. The first is simply that it is the area of Franco-Ontarian life that I know best, and that as a result affords me the best possibility of linking broad social, economic and political processes to everyday life in some domain. Since arriving in Toronto I have worked at the Ontario Institute for Studies in Education (OISE), a somewhat anomalous institution which has as its mandate the provision of graduate studies programs, research and "field development" (which I understand as collaborative work with practicing educators) in the field of education. I have worked specifically in the area of Franco-Ontarian education, and through all three avenues of work at the Institute I have come to know Franco-Ontarian educators in all parts of the educational system. My closest ties have been to the francophone community in Toronto, and these ties have been both professional and personal.

Second, Franco-Ontarian education has been central to the development of the Franco-Ontarian community. As a system, of course, it contributes to the production and reproduction of the economic and political relations which underlie ethnic boundaries and ethnic stratification. As a result, it has been the site of struggle between the Catholic Church, the francophone lay community and the anglophone state for control over the definition of Franco-Ontarian social, economic and political goals. An examination of Franco-Ontarian education allows one to unravel a number of different threads which contribute in various ways to understanding what it means to be Franco-Ontarian today. These include the role of the state in Franco-Ontarian social institutions and the changing class profile of Franco-Ontarians as these are linked to the integration of Franco-Ontarians into national and international economic networks.

Central to these processes, as I shall argue, is the value attached to French (indeed, to specific varieties of French) as a form of what Pierre Bourdieu (1977a, 1982) has called *linguistic capital* (this argument is taken up at greater length below and in Chapter 3). Language, a form of *cultural*, or, more generally, *symbolic*, capital, is exchangeable in the marketplace of social interaction. One's ability to use language appropriately (i.e. according to conventions established in the interests of dominant groups) affects one's chances of gaining access to situations where valuable resources are produced and distributed, and, once there, to participate in the processes of production and distribution, indeed, to benefit from them. As a result, linguistic and cultural capital acquire a value of their own, and become sources of power and prestige in their own right.

Bourdieu argues that it is necessary to "extend economic calculation to *all* the goods, material and symbolic, without distinction, that present themselves as *rare* and worthy of being sought after in a particular social formation" (1977b: 178). However, "symbolic capital, a transformed and thereby *disguised* form of physical "economic" capital, produces its effect inasmuch, and only inasmuch, as it conceals the fact that it originates in "material" forms of capital which are also, in the last analysis, the source of its effects" (1977b: 183). In other words, symbolic capital functions to disguise, and thereby legitimate and in turn contribute to, the accumulation of material wealth and the exercise of power based on that wealth. It can also, as I shall argue, serve as the terrain for contesting the distribution of wealth.

Education has an important role to play in the definition of the value of symbolic capital, in its legitimation and in mediating access to it. By objectifying forms of cultural knowledge (for example, by representing them through credentials), it contributes to disguising the exercise of power through the institutionalization of relations of dominance. At the same time, it helps to set up the system of values to which all must subscribe if they are going to be able to participate as producers in a system of social production and reproduction (Bourdieu 1977b: 187–188). Education is currently a major site of the struggle waged between anglophones and francophones, and within each group as well, over whether or not bilingualism should be valuable, and if so, whose property it should be. As such, it represents a struggle over the distribution of wealth and power.

Finally, in order to understand ethnic relations in Canada, it is important to look not only at the sources of power within francophone Quebec and anglophone Canada, but at the places where those different forms of power meet and are articulated. In that respect, Franco-Ontarian education is but one of many such loci. Nonetheless, it is one which plays an important role and which illustrates well some of the major processes involved in the distribution of resources and of prestige among ethnolinguistic groups in Canada.

1.1. Franco-Ontarian education and problems of difference and dominance

Because of the work I do, I frequently get asked for advice about where parents should send their children to school. Sometimes people call me in the office, looking for an informed but impartial point of view, or, on occasion, an "expert opinion". Sometimes friends, relatives or acquaintances will bring the subject up at dinner parties or sitting around the garden.

English-speakers (and most of the ones who consult me are middle-class) generally want to know whether I think it is important for their children to learn French at an early age, and if so, what the best way is to accomplish this. Should they send their child to French immersion, those by now well-known programs in English-language schools which teach French as a second language by using it as the language of instruction? Should they attempt to enroll their child in a French-language minority school? Or will all this be too confusing and difficult for a child already learning to adjust to school?

French-speakers usually want to know whether their children are likely to lose their French if they send them to English-language schools. Very often, the child is in a French-language school and wishes to leave, because everyone else in the mainly English-speaking neighbourhood is in an English-language school around the corner. Being bussed for hours to a far away French-language school has lost its allure. Parents fear that they will lose the investment they have made in French and that a gulf will open between them and their children; the resulting tension can rip families apart and cause sleepless nights of anxiety. One mother begged me to help her find a way to convince her only child to stay in a French-language school; as a single parent, her emotional investment in her child was high, and she felt that no matter what decision was made a wall was going up between the two of them. In other cases, francophone parents are concerned that their children learn English adequately in order to make it in Ontario society: they worry that if they send their children to French-language schools, their children will never speak English well enough to get ahead.

In many of the interviews I and my colleagues conducted with parents and students in Toronto's French-language schools, other related concerns arose. In some families where parents were of different ethnolinguistic backgrounds, parents attempted to compromise. For example, some would send their children to French-language schools at the elementary level (kindergarten to grade 8, or roughly age 5 to age 13) and English-language or immersion schools at the secondary level. In addition, some children, such as one son of a German father, attended third language programs after school or on weekends. Immigrant families quickly recognized the value of bilingualism in Canadian society, and sought ways to achieve that. In Catholic families, some parents and students worried whether to attend Catholic or public schools. While involvement in religion was clearly important in this decision, it also frequently had to be balanced off by language, or language-related, factors. Indeed, while in the past it could fairly safely be assumed that all francophones were Catholic, that is no longer true: some have left the Church, and there are increasing numbers of francophones from outside Canada who have other religious affiliations.

Many of these concerns arise because, in most parts of the province these days, several educational options are open to parents deciding on where to send their children to school. While for some the decision among these options is clear, for many it is no longer always so straightforward. Instead, the increasing involvement of the government and the changes in social boundaries which Ontarians have been experiencing since the 1960s make such educational decision-making complex and often difficult.

The decisions people have to make mainly involve religion and language of instruction. As will be described in greater detail in Chapter 2, the government of Ontario now fully funds both Catholic confessional (so-called "separate") schools, as well as secular or non-confessional (so-called "public") schools. In addition, in many areas of the province, both English and French may be used as languages of instruction (although usually not in the same school). Franco-Ontarians thus rely on the English-dominant government for the provision of education in their language. At the individual level, they do not have the option of sending their children to (or finding employment themselves within) private, community-run schools (although there are one or two exceptions to this). Within the state-run system, they must choose between separate or public schools and between French and English as languages of instruction. Within the English-language system they may also have access not only to French immersion programs but also to so-called "Heritage Language" programs: classes focussing on the instruction of (and sometimes in) the language of one of Ontario's other minorities. Also, as we saw above, some children of mixed marriages may be involved in education run by a non-French minority community; for example, in Toronto, the Italian, Polish and Ukrainian communities (where, due to shared religion, intermarriage with francophones is most likely) have well-established programs which children attend in addition to their publicly-funded school.

Some of the uproar of early 1990 in Ontario municipalities was directly connected to the particular manifestation of these sets of options in specific communities. Thunder Bay (1991 population 124,430) and Sault Ste. Marie (1986 population 80,088) are multi-ethnic cities at either end of Lake Superior. They have small francophone populations (only 3,675, or 2.95 percent of the population in Thunder Bay; 4,260 or 5.3 percent of the population in Sault

Ste. Marie),[2] but they also serve as provincial government administrative centres for northwestern Ontario, an area which includes, in addition to a large Native population, several areas of high francophone concentration.

There are French-language schools in both cities, but all of them are Catholic. Some parents have lobbied the public boards for the provision of French-language education, on the grounds that it can no longer be assumed that all French Canadians are Catholic, and, indeed, they themselves no longer identify themselves as such. (Of course, as mentioned earlier, in other communities, notably the major urban centres of Toronto, Ottawa and Sudbury, there are an increasing number of francophones who have never been Catholic. These include Moslems and Jews from Africa and the Middle East and Buddhists from Vietnam.) The public boards have refused these parents' requests on the grounds that it is too expensive to provide "special" educational services to a small number of children. At the same time, the provincial government had recently (November 1989) begun to implement its legislation guaranteeing French-language provincial government services. While this law does not in fact directly affect municipal governments, many feared that it was a harbinger of things to come. The request for increased educational services was seen as merely the first in what might be an increasing number of demands for French-language services in any of the areas which are supported by municipal funds, in whole or in part. In order to prevent any further occurrences of the request for public French-language education or any other service provided on a local level, the municipal governments decided to declare that English is the only official language of city administration.

The role of the state, of religion and of language in Ontarian education can be seen as reflecting strategies different groups have adopted over time to set their own agenda within the educational process. Within that broad context, individuals must take their own position; under current circumstances, it is not possible to make a neutral educational choice on behalf of one's child. At the same time, it is possible for groups to mobilize themselves in order to use the educational system for their own ends, thereby changing the conditions in which any individual decision may be made. At any given moment, language or religion may emerge as more salient to the ways in which groups and individuals seek to maintain, change or cross over ethnic boundaries in the pursuit of a decent life.

While religion remains an important factor in people's lives, however, it is language which is currently at the heart of ethnic boundary formation and ethnic stratification in Canada. The distribution of resources now falls primarily along linguistic lines: language has become the major source of access to valued resources, and as such, it has become an increasingly important field for the definition and exchange of symbolic capital. Education is important insofar as it constitutes an arena where valued linguistic capital is, in fact, distributed. What is remarkable is the way in which the value of different forms of capital has shifted. Whereas once cities like Thunder Bay took the dominance of English for granted, now they feel compelled to defend that privileged position. Whereas once it would never have occurred to francophones to speak French in public, now it is sometimes actively encouraged. Whereas once an English-speaker would not have been caught dead speaking French, now anglophones battle francophones over access to bilingualism.

In Canada, the distribution of economic and political power can be seen in the first instance to be linked to material resources and to an ethnic division of labour. As I will discuss more fully in Chapter 2, the power of English-speakers in Canadian society has traditionally been based on their ownership of the means of producing wealth (mainly primary resource extraction and related industry) and economic power has been intimately tied up with political power. The powerlessness of other groups (Native Canadians, francophones, immigrants) is connected to their position with respect to those ways of producing wealth. Either the group has been marginalized and their own means of producing alternative forms of wealth has been suppressed (as has most notably been the case of Native Canadians), or their labour has been exploited within the dominant wealth-producing system. While the use of brute force in maintaining this set of relations of dominance is by no means unknown in Canadian history (cf., e.g., Wolf 1982; Choquette 1977), it has been far from the only way in which the system was maintained and, later, changed.

The economic and political power of English-speakers has also contributed to the prestige of their language and the high status accorded to their way of doing things. These forms of symbolic capital have been deeply embedded in relations of dominance in Canadian society. In order to gain power, it was necessary to gain access to the network of English-speakers who controlled Canada's valued resources. In order to gain access to that network, it was necessary to act like one of them. As Bourdieu has pointed out, it is almost impossible to learn fully how to act like a member of another group without having been properly socialized; however, in some cases individuals managed to pass, not, one assumes, without cost (there are remarkably few accounts of people who tried to assimilate, whether successfully or not, nor of those who were able to act as brokers between members of their own group and the dominant élite). Still, it was English-speakers, and, more specifically, members of the English-speaking mercantile class, who were able to define what forms of knowledge and behaviour were to be considered not only acceptable, but essential for the accomplishment of their goals and the protection of their interests.

In order to understand why education is a bilingual battleground at this moment, it will be necessary to explore the changing value of French and English as forms of symbolic capital, specifically as this shift is linked to what Barth (1969) would call the *ecology* of the relationship of dominance between anglophones and francophones in Canada. The argument is that those relations are tied to specific material conditions and ways of exploiting or responding to those conditions. Any change in conditions or in collective ability to continue responding to them as in the past is going to have an effect on the extent to which an ethnic group can remain generally effective in its practices. Thus, in addition to exploring the material underpinnings of the hierarchical dominance of English-speakers in Canada, it will be possible to explore what changed, both in the value of those material resources as sources of wealth, and in the ways in which it was possible to exploit them. If English is no longer the only form of linguistic capital honoured in Canadian society, what happened to undermine the sources of its power? Or is it simply that that power must now be shared? If French has suddenly become sought-after, what are the bases of its new-found prestige? In both cases, how are the economic, political and symbolic arenas of activity related to the value of languages as linguistic capital and to the possibilities its speakers have open to them? In particular, how and why has education emerged as an arena where valued capital is distributed and where members of different groups can struggle over defining what it is and who gets access to it? These questions will be further explored in Chapters 2 and 3.

The other side of this coin has to do with the impact of such changes on the possibilities for maintaining ethnic differences. For marginalized and exploited francophones, the changes of the post-War period have raised a number of questions unheard of in their history. If there was a tension to be managed in the past, it was the tension between alternative sources of prestige (and, yes, economic and political power, albeit of a different order) within and beyond the borders of the group. Today, the tension has to do with the very nature of those borders: the question of who is a francophone is crucial to the development and future of the group.

This question is tied to the ability of francophones to constitute themselves as a group, to retain exclusive control over certain resources and to define the practices which are meaningful and effective in social interaction. The irony of the success of francophone mobilization has been the unintended consequence of attracting to the group people of other origins, not only anglophones interested in bilingualism, but also immigrants. In Quebec, the new power of francophones has turned the old order on its head, and francophones must worry about the consequences of their actions for minorities within the population. While it may be argued that anglophone Québécois are scarcely disadvantaged, the issues are less clear for immigrants and the Native population, who remain without power.

In Ontario, francophones have less power than they do in Quebec, but the same kinds of issues emerge in certain zones, notably in Franco-Ontarian lobbying groups and in the now francophone-controlled schools and school boards. For francophones across Canada, then, there is a tension between fighting against powerlessness and handling new-found power. Fighting an unequal distribution of power is associated with mobilization on the basis of commonalities. What gains there have been, paradoxically, undermine the conditions which underlie those commonalities: the basic experience of being a francophone is no longer what it used to be, and the ways in which francophones have gained power entail new relationships with people who are no longer so clearly outsiders. For Franco-Ontarians, decisions about who can control key areas like education, and who can gain admission to schools, have long-term consequences not only for their ability to gain access to the resources distributed through education, but also for what it means to be Franco-Ontarian.

1.2. Minority-language education

Most of the literature on the education of minorities focusses on the problem of school achievement. Initially, much work in the United States and Britain documented the chronic underachievement of members of certain groups, sometimes defined by class (as in the work of Bernstein (1975), Bowles and Gintis (1976), or Willis (1977)) and sometimes defined by race or ethnicity (as in the vast literature on the underachievement by Black and Hispanic students in the United States; cf. Bereiter – Engelmann 1966; Labov 1969, 1982; Ogbu 1978; Jacob – Jordan 1987). In Western Europe, attention focussed mainly on the school problems of the children of guest-workers and immigrants (cf. Skutnabb-Kangas 1981; Saifullah Khan 1980; Edwards 1986), although class differences received some attention, especially in France (cf. Dannequin 1976; Bourdieu – Passeron 1977; François 1983). More recently, attention has been paid to the unequal representation of females and males in certain types of program, notably at the high school and post-secondary levels, where females tend to be over-represented in the humanities and social sciences (Bourdieu – Passeron 1977).

However, it has been pointed out that it is not possible to separate out class differences from race and ethnic differences in many cases; what is at issue is the way in which race and ethnic differences may be bound up in class stratification (Ogbu 1987; Grillo 1989). Indeed, not all minorities do badly in school; as is well-known, some do extremely well (Ogbu 1987; Shamai 1992; Gibson 1987). What needs to be explained, then, is the overall pattern of ethnic stratification, and its association with class and gender differences.

Many of the patterns noted in the United States and Europe hold true for Canada. Using as an index the level of education attained as reported for ethnic groups in the Canadian census since 1921, Shamai (1992) has shown that there has been a consistent pattern of ethnic educational stratification over the course of close to seventy years. The overall level of educational attainment may have risen, but the position of ethnic groups with respect to each other has changed little. Jews and Chinese have consistently been the most educated, followed by the so-called "charter groups", the English and then the French. At the bottom one finds other immigrant groups, and the Native population. The major change has been a recent one: the decline in the level of anglophone education, which has dropped slightly to meet the rising level of education of francophones.

The general pattern of ethnic stratification shown in the area of education is paralleled in other traditional indicators of class, such as income levels and occupational categories. Various studies in the 1960s, including those conducted for the federal and Quebec provincial governments' commissions of enquiry into ethnic relations in Canada, revealed that francophones were close to the bottom of the scale in terms of income (see Porter's classic 1965 study of ethnic stratification, as well as Government of Canada 1967-1969; Gouvernement du Québec 1972; Lacroix – Vaillancourt 1981). Within Quebec this situation began to change over the course of the 1970s (Lacroix – Vaillancourt 1981; Vaillancourt 1985).

During the 1960s, a minority of Franco-Ontarians may have achieved higher levels of income than the national average for francophones; nonetheless, ethnic stratification persisted, and worked to the particular disadvantage of francophones at the bottom of the scale (Bernard 1988:32). A demographic survey of Franco-Ontarians published in 1985 by the major Franco-Ontarian lobby group, *l'Association canadienne-française de l'Ontario* (ACFO), showed that on the whole Franco-Ontarians had lower income levels than the Ontario average, and were concentrated in certain sectors of the economy, notably the primary sector (resource extraction) for men, and the tertiary sector (services) for women. Men and women both occupied relatively unskilled, low-paying jobs in each sector. Of course, historically, in Ontario as in other parts of Canada, alongside the francophone labour force there has long existed a francophone élite, highly educated in private institutions, but concentrated in the humanities and the professions of medicine and law, as well as a small petty bourgeoisie (Ossenberg 1970; Choquette 1977, 1987).

The ethnic stratification of educational attainment in Canada is bound up in some ways with the class profile of ethnic groups. If there has been a rise in francophone attainment, it is related to the emergence of a new middle class. But this relationship is complex. It is unlikely that francophones stay in school longer because they have entered new sectors of the economy. Rather, it has everything to do with the way francophones have chosen to use education as part of a broad strategy of social mobility, a strategy which has to be seen as a response to ecological shifts in the basis of ethnic stratification in Canada.

Participation in educational systems run by the state is today perceived as opening up opportunities that formerly were closed. Indeed, debate within the Franco-Ontarian community about Franco-Ontarian education concerns the best way to profit from the current basic educational arrangements, not about alternate paths to different goals. Franco-Ontarians generally do not feel the degree of tension that, for example, the Native population feels with regard to state-run schools. For most Native Canadians, going to school is in the first instance an act of boundary-crossing: one can either stay out of school, and act like a proper Cree, or Inuk, for example, or one can go to school and invest in another way of life. There is no guarantee, however, that the investment will pay off, since structural discrimination in Canadian society can close doors that would have been open to a white person with the same qualifications. Thus attending school is a complex balancing act for Natives, and the drop-out rate is high. The drop-out rate is high for Franco-Ontarians also, and for some of the same reasons, but to a much greater extent Franco-Ontarians have been able to use the educational system to achieve some of their goals, indeed, they share to a much greater extent the goals defined by dominant society as the primary objectives of education.

Thus class is related in a problematic way to ethnic boundaries and educational attainment; the central question is how participation in educational structures does or does not lead to opportunities of access to valued resources, whether those resources are controlled by dominant or by dominated ethnic groups. That question only takes on real meaning when it is linked to specific circumstances, and those circumstances can be variable. Dominated ethnic groups do not always share the system of values of the dominant group. Individuals may succeed or fail as members of their own or of a host group; assimilation can skew the statistics, if, say, a francophone who has a Ph.D. has had to become an anglophone in order to get it.

The problem of educational underachievement has also been approached as a problem of cultural difference. Here the focus has been directly on the ways in which schools define what counts as knowledge and regulate access to it by favourably evaluating certain kinds of behaviour, that is, certain kinds of performances, over others. The problem that minorities encounter is that they have no control over what counts as valuable knowledge, and frequently the kinds of performances they provide are not the ones valued by the school.

Bourdieu has argued that this is one way in which education participates in social and cultural reproduction: students have to possess certain kinds of knowledge *before* they get to school in order to provide the kinds of performances which will be favourably evaluated *in* school. Educational systems, he argues, then use approved performances as the criteria according to which one judges a student's capacity to handle further knowledge, or specific kinds of knowledge. However, only those students from social groups which control the school as a social institution ever regularly possess that prior knowledge: society's dominant groups define what counts as valued knowledge in terms of the knowledge which counts for them. This exercise of power, in order to be legitimate, must be hidden; it must be made to appear to rest on universal values. Thus the knowledge of the dominant group becomes the only way in which to understand the world: it becomes taken for granted, routine, normal, neutral. It is this process which constitutes *hegemony*, and which makes resistance and contestation so difficult. This is reinforced by the fact that some of the disenfranchised may indeed succeed; the best and the brightest of their group or class, they will inevitably be among the stars of their chosen fields. However, Bourdieu does not explore how these highly-selected few come by their cultural and linguistic capital in the first place, nor, indeed, how relations of power get constructed, that is, how they may be subject to resistance, contestation and change.

Some work in the United States has tried to address the problem of disadvantage, primarily by arguing that school failure can be attributed to cultural differences in conventions of behaviour and to socially-variable distributions of knowledge and ways of gaining knowledge. It is argued that schools can broaden the range of performances they value and thereby facilitate the access of minority children to the knowledge valued by schools (cf. Heath 1983; Philips 1983; Vogt et al. 1987; Moll – Diaz 1987; Erickson – Mohatt 1982). Most of this work has not, however, questioned the nature of the knowledge defined as valuable by the school, nor have researchers questioned how the participation of minorities in the control of education might change that resource.

In addition, this work has been criticized, notably by the anthropologist John Ogbu (1987), on the grounds that it cannot account for minorities who do well in school even in the face of cultural differences, nor for minorities who do poorly even if cultural differences are minimal. Instead, he argues, one has to understand what is at stake in participation in education for members of minority groups, that is, what there is to gain and what there is to lose, what is possible and what is not. Participation in mainstream educational institutions is worthless if it leads nowhere. It is problematic if it requires giving up social relations and access to alternative resources.

The cultural difference model also assumes that those differences spring from historically separate forms of experience. While in some cases, to some degree, this may be true, it may also be the case that what appear as cultural differences are in fact oppositional, that is, they spring from the contest between dominant and dominated groups (Williams 1973; Willis 1977; Woolard 1985). It is therefore not possible, it is a contradiction in terms, to simply incorporate such cultural forms into a process controlled by the dominant group.

Finally, the model does not account very well for how the process of the maintenance of relations of dominance in and through education actually occurs, nor for how change may begin and unfold. Clearly, as Giddens (1984) has argued, that is because no simple theory of social structure will allow us to understand how power works in social life: structural explanations cannot account well for change or for variability at the level of individual experience. At the same time, more is going on than the sum of the actions of individuals. Instead, it is necessary to explore the material, ecological underpinnings of power and its distribution among social groups, and the ways in which those are made use of strategically by individuals, acting alone and acting collectively. In the particular case that concerns us, the question is what role education plays in the ecology of ethnic relations and ethnic stratification, and how it can be used as an arena to maintain or change the status quo.

The problem that Franco-Ontarians (and francophones elsewhere in Canada) face is how to participate in an educational system controlled by the majority without losing their identity as francophones, without losing their collective ability to define and accomplish their own goals. But the very formulation of that problem rests on an interesting historical phenomenon, namely the fact that some Franco-Ontarians have chosen to mobilize collectively to achieve their goals through the state-run educational system, while others have chosen the individual path of assimilation, but all share the same goal of access to the valued resources controlled by the dominant group. At the same time, nowhere is the radical alternative of non-participation even raised, as it has been, for example, in Native communities.

A recent item in *The Toronto Star*, a major daily newspaper, captures this nicely. At a press conference held in Quebec City in early February 1990, Jacques Parizeau, the leader of the *indépendantiste* Parti Québécois, was asked what he thought of a recent poll "indicating that a majority of English Canadians think Quebecers will always ask for more" (no matter what legal provisions are made for recognizing the special status of Quebec). Parizeau replied that this reflects "a 'healthy realism' on their part... Quebec sovereignists...' want everything'" (*The Toronto Star*, 8 February 1990).

Franco-Ontarian education is thus but one part of the picture of ethnic relations in Canada. But it is a central arena for the playing out of individual and collective strategies, a major domain where class stratification and the maintenance of ethnic boundaries intersect. As a result, it affords one avenue of approach to the general problem of pluralism and power.

There is one area I have not yet touched upon: the role of gender. It is often argued that Franco-Ontarian women are doubly minorities, because of their gender and because of their ethnicity (Coulombe 1985). Obviously, the class structure of francophone society cuts across the two other forms of social difference and social inequality. While a strong francophone feminist movement exists, centred in Quebec, little is known of the particularities of the experience of francophone women outside Quebec, beyond their concentration in the service sector of the economy (see, however, Cardinal – Coderre 1990, for a general discussion of the history of the education of francophone women outside Quebec and its place in the development of francophone feminism in those regions). Nonetheless, it will be important to account as much as possible for the different roles that francophone men and women play, in terms of their own participation in French-language education and francophone society in general and in terms of the decisions they make for their children. It is possible that francophone women in different communities are involved in the economy and in social forms and institutions in different ways from francophone men, particularly with respect to their position vis-à-vis the linguistic boundary. As a result, they may have differential access to French and English, and those languages may be connected in different ways to economic and social opportunities; as a result they acquire different values for men and for women, with different consequences for the strategies they adopt, not only for themselves, but also for their children. To raise only one example, in addition to the different things that French and English may represent for them, men and women may have different roles in educational decision-making within the family; this may contribute to a family dynamic which has an impact on the language of instruction and ethnic affiliation of children. The picture that will emerge is even less complete than that which touches other facets of francophone life in Ontario, and, in particular, in Toronto, but it will be a start.

1.3. Outline of the book

The remaining chapters of this book will approach the problem of the bilingual battleground which Franco-Ontarian education has become from a number of different angles. Chapter 2 begins by framing the problem from both an ecological and a historical perspective. While I intend eventually to focus on the French-language schools of Toronto, I cannot adequately describe or explain what goes on there without conveying a sense of how that current and local experience is tied to francophone experience elsewhere in Canada, and how it emerges from a history of contact between francophones and non-francophones within specific sets of social, economic and political relations.

Chapter 2 is divided into two major chronological sections. I have taken the 1960s as my dividing point on the grounds that it was then that the social, economic and political changes most affecting contemporary Franco-Ontarian education came to the surface most clearly. The history of Franco-Ontarians from their arrival in the sixteenth century in what has become Ontario to the 1960s focusses on the place of francophones in the regional economy, and on the place of the region in the economy first of the French and then of the British empires, and finally in the development of the Canadian confederation. Readers more familiar than I with Canadian history may find the account over-simplified, but I have tried to convey the essence of the central processes for readers who bring no background knowledge to this text.

As colonizers, new arrivals in what was then *Nouvelle France* engaged mainly in agriculture in semi-feudal settings under the control of the colonial administration and the Catholic Church, and in the fur trade as merchants, *voyageurs* and *coureurs de bois*. There was also a small urban population of artisans and merchants. While most of this population was concentrated in what are now Quebec and New Brunswick, there were also pockets of settlement elsewhere in the Atlantic region and around the shores of the Great Lakes in what are now Ontario and Michigan.

After the British conquered *Nouvelle France* in 1763, some of the governing élite and some of the merchants went home, leaving the remaining farmers, artisans, small merchants, workers, *voyageurs* and *coureurs de bois* under the aegis of the Church and the professional élite. Those involved in the fur trade often had to deal directly with British merchants; otherwise, the French remained relatively isolated from the new British rulers. Beginning in the mid nineteenth century, an agricultural crisis due in part to population expansion drew large numbers from the French rural population to new industrial centres in southern Quebec and New England. The Catholic Church took the initiative of turning this tide towards the colonization of what is now eastern and northern Ontario; this served the interests of the ruling English-speaking merchant élite, since the French provided most of the labour required to exploit the other resources of the area (providing both food and labour for the lumber industry in both areas and for the mines in the north) and eventually to build the railway through that area across to the Prairies. The railway, of course, was an important adjunct to inland waterways as a way of transporting the primary resources (fur, then wheat and lumber) on which English Canada built its wealth.

The Quebec Act of 1774 is widely considered to have consolidated the power of the Church with regard to French Canada; it can be seen as a strategy on the part of the British to use the French élite to guarantee francophone loyalty against American insurrectionists. The arrival of Loyalist settlers after the American War of Independence changed the demographic balance in many regions, although they mainly settled Upper Canada, the area north of the St. Lawrence and Lake Ontario, and west of the Ottawa river. Immigrants continued to arrive, of course, from England and Scotland. Mainly English Protestant Upper Canada and mainly French Catholic Lower Canada were joined by the Act of Union in 1841, at about the time that Irish Catholics began arriving and the rural exodus of Quebec got underway. Thus began a long process of conflict and accommodation among French and English Catholics and English Protestants (Choquette 1977, 1987; Jackson 1988).

The British North America Act of 1867, which gave Canada its independence, created the provincial boundaries and powers which underlie modern political processes. At the same time, it established the notion (central now to a certain ideology of the Canadian state) that the English and the French constituted two founding nations, a concept that went beyond, and later came into conflict with, the strength of provincial boundaries. However, as part of these processes, it guaranteed educational rights on the basis of religion, not language, leaving the door open to local or regional interpretation of rights to minority language education, and ensuring the continued importance of the Church as well as of the state in that area. It thus sowed the seeds of conflict between a centralizing federal government legitimized through recognition of linguistic (or ethnic) duality and decentralizing provincial governments which could appeal to monolingualism; between concepts of nations as crossing political boundaries and nations which are intimately bound up with processes of legitimizing state formation; and between language and religion as legitimate bases of ethnic mobilization.

In eastern, and then northern, Ontario, francophones lived in largely homogeneous communities, engaged in a combination of agriculture and lumbering. When mining operations opened up in many northern Ontario communities, many rural francophones, from the surrounding regions as well as from elsewhere in Canada, moved to these small centres to provide labour in the anglophone-owned mines. Others moved to the southern parts of the province, at first to settle and farm, and then, starting in the late nineteenth century, to work in the new factories. For example, the southern Ontario community of Welland has a sizeable francophone community dating from the establishment during the First World War of a branch plant of an English-owned, Quebec-based, textile mill, for which francophone labour from Quebec was imported (Choquette 1987:138). During and after the Second World War, a second wave of francophone recruits from Quebec arrived to work in armaments factories and steel mills (Beniak et al. 1985; Lapointe et al. 1987). In such centres, francophones were often able to maintain separate and cohesive communities, with all services provided from within. There was a small merchant class, and a small élite, engaged in the liberal professions and sustaining the Church. The Church played a key role in the community, and was responsible for education. In other urban areas, such as Toronto, however, it was harder to establish community links, frequently because immigrants came from a variety of regions and for a variety of reasons; they worked in multi-ethnic factories and lived in multi-ethnic neighbourhoods. It was difficult under those circumstances to establish and then maintain francophone structures of reception which would serve as the basis for ethnic (rather than class) affiliation.

After the Second World War, major social changes shifted the basis of ethnic relations in Canada. Industrial expansion, particularly in the area of manufacturing, provided a new resource base for the state, particularly for provincial governments, in the form of commercial taxes. Those governments were able to use this resource base to consolidate their control of provision of basic services. An immediate consequence of the extension of the power of the state in Quebec, a province where approximately 80 percent of the population was French, was the creation of a much larger civil service than had previously existed. In order to staff that civil service, the government required educated candidates, and indeed it moved quickly to expand and democratize the educational system. This most central process of the Quiet Revolution had as its effect the creation of a new francophone middle-class. When the civil service became saturated, however, in the late 1960s, the state was faced with the problem of new ranks of educated francophones with limited opportunities: there were not enough jobs to go around in the public sector, and only those who had assimilated could gain access to the anglophone-controlled private sector.

At the same time, the centre of control of the private sector, which remained in the hands of anglophones, began to shift from Montreal, which had been the financial centre of Canada since the establishment of *Nouvelle France*, to Toronto. Some companies moved lock, stock and barrel, but most simply shifted their head offices to Toronto. This in itself left openings at the management level in Montreal. In the late 1960s and early 1970s, it was possible to imagine that the collective mobilization of francophones would enable them to gain access to management levels of private enterprise as francophones. One can read the nationalist movement in Quebec as just such a strategy of mobilization, and as such, it has been remarkably successful. Indeed, in order to keep the newly powerful Quebec within Canada, the federal government had to make major changes in its own mode of operation and in its official policy; hence the ideology of bilingualism and biculturalism of the Trudeau years, an ideology which is still central to Canadian federal politics.

This has had a number of consequences for francophones outside Quebec, and in particular for Franco-Ontarians. Franco-Ontarians too have participated in this mobilization, but for them it has been more difficult to participate in private enterprise as francophones, or to take any measure of control over that sector. Nonetheless, the 1970s and 1980s have seen the rise of a new, educated middle-class. Some members have arrived recently from Quebec: they came to settle when the economic situation of their home province took a turn for the worse in the late 1970s and early 1980s, or they have come to spend a few years working in their companies' head offices and learning English. Eventually, usually within three to five years, they return to Quebec. Others are home-grown, and many of these find employment in the public sector, as first the federal government in Ottawa and then, twenty years later, the provincial government in Toronto, began to recruit increasing numbers of bilingual civil servants.

The increase in the importance of French in Ontario is clearly directly related to the economic and political importance of French Quebec; Franco-Ontarians do not themselves have the kind of control over important resources which would occasion a similar change in their fortunes. Thus while for the Québécois the basis of power remains an investment in French monolingualism, for Franco-Ontarians this cannot be the case: they remain dependent on the power of the English-dominated state and on the wealth of the English-dominated private sector. For Franco-Ontarians, what is important is to be bilingual. The contradiction which they have to resolve is that bilingualism is predicated on some social division of labour which might be articulated through separate zones of activity, but what they are using bilingualism for is full and free entry into provincial, national and indeed international economic and political networks.

Of course, the Québécois are also caught in a similar contradiction, albeit at a different level, having succeeded in creating a regional network of business and commerce that functions largely in French, but is embedded in national and international networks that function in English. Consequently, the success of Quebec's regional economy depends crucially on the ability of some Québécois to mediate between the French economy of Quebec and the English economy outside Quebec. It is French Canada's fate to be up against an international lingua franca. But it is also because of that fate that so many Québécois, and indeed, francophones from other parts of the world, come to Ontario; while they learn English, they also participate in the local francophone communities, sending their children (sometimes) to French-language schools, joining social clubs, and supporting francophone activism.

Francophones from other areas of the country, and, indeed, of the world, also come to Ontario for economic reasons; some also come for political ones. As the area of the country with the lowest rate of unemployment and the strongest economy, it needs and attracts immigrants, some of whom happen to be francophone, or come from regions where French is widely used and may even be the language of instruction. While not all such immigrants expected to find a francophone community upon their arrival, many choose to affiliate with it when they discover its existence. As with the movement of francophones from other parts of Canada (and indeed within Ontario itself), it is mainly the urban areas, and in particular Toronto, which act as the pole of attraction. This has obvious consequences for the local francophone communities: suddenly Franco-Ontarians, with a shared background and experience, find themselves together with francophones from other parts of Canada and other parts of the world.

The final major consequence of the Québécois nationalist mobilization of the 1960s and 1970s has been, of course, that anglophones began to be interested in French. This has mainly taken the form of educational programs, notably French immersion. But many anglophones have also become interested in francophones, their culture and their community, and in places like Toronto many of them fought hard to open French-language schools. Then they enrolled their children there. As a result, Franco-Ontarian education has become a meeting ground for francophones of many backgrounds, some more or less already assimilated to English, some monolingual in French, as well as anglophones of various interests and backgrounds. This is the backdrop to the subsequent chapters, which take up the problem of the social value of French and English, their roles as emblems of ethnic identity, their relationship to questions of access to valued resources, and the different and often opposing interests of members of different groups with respect to the valued resource of language.

Chapter 3 deals with the role of language in the ideology and politics of ethnic mobilization, primarily in Ontario, but with necessary reference to Quebec. It discusses the evolution of the identity of francophones in Canada, primarily in terms of the change in the relevant contrasts. While at first francophones in Canada could speak of themselves as *Canadiens*, in opposition to Europeans (whether French or British), they then became *Canadiens français*, in opposition to the English-speakers who also, in time, became Canadian. This label is one that is still in current use, but its usage has shifted; it now forms part of a set of terms which include a variety of labels based on regional, rather than pan-Canadian identity. In Ontario, there are two such terms in use: *Franco-Ontarien* and *Ontarois*, each signalling a different political stance with respect to the degree of autonomy from the English province (Bernard 1988). As a result of the expansion of these terms, the term *Canadien* has come back into circulation, only this time it refers to a national identity crossing ethnolinguistic lines.

These labels index not only ethnic boundaries, but also the nature of the ideology underlying ethnic mobilization and ethnic relations. The theme underlying them all is the theme of nationalism; the difference is in the way that national identity is conceived. The individual inhabitants of this territory have variously thought of themselves as parts of an empire, as citizens of a Canadian state, in terms of religious categories or as members of nations defined by ethnicity cross-cutting the formation of states, and as citizens of nation-states wherein ethnicity is the primary source of the legitimacy of the state. While the strength of the concept of empire has certainly waned in recent years, it has by no means disappeared; the other ways of conceiving national identity are all currently present in debates on language rights and the nature and future of Canada. At issue in particular is the overlap of citizenship (affiliation to a polity) and ethnicity.

Language is taken up in these debates in a variety of ways, but it is generally used to appeal to the notion of national unity. In most of these debates, some people argue that national unity will best be achieved on the basis of bilingualism. They argue that it is in everyone's best interests to maintain the Canadian state; in order to do so, anglophones and francophones must be able to achieve their goals within the same structure. Others argue that English monolingualism is the privileged path to national unity. Their power base allows them to see English as neutral (Jackson 1988); it is thought to provide equal access for all to full participation in Canadian society, giving no advantage to any one group (such as English-speakers, for example) over others. To the extent that speakers of other languages than English share this belief (and many do), English is truly hegemonic.

However, francophones do not see English as neutral, and it is not clear to many of them that bilingualism works. If it is not possible for francophones to achieve their goals within the Canadian state, they have an option to consider, a different strategy for achieving social and economic goals as francophones, namely, the establishment of Quebec as a nation-state where French is the privileged path to social and economic success. There are echoes of this strategy in the other provinces as well; the concept of *"Ontarie"*, for example, reflects just such a nation-state, which, however, happens to be territorially contiguous with

"Ontario". The possibility of such an overlap in turn raises questions concerning ethnic boundaries: if the state is defined in terms of ethnic affiliation, then surely ethnic affiliation is defined in terms of citizenship and residence. Eventually, it becomes necessary to guard against the effects of the legitimacy and hegemonic status that French may acquire within its own zones of influence.

The second theme that usually emerges in debates over language rights is money. What is at the heart of these arguments is whether or not people are willing to invest in particular strategies for achieving certain measures of social equality. The dominance of English led to fixed systems of ethnic stratification; francophones had to mobilize as a group to break out of that hierarchy. The federal government, and some provincial governments, have adopted strategies of supporting that mobilization in the hope that they will remove the economic and social grounds for Quebec to separate from Canada (and take with it its labour, its resources and its market, representing close to 25 percent of the Canadian population and a slightly smaller, but nonetheless significant, proportion of its wealth). To accomplish that costs money, since most government systems began and developed as English-speaking domains. It also requires, on the part of those who speak no French, an at least potential investment of the time and energy it takes to learn that language in order to participate in the areas of the public (and to the extent that francophones are successful in presenting themselves as a monolingual bloc, the private) sector where the use of French has become important.

Nonetheless, public discussion of language rights rarely overtly deals with the goals underlying the various strategies individuals and governments adopt. These goals vary from the rectification of historically-entrenched social and economic equalities, to its obverse, the protection, whether by resistance or by adaptation, of historically-entrenched privileges that are now being threatened, or, more recently, to the protection of the new-found privileges of being francophone. As a result, most people find themselves caught in unresolvable contradictions between social equality and the protection of privileges based on ethnic affiliation, all veiled in the legitimating language of "national unity", "*la cause*" or "simple economics".

In order to pierce this veil, I will take up the problem of the relationship of linguistic capital to access to valued resources, and how the shift in the nature of the ecology of ethnic relations has had an effect on the resources controlled by different groups and hence on the ways in which language can be used to regulate access to them. At the same time, it will be necessary to explore how language takes on value as a resource in itself, and how access to that resource is itself regulated through social institutions, notably the school, and through social interaction. I will use the example of the bitter debates over francophone rights which shook Sault Ste. Marie in early 1990 as a way to explore these issues. I will then go on to explore the various ways in which educational policy constrains the use of the school as a means of access to valued linguistic capital. The major issues involve the use of educational systems to maintain minority languages, in particular, French, and the use of those systems to gain access to bi- or multilingualism.

In Chapter 4, I will take up the particular problems of regulating access to French and English manifested in the Franco-Ontarian educational system. These problems are articulated through four themes. The first theme is the theme of what is called "*la gestion*": governance. Franco-Ontarians, whose schools used to be run by the Catholic Church, have long been attempting to use the state in order to have access to improved educational facilities and programs. Since the beginning of that attempt, they have been struggling to gain control over their own schools, through the mechanism of the state. The Catholic Church itself has been engaged in a similar struggle. The question of governance foregrounds this relationship between the Franco-Ontarian community, the Church and the state, and poses the problem of how ethnic and religious interests may be met within the mechanisms of a state controlled largely by Protestant English-speakers.

The second theme concerns a group of students in Franco-Ontarian schools who have become known as "*les non parlants*". This somewhat unfelicitious term refers to students who enroll in French-language minority schools, but whose proficiency in French is limited. Their presence points to some important processes within the Franco-Ontarian community and to problems related to the regulations surrounding minority-language education in Ontario. Some of these students are of French background, but they, or their parents, have become so assimilated that they no longer (or perhaps never did) speak French fluently, or even moderately well. (These assimilated francophones are sometimes called "*francogènes*", that is, people who have some historical, one might say almost biological link, to the community, even if they do not currently actively participate in it.) Other students are not of French background; their parents send them to Franco-Ontarian schools because they consider it the best way to gain access to French.

Many schools feel it necessary to admit these students. The admission of *francogènes* is often argued for on moral and demographic grounds, as a way of recouping those who were almost lost to the fold. But admission of *non parlants* is also often deemed necessary by schools because otherwise they do not meet government enrollment quotas. These quotas, which apply identically to majority and minority schools, are the basis for obtaining permission to open a school in the first place, and then to keep it open, and for obtaining specific services (full-time librarians, special education teachers, psychoeducational consultants, etc.).

However, the presence of these students has also frequently caused bitter disputes, since many francophone parents feel that they promote assimilation to English from within the major institution charged with fighting it.

Schools and school boards have adopted a variety of strategies in response to the issue of the *non parlants*, and this is the third theme to be taken up in Chapter 4. On the one hand, school boards must operate within federal and provincial legislation regulating rights of access to their minority-language schools, and within provincial regulations surrounding the operation of all schools; on the other hand, they are free to adopt a variety of strategies within those regulations. Among them, schools and school boards have debated admissions criteria, and special programs within their school boards for students whose French they consider weak. These gatekeeping mechanisms are important means of defining what counts as valued linguistic capital (what is an adequate command of French in this case?) and in regulating access to it, and hence in regulating access to ethnic affiliation. They can be looked at as a form of border patrol.

The final theme is a related one; it concerns the consequences for Franco-Ontarian ethnic boundaries of the presence in their schools of students from other regions of Canada and from other countries altogether. In some cases, these are students from other francophone countries. In others, students come from areas where French is a second official language, a language of instruction or simply the most commonly learned language of wider communication. In still others, parents come to Canada speaking neither English nor French, but choose either to affiliate with francophones or see enrolling their children in French-language schools as the most effective means of achieving bilingualism. Finally, some students are the products of mixed marriages. The presence of these students has made salient both the question of who counts as a Franco-Ontarian, but also the important question of how that identity is constituted. It raises the issue of participation in the governance mechanisms of Franco-Ontarian schools, and the definition of what counts as appropriate Franco-Ontarian behaviour.

In Chapter 5, I will explore what these four themes look like in one particular set of Franco-Ontarian schools, those of the metropolitan Toronto area. Metropolitan Toronto currently has eleven elementary and three secondary French-language minority schools, divided between a public French-language board and a Catholic board which includes a vast number of English-language schools in addition to its seven French-language schools. This particular administrative arrangement is recent; its history will illustrate many of the governance-related issues raised in the previous chapter.

A demographic profile of Toronto's French-language community and of its schools will also reveal some of the ways in which major social and demographic trends are reflected in the creation and development of the schools, notably the trends of migration (related to the growth of Toronto's importance as a financial and administrative centre) and assimilation (related to the importance of English and the weakness of the francophone social network in Toronto). It will also provide the backdrop to a discussion of the debates and practices surrounding the regulation of access to those schools.

First, I will discuss the ways in which the schools define the linguistic and cultural aspects of what is often referred to as their *mission*. The discussion will be based on the efforts observed within schools to transmit certain specific values, and to legitimate certain ways of using language and certain linguistic forms over others.

Second, I will take up the ways in which parents of different backgrounds formulate their educational decision-making, focussing in particular on two disputes within the public schools. The first is a dispute over the place of English and of English-speakers in those schools; the second is a dispute over the access of francophones of non-Canadian background to participation in governance. The different positions that parents take on the questions of access and governance can be seen to be related to the value they place on access to French and English, and within that, to access to different forms of French (variously referred to as "*le français européen*" or "*international*", "*le français canadien*", "*le québécois*", "*le français ontarien*" or the distinctly pejorative "*joual*"; and sometimes simply as "*le bon/mauvais français*"). In turn, those positions can be related to the social position of the parents themselves, that is, the extent to which they and their children have access outside school to French and English and the extent to which an investment in those languages (and their different forms) might actually pay off in terms of access to other valued resources (such as a university education or jobs). Their expressed positions can be seen as strategic responses to the problem of achieving valued resources; differences arise due to the fact that not all parents and children come to participation in school affairs already possessing the same knowledge and resources, and not all have the same avenues open to them to maintain the resources they already have or to gain access to new ones.

The chapter also takes up some of the ways in which language is used to regulate access to resources within the school. It focusses in particular on access to knowledge, controlled by teachers and other school authorities through the use of particular forms of French, and access to friendship networks, controlled mainly through the use of English. I will discuss how language choice is used strategically by students of different backgrounds to gain access to both those forms of valued resource, and to neutralize the tension between them when the two opposing frames overlap.

Finally, I will discuss what the ideologies and practices of parents and students mean for the ability of French-language schools in Toronto to accomplish their explicit goal of maintaining French language and culture in this English-dominant area. In particular, I will focus on two major challenges. The first major challenge has to do with resolving the tension between using Franco-Ontarian schools to maintain ethnic boundaries and using education to facilitate francophone access to national and international economic networks. The second has to do with resolving the tension between challenging relations of dominance in which francophones are rendered powerless, and constructing relations of power within francophone institutions which create their own inequalities.

Chapter 6 is an account of an explicit pedagogical intervention which attempts to address a small part of this array of concerns. In particular, it focusses on ways in which Franco-Ontarian schools can manage the double problem of maintaining French in minority contexts and the problem of the heterogeneity (in linguistic, cultural and social terms) of the student body.

Projet "Coopération et découverte" is a pedagogical approach which a team of us developed in order to act on the analysis which emerged from several years of ethnographic study. While the problems facing Franco-Ontarian education today can only be resolved through changes in a number of different arenas, it is possible, we felt, to use pedagogical practice as one point of intervention. Our specific goals were to help students expand their repertoire within French by involving them in a wider variety of communicative contexts than they usually participate in, creating the conditions which would permit them to discover and reflect on the value of English and of different forms of French as well as the source of that value, and allowing them to share the different linguistic resources which they bring to the classroom. Chapter 6 describes the motivations for this pedagogical initiative, its social goals as translated into classroom practice, the specific pedagogical techniques involved, and what happened when this approach was used in a variety of classrooms across Toronto.

Chapter 7 presents a synthesis of the issues raised by Franco-Ontarian education, in terms of what it tells us about the role of minority-language education in maintaining ethnic boundaries and facilitating access to power. It also focusses on the problem of successful mobilization: when power is gained, how is it to be used? Finally, it explores the complex relationship among various forms of social difference, and what that relationship reveals for the possibilities Franco-Ontarian education has to contribute to a plural but egalitarian society.

1.4. Sources of data

The material for this book comes from a variety of sources. Much, of course, comes simply from living and working in Quebec and Ontario, reading the newspaper, listening to the news, participating in social institutions. However, my analyses and positions have also been informed by a variety of more formal enquiries.

Much of my material on Quebec comes from my masters' and doctoral theses based on ethnographic studies there, the first on public negotiations of language choice and the second on the implementation of Bill 101, the 1977 language law, in a private enterprise in Montreal. My doctoral work was financed in part by the *Office de la langue française* (Gouvernement du Québec), and I gratefully acknowledge the help I received from the members of my team: Jean-Paul Bartholomot, Laurette Lévy and Luc Ostiguy.

My work in Ontario has been funded by the Social Sciences and Humanities Research Council of Canada, the Multiculturalism Directorate of the Secretary of State (Government of Canada), the Ministry of Education (Government of Ontario), either directly or through the Transfer Grant to the Ontario Institute for Studies in Education, and by the Toronto Board of Education. I owe a large debt to the colleagues who, one way or another, participated in this research: Graham Barker, Monique Bélanger, Mary-Ellen Campbell, Michael Canale, Jacinthe Fraser, Laurette Lévy, Raymond Mougeon, Françoise Pelletier, Carole Roy-Harrison and Merrill Swain.

This work, conducted since my arrival in Toronto in the fall of 1982, has been mainly ethnographic in nature. I have spent many months in most of Toronto's French-language schools, sitting in classrooms, talking to teachers and principals in their offices and staff rooms and to students in the playground and the hallways. I and my colleagues have conducted formal interviews with students, parents, teachers, school board administrative personnel and community leaders involved in educational issues, focussing on their backgrounds and their goals, and their formulation of what they see as the most important issues facing Franco-Ontarian education. Questionnaires have been used to gain basic demographic information, or to survey the distribution of program types. I have drawn on published sources for demographic data (mainly from Statistics Canada) and for my analysis of historical and ecological aspects of the position of Franco-Ontarians and Franco-Ontarian education. In the latter case, some of these sources are primary (principally documents produced by government and para-governmental agencies, school boards and community organizations) and others are secondary.

1.4 Sources of data

In addition, I have drawn from my experience of curriculum development and implementation in collaboration with a number of teachers and other school board personnel. I would like to acknowledge here the important roles that the following people played in teaching me about the realities of classroom practice and in working with me and my colleagues to elaborate our approach and develop materials to support it: Suzanne Arsenault, Gérard Boulay, Liliane Brown, Anne-Marie Caron-Réaume, Denise Drago, Bernard Lachapelle, Céline Lacroix, Anne Leroy-Audy, Pierre Nadeau, Line Pelletier, Maryse Roussel, Arthur Roy, Jacques Samson and Christiane Turgeon.

The challenge for me will be to use the insights that I glean from writing this book in the development of my own practice, in teaching, research and field development. In particular, I will have to use it to articulate the role that I think I can continue to play in Franco-Ontarian education, and to develop ways of resolving the tensions and conflicts which I see developing there, and in which I fully participate. My own position as someone who is difficult to classify, or at best will continue to represent difference within any otherwise homogeneous population, clearly informs my commitment to making some kind of pluralism work. While my own interests are clearly served here, the question remains of how those interests coincide with, overlap with or enter into conflict with those of others.

A final word about the politics of writing in English. Anyone who has lived on the Canadian linguistic frontier as I have knows that the only choice of language which can in any way be construed as neutral is codeswitching. While codeswitching as a mode has a precedent in fiction, to my knowledge it has no such precedent in academic discourse. I might have taken up the challenge of setting that precedent, and some day I may still. As it stands, I am caught in the contradiction of writing for many audiences in a world where the major language of wider communication is English. I have tried to cope by writing sometimes in English and sometimes in French, publishing sometimes in Canadian networks and sometimes in American and European ones (which both have a wider circulation and overlap the Canadian networks). I am not convinced that I have coped well; rather, these thoughts are offered in order for the reader to know that I am, at least, aware of the irony of my actions.

Chapter 2
The French in Canada: A historical overview

2.0. French ethnicity: Stratification, assimilation and mobilization

In the fall of 1989, I found myself having lunch in the Banff Springs Hotel, an elegant sprawling Victorian masterpiece in the Alberta Rockies. The hotel is part of Canadian history, one of a chain built in the late nineteenth and early twentieth centuries by the Canadian Pacific Railway company along its nation-wide and nation-building rail line. I was attending a conference in Calgary, and five of us, three from Ontario and two from Alberta, had gone to Banff for the day to see the mountains and soak in the hot springs. We entered the nearly-empty restaurant, and settled ourselves. We had been chatting in French for a while when the waiter finally approached our table. He gave us a big smile and said: "So, are you folks from Quebec?"

Two months later I was with my husband and daughter on a flight from San Francisco to Toronto; the flight was ultimately destined for Montreal. In the San Francisco airport lounge, we had struck up a conversation with the Montreal-based, francophone flight crew, and we continued to chat periodically with some of the attendants throughout the flight. As we collected our things in preparation for leaving the airplane in Toronto, one of the flight attendants looked at us in surprise and asked: "*Mais vous n'allez pas à Montréal?*" ["But you're not going to Montréal?"]

Within a short period an anglophone Albertan and a francophone Québécoise had both given me the same message: anybody who speaks French must be from Quebec. This popular conception is belied by the facts: not all French speakers in Canada are from Quebec. In 1991, when the most recent census data for which figures are available was taken, Canada had a total population of about 27 million, of whom about 16.5 million claimed English as their mother tongue, and about 6.5 million of whom claimed French as their mother tongue (see Figure 1). About 900,000 of those francophones lived outside Quebec (while about 600,000 anglophones lived in Quebec).[3] French-speaking populations exist in every province and territory, and persist, despite the ravages of assimilation, in part because of successive waves (or sometimes continuous trickles) of migration from Quebec and Acadia. While these "minority" populations are not huge, they are nonetheless reasonably large (although they have declined by about

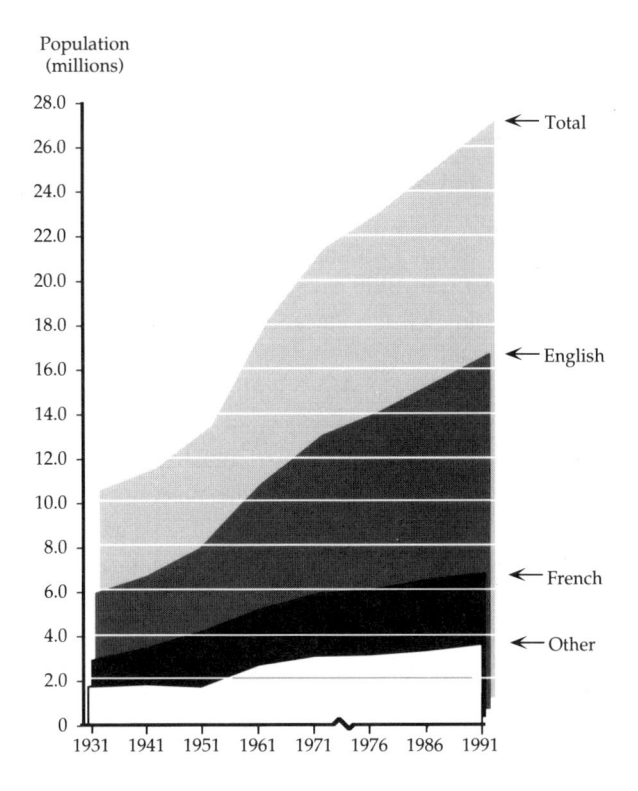

Figure 1. Population of Canada by mother tongue, 1931–1991.
Source: Statistics Canada. Lachapelle and Henripin 1980: 336

100,000 since the 1986 census). At least in theory, they are protected by Canada's 1969 Official Languages Act, an act designed expressly to keep the country together by guaranteeing bilingualism across its territory. Of course, over the last thirty years there has been almost constant discussion of the possibility that Quebec might separate from Canada. As of this writing that has not happened, but in the popular imagination it sometimes seems as though it has, bringing into focus two monolingual regions: French in Quebec and English everywhere else.

Certainly recent debates about the role of Quebec in Canada underscore this tension between ideologies of bilingualism and ideologies of territoriality. In 1982, the Canadian government "repatriated" the constitution, that is, it brought to Canada the legislation (the British North America Act) by which Britain had created Canada in 1867, and which had resided in London ever since. This nation-building gesture immediately ran into trouble. According to the arrangements between the federal and the provincial governments in Canada, the constitution had to be ratified by all the provincial governments. However, Quebec refused to sign on the grounds that the Constitution did not give it enough control over its own territory. Specifically, Quebec argued that it could not be treated as a province like the others; rather, it had the special mission of protecting the French language and culture in Canada, and needed the power (for example, in the areas of immigration and education) to accomplish that mission.

Several years of negotiation followed, aimed at finding a way to permit Quebec to sign the Constitution. Elections came and went, and new governments continued the debate. Finally, in 1989, an agreement was reached which satisfied Quebec (the agreement is known as the Meech Lake Accord, after the lake on the shores of which sits the hotel where the accord was negotiated). This agreement recognized Quebec as "a distinct society", and gave it the freedom it wanted in certain areas. The accord itself became the source of controversy, however, not because of the recognition it granted Quebec, but because of ancillary issues. Foremost among them, for our purposes, is the perception that the rights of linguistic minorities are not sufficiently protected, that is, in opting for Quebec's territorial strategy, francophones outside Quebec and anglophones inside Quebec are abandoned to their fate. In the end, the agreement was never adopted, and instead there followed several more years of negotiations culminating in a new agreement (the Charlottetown Accord) reached in August 1992, and touching on a broad range of issues including Senate reform and aboriginal rights. A referendum held in October 1992 to ratify the accord was defeated. The reasons for that defeat are complex and go far beyond the issues of Quebec nationalism and minority rights. Given the events of this ten-year period, it seems that discussions will continue through moments of greater and lesser tension.[4]

If I dwell on these issues now, it is to demonstrate how deeply notions of language and identity are bound up with the politics of nation and state in Canada. We are living now through a period where the welfare of members of different ethnolinguistic groups is said to rest on two conflicting ideologies, the ideology of bilingualism and the ideology of territoriality. This conflict, however, is but the most recent manifestation of a tension that has been part of Canada ever since the British conquered New France in 1759.

In order to understand the value and significance of French and English today, it is necessary to understand how those languages are caught up in processes of distribution of material and symbolic resources. The question is what the use of French and English allow you to do, and what they allow you to be, as well as what circumstances (political, economic, social) provide the conditions which allow you to achieve what you want the way you want to. There is no simple answer to that question, since individuals and groups are constantly using languages in order to define and redefine, as well as accomplish, their goals, under

2.0 Stratification, assimilation and mobilization

changing social and material circumstances. However, it is possible to grasp some of the processes involved, processes which have historical bases.

In this chapter, I will explore the historical development of the economic and political processes which underlie the persistence of the boundary between French and English in Canada, and the consistent tension between assimilation and separation which has marked the contact of the two groups. At the heart of these processes is the particular form ethnic stratification has taken in Canada: ever since the Conquest, French-speakers have been subordinate to English-speakers in a variety of ways. The two groups have been, however, both divided and linked through language, ethnicity, religion and class; furthermore, ethnic interests, religious interests and class interests have not always entirely coincided. Instead, these have often been competing tensions. In addition, access to valued resources has come sometimes through individual assimilation and sometimes through collective mobilization. Sometimes, such access has been gained (or at least fought for) through the strategic use of social institutions which cut across ethnic lines, such as the Catholic Church or labour unions. More recently, ethnic nationalism has provided a means of taking control of the state. There has been competition for material resources and competition for symbolic ones, and the relationship between the two has usually been complex. French and English have sometimes confronted each other in the same arenas, and sometimes have moved in separate ones. However, once the French lost the Battle of the Plains of Abraham in 1759, it was the English who set the broad rules of the game within which groups and individuals manoeuvred, and continue to manoeuvre, for their share.

In what follows, a chronological narrative focusses at different moments on different levels of Canadian society. In the next section, I describe the origins of the French presence in Canada, during the period (1534–1759) when France possessed a colony covering most of what is now Quebec, as well as parts of New Brunswick, Nova Scotia and Ontario, with excursions to the north and west. The following section discusses the period from the British Conquest to the beginning of Confederation (1763–1867). Here, the focus is national, but particular attention is paid to Quebec, as the centre of French settlement, and to Ontario, which, after all, is the focus of this book. It was during this period that the distinction between Quebec and Ontario began to take form, and the different histories of ethnolinguistic contact in the two regions, as well as their relationship to each other, still inform the lives of Franco-Ontarians today.

The fourth section begins to focus on Ontario, discussing the French settlement of Ontario in the late nineteenth and early twentieth century, and subsequent migrations in the course of the economic transformations of the twentieth century through the post-War boom. The fifth section examines the relationship between the economic and political organization of ethnic relations during this period and the distribution and value of French and English.

The sixth section concerns the francophone ethnic mobilization of the 1960s. This central process in the evolution of French-English relations in Canada is centred on the control by francophones of Quebec as a nation-state, and so the discussion must focus first on events within Quebec, before turning to the consequences for francophones elsewhere of Quebec nationalist mobilization. By defining Quebec as the francophone stronghold, Quebec nationalism has effectively undermined pan-Canadian French nationalism and ethnic ties, leaving francophones outside Quebec to redefine their frames of reference, that is, to try to reconstitute an identity for themselves which recognizes the new political reality splitting the population.

The last two sections turn to the consequences for francophones in Ontario in particular. I will first discuss the ways in which francophone mobilization in Quebec led to processes of (and possibilities for) francophone mobilization within Ontario since the 1960s. I will then consider the major trends and areas of discussion which seem likely to inform the collective life of Franco-Ontarians in the decade to come.

Throughout this chapter, where possible, I have also tried to situate Toronto within broader provincial and national processes. Since later chapters (Chapters 5 and 6 in particular) deal with the use of French and English in Toronto's French-language minority schools, it is important to begin immediately to locate Toronto's francophone population within the economic, political and social transformations of French-English relations in Canada over the course of the last century. Toronto is not typical, in any sense of the word, but it represents certain basic aspects of what it means to be francophone in Canada today. Since the majority of Toronto's francophones are recent arrivals, most of this information concerns the period since the 1950s, when the increased integration of francophones into the modern industrial world, the development of the francophone middle class, and the emergence of Toronto as Canada's financial centre together brought increasing numbers of francophones (from Canada and elsewhere) to Toronto at the same time as ethnic mobilization rendered them more and more visible on the local scene.

This chapter, then, is an attempt to link up local, regional and national aspects of the development of French ethnicity in Canada, and in particular in Ontario and in Toronto. It goes without saying that those aspects are in turn linked to global processes which account for colonialism, imperialism, and then the development of nation-states and the increasingly integrated global economy which affects the lives of each of us. My purpose here, however, is more narrowly defined: it is to understand the roots of the value of French and English in both material and symbolic terms, in order to understand the role of the school in defining that value for francophones in Toronto, and in order to understand what those values and institutional processes can tell us about the possibilities for social mobility and social equality in an ethnolinguistically diverse society.

2.1. Colonization and *la Nouvelle France* (1534–1763)

The history of the French in Canada generally begins with the expedition in 1534-1536 of Jacques Cartier from his home port of St-Malo, on the northwest coast of France, across the Atlantic and up the St. Lawrence river to the village of Hochelaga. Cartier was able to scale the rise in the middle of the island on which Hochelaga was situated, and, re-naming it Mont-Royal, he claimed it for France. The present-day city of Montreal dates itself to that moment in 1534, and a large electrically lit replica of the cross Cartier planted on the summit now lights up the night over the city.

France was able to hold the claim Cartier had made in the name of the king, François I, but unable to do much about it until the early part of the seventeenth century, when Spain lost the ability to control ocean travel in the northern Atlantic (Wolf 1982). French exploration and colonization began in earnest with the arrival of Champlain, who in 1604 established a settlement in what is now Acadia (Daigle 1982); in 1608, he established the city of Quebec at the mouth of the St. Lawrence, and explored that river and its tributaries. Slowly, over the course of the seventeenth and the early part of the eighteenth centuries, trading posts, forts and settlements were established along the coasts and waterways.

As Wolf (1982) has pointed out in his analysis of the fur trade (from which much of the following account is taken), the European presence in North America was principally due to the need of the new European states to find new sources of valuable goods, since they had exhausted local capacity to produce adequate surplus to sustain the crown. Indeed, European presence in North America was only part of the global expansion of European empires. Significantly, British and French interest in North America was primarily in furs, which were used exclusively as luxury items. The major target, the beaver, was hunted for the fur underneath the pelt; this was used to make the felt hats which came to distinguish the wealthy from the woolen cap-wearing poor, and the form of which came to signal a wide variety of social and political distinctions (Wolf 1982: 159–160).

The local beaver populations of Eastern North America rapidly declined, and so both the British and the French expanded farther inland in search of new supplies. The arrival of the French in what is now Ontario was part of that expansion, as explorers, traders and missionaries moved up the St. Lawrence and through the Great Lakes. Trading posts were established, and the shores of the Great Lakes were settled, principally on either side of Lake St. Clair, at the juncture of Lake Erie and Lake Huron. The British established themselves along the seacoast to the south, gaining access to the interior up the Hudson River. They were eventually able to gain access to the north through Hudson's Bay.

The French in North America were in a constant contest with the British for control of the lucrative fur trade, and this contest also directly involved the indigenous population. Through alliances cemented by gift-giving, both French and British sought to bring under their control different indigenous groups, since they relied on the indigenous population for their supply of beaver pelts. Indeed, the indigenous population were not only the primary producers (i.e. the hunters and trappers), but also acted as middlemen. The French with whom they had direct contact were *voyageurs* (literally, travellers; in this case, canoeists) and *coureurs de bois* (literally, runners of the woods), fanning out through the forests and along the rivers and lakes and bringing the furs into the trading posts and settlements. Conflict between the British and the French also directly involved the indigenous groups within their spheres of influence. However, this conflict has to be understood not only as local conflict over privileged access to the supply of furs, but also as part of a conflict among expansionist European powers for control of valued resources all over the globe. European incursion had a direct effect on the social, economic and political organization of the indigenous population, which, while it sought to gain from alliances and was occasionally able to play one power off against the other, nonetheless, as we know, was exploited and then marginalized when its usefulness had run its course.[5]

The fate of the French in North America was equally tied to the fur trade and its role in the contest between European powers for access to valuable resources worldwide. France attempted to solidify its hold on its North American colony not only through the fur trade (with the European contribution of gifts in the forms of blankets, firearms, alcohol, and the like) but also through conversion of the indigenous population to Catholicism and through direct colonization of "unoccupied" areas. While the number of colonizers was never very high, this process undoubtedly also had the effect of helping France place some of its surplus population, including those most marginal to French society. Tracts of land on either side of the St. Lawrence and along some of its tributaries were granted to *seigneurs*, and settlers were brought into these *seigneuries* to farm them, entering into a semi-feudal relationship with the *seigneur*.

The Annapolis Valley, the site of Champlain's first attempt to colonize, was another centre of settlement; it was disrupted in 1755 when the British, having established themselves in nearby Halifax, deported the Acadians who refused to take an oath of allegiance to the British crown (Daigle 1982). Some eventually made their way back, but in the meantime the area became heavily settled by the British, especially by Loyalists fleeing the American War of Independence. Since that time, the francophone population of the Atlantic region has had a history, and sense of identity, separate from those of the population centred in Quebec, although migration out of the Atlantic region and the necessities of political alliances have brought the two closer during the twentieth century.

The British were, finally, able to conquer *Nouvelle France*. In 1759, during what has variously been called the Seven Years' War or the French and Indian War (one of the series of armed conflicts among European powers which marked the eighteenth century), they won the now-famous Battle of the Plains of Abraham, outside Quebec City. The British were officially granted the territory of New France by the terms of the Treaty of Paris in 1763.[6]

Most historians agree that French administrators and soldiers went back to France following the Conquest. While it has been argued that what remained was a fairly undifferentiated, rural society of peasants dominated by the landowning *seigneurs* and the Catholic Church, it seems clear that French Canadian society also included a relatively large proportion of merchants and professionals (Ouellet 1966, 1972; Ossenberg 1970). Ossenberg (1970) argues that at least one quarter of the French-speaking population was located in urban centres at the time of the Conquest; however, there followed a process of de-urbanization, or at least a period during which the French in rural areas were unable to move to the cities, and it is this which may in part account for the image of a rural society which does tend to dominate constructions of post-Conquest French-Canadian society. In sum, that society was likely fairly differentiated both in terms of rural and urban activities and in terms of social class, including rural peasants and *seigneurs*, the Church hierarchy, urban-based small merchants and professionals, as well as artisans and an incipient working class. In addition, there remained the *voyageurs* and *coureurs de bois*, some of whom combined their fur-trading activities with agriculture.

The British, in any case, moved into the positions vacated by the military and administrative élite, and, based in the urban centres, particularly in Montreal, took over control of the fur trade and other commercial activities. The *voyageurs* and *coureurs de bois* had expertise that was valuable to them, and so found a niche in the new régime. The agricultural population, engaged in part in subsistence farming but also supplying the towns, remained relatively isolated from the British. Concentrated in the area of what is now Quebec, the French-speaking population nonetheless included both the Acadian population of the Atlantic region, and agricultural settlements in southwestern Ontario near Lake Erie and

40   2   The French in Canada: A historical overview

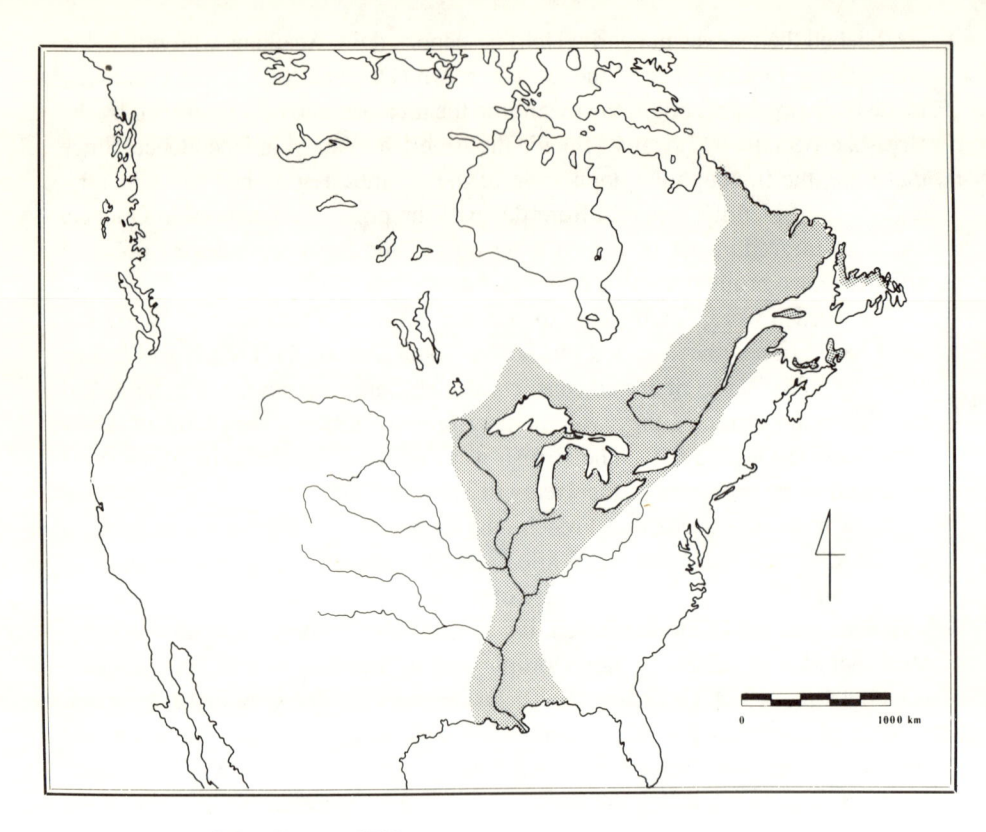

Map 1. Map of New France, 1713

2.1 Colonization and *la Nouvelle France* 41

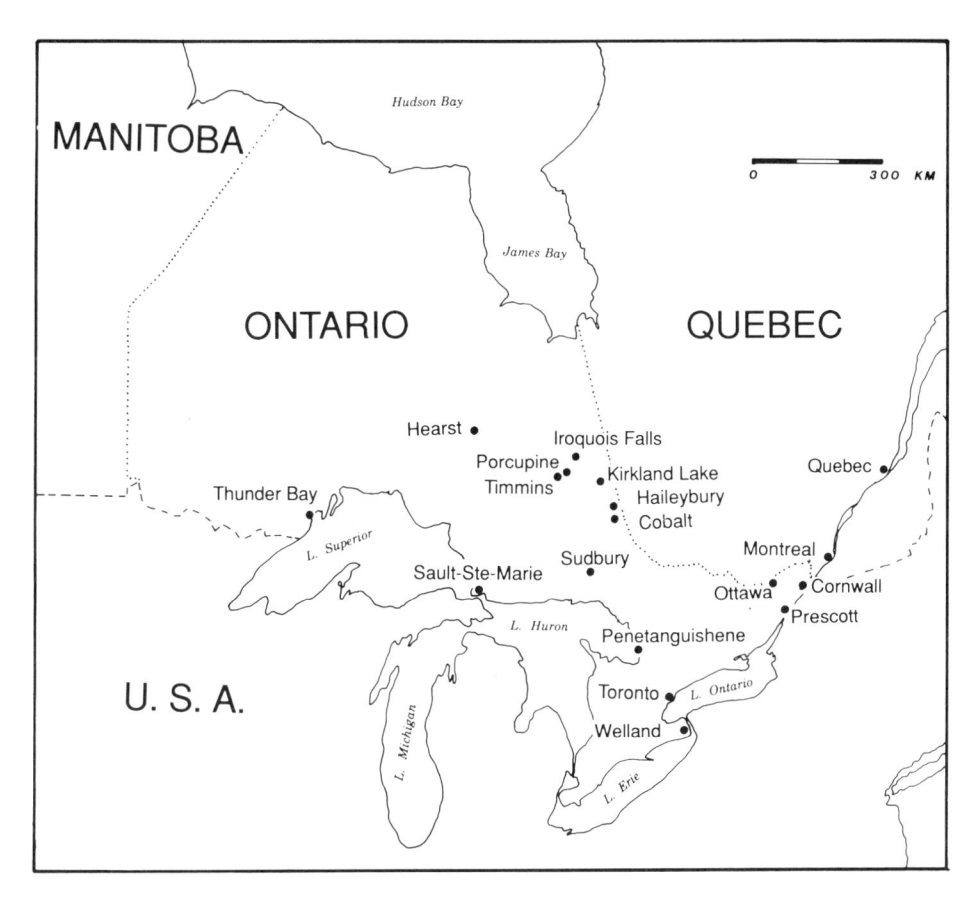

Map 2. Map of Ontario, places cited in text

Lake St. Clair. In all these regions, the French élite and the Church provided the points of articulation between the conquerors and the majority of the population, and developed a power base which it was in their interest to preserve (Ouellet 1972).

2.2. Conquest to Confederation (1763 – 1867)

The British adopted a variety of stances towards this subjugated population. It seems clear that, while a current of thought favouring immediate assimilation of the French certainly existed, it was quickly overridden by more pragmatic political concerns. As relations with the thirteen colonies to the south worsened, the British concentrated on obtaining French loyalty. Institutionalized through the Quebec Act of 1774, this strategy involved letting the French retain their social and economic institutions, which were left, for the most part, under the control of the Catholic Church and the French land-owning and professional élite. While largely successful as a strategy, it was by no means left uncontested by certain members of the French population, who indeed saw that they shared interests with the American rebels.

British small business grew up in the towns. Montreal became the centre of the fur trade, as furs were shipped down rivers, through the Great Lakes and into the St. Lawrence river. As a result, Montreal also became the new British colony's financial centre. Indeed, even near the end of the nineteenth century, Montreal was primarily inhabited by people of British origin (Keyfitz 1960). After the American War of Independence, many Loyalists fled to Canada, settling in Acadia (Nova Scotia, Prince Edward Island, and eventually New Brunswick) and Ontario, but also some parts of southern Quebec. Their arrival changed the nature of British-French relations, adding a large and militantly British population, especially in Acadia and what was to become Ontario. The rural areas settled by the Loyalists tended to be largely ethnolinguistically homogeneous. Even where they became more mixed, the populations were still economically and geographically divided. For example, in the eastern Ontario counties of Prescott-Russell, the English, arriving first, were able to settle the high, more productive lands in the middle of the counties, while the French were relegated to the swampy lowlands on the river's edge (Gaffield 1987).

In 1791, the Constitution Act split what was then known as Quebec into Upper Canada (now Ontario), largely Loyalist (hence Protestant and English-speaking), and Lower Canada (now Quebec), where the rights of the French and of the Catholic Church were retained, despite the presence of the British in Montreal (the heart of the fur trade) and of Loyalist settlements in the south. The French were thereby able to find political means for pursuing their interests, through the legislative structures set up in each province. Thus, by the end of the eighteenth century, social, economic and political structures reinforced the separation of French and English, and strengthened the power of the French Catholic Church and of the lay élite, especially of the urban professionals (Gagnon 1989).

Over the next fifty or so years, the balance between Ontario and Quebec, Montreal and the hinterland, French and English, swayed back and forth, as Canada lived through the long aftermath of the American War of Independence, the French Revolution and the rise of Napoleon. At the same time, while the fur trade remained an important source of wealth, conferring power and authority on the English traders based in Montreal, the Canadian economy diversified, and the industrial revolution began to have an effect. Part of this effect was expressed in the political turmoil of the 1830s, leading to a bourgeois rebellion in 1837.

Significantly, while the French and the English bourgeoisie were able to make common cause, for the French, mobilization rested also in part on a sense of ethnic, or national, rather than purely class interests. This was a rebellion which was in part about the diverging interests of the bourgeoisie as opposed to those of the old élite, but it also concerned francophone resistance to English capitalism (Clift – Arnopoulos 1979). Of course, the English began to feel that their path to profit and expansion was blocked by the presence of the French. In the 1830s, the then governor filed a report which, among other things, called for the adoption of means to assimilate the French. One of these means included the unification of Upper and Lower Canada. The 1840 Act of Union brought French and English into much closer political contact than they had been in before, but the English began to make concerted efforts to control the power of the French.

The Act of Union scarcely resulted in the assimilation of the French; as might be expected, it probably helped strengthen a sense of identity among the French, at least those of Lower Canada (now called Canada East, as opposed to Upper Canada, renamed Canada West). By the early 1860s, when Canada began to consider establishing its independence from Britain, the French were certainly a distinct political force. Their participation in Confederation in 1867 was a deliberate strategy, designed in part to help preserve the distinctiveness of French society, which might otherwise, it was felt, be threatened by the United States to the south (McNaught 1969). Certainly, the British North America Act (1867), by virtue of which the Dominion of Canada was created, recognized certain principles underlying the political separation of French and English. It did this in two ways. First, it set the terms of a relationship between provincial and federal governments which provides for significant scope of action at the provincial level. Thus, as long as francophones could make use of their numbers, the apparatus of the Quebec provincial government remained available to them as a means of furthering their interests (or, at least, those of their spokespeople). Second, the BNA Act guaranteed rights (notably to state-funded education) along religious lines, which, at the time, coincided partly with linguistic ones (there were for all intents and purposes no francophone Protestants, and Catholics were mainly, if not exclusively, francophone). Thus the Catholic Church was assured continued importance in the organization of Canadian society, and a central role in the development of ethnic relations.

The political processes of the nineteenth century can be read as a debate between those who wish to strike a balance between a French Catholic Quebec and an English Protestant Ontario, and those with broader nationalist aspirations, whether French or English. Certainly, French nationalism aspired to the spread of French Catholicism across the country, while many anglophones argued for the rapid assimilation of francophones. Of course, since Canada was a British colony, the British in fact held political power; the question was how the colonial administration used it to advance the interests of the local English-speaking population, or the extent to which they felt it necessary to grant some degree of power to the francophone élite in order to keep them under control. The political compromises of the era, which in fact granted francophones a certain degree of power within Quebec, created some difficulties for anglophones in Quebec and francophones outside Quebec. However, while Quebec anglophones were able to mobilize support for their economic and political interests based on their economic power (McNaught 1969), francophones outside Quebec had largely to rely on the Catholic Church for the advancement of their interests.

Indeed, the political processes of the nineteenth century need to be understood in relation to the hierarchically organized social division of labour which also characterized ethnic relations. In the late part of the eighteenth century and the early part of the nineteenth, this division of labour took the form of British control of trade in valued primary resources (first, furs, and later, lumber) and use of the French as *voyageurs* in the fur trade, as producers of food and in the lumber industry. Isolated on their *rangs*, interacting with the British mainly through the intermediaries of their own middle class and élite, the French had little access to the British, or the British to the French.[7] What interaction there may have been (for example, in the fur trade and the lumber industry) was clearly circumscribed by the unequal economic relations which prevailed there.

In Quebec and eastern Ontario, agriculture was combined with the lumber industry, which, like the fur trade, was controlled by the British.[8] From the point of view of the lumber industry, agriculture provided needed supplies; from the point of view of farming families, the lumber industry provided a supplementary source of income (Gaffield 1987; Welch 1988: 123–125). While the fur trade remained active well into the nineteenth century, it was no longer the sole, nor even the most important, source of wealth in the colony (indeed, it remains a small, if highly visible and controversial, element of the current Canadian economy). Nonetheless, the French retained the same general position in the economy, that of providing food and labour in economic activities controlled by English-speakers; the French élite played the role of broker. Even if the geographical boundary was not as clean as politics would sometimes have it, the social boundary remained hard to cross, and the political use of the geographical distribution of the populations laid the groundwork for the use of the state as a basis for collective mobilization in the future.

Beginning in the 1840s, several processes combined to shift the ecology of ethnic relations in Canada, with major consequences for the French-speaking population of Ontario. First, the Catholic rural families of Quebec had been producing large numbers of children. The population was expanding at a tremendous rate (indeed, the birth rate of Quebec was to remain the highest in North America, and one of the highest in the world, until well after the Second World War). However, the stony soil of the Canadian Shield was unable to produce enough food to support this population (Vallières 1982: 185). At the same time, industrialization had come to North America; in particular, the new textile mills of New England were in great need of labour. The middle part of the nineteenth century saw a large emigration of French-speakers from rural to urban areas, within Quebec, but mainly to urban New England.

Large numbers of Scottish and Irish immigrants began to arrive in Canada, pushed off the land as England began industrializing. The arrival of the Irish was to have a particular impact on the French, and especially those of Ontario. Throughout the nineteenth century and into the twentieth, the Irish and the French battled over the role of the Catholic Church and over their place in it, alternately forming class and religion-based alliances and developing ethnic tensions within the Church and the working class (Choquette 1977, 1987).

The period between the Conquest and Confederation laid the groundwork for the tensions between French and English which have characterized Canadian history ever since. In the context of British economic and political domination, francophones were nonetheless (or perhaps, therefore) able to develop their own sources of political power within Canada, and to create, through the Church and through the political domain, their own symbolic resources and their own avenues of social mobility. The boundary also served the interests of those who became brokers between English owners and rulers and francophone labour. However, this boundary was also contested and crossed at various moments by proponents of assimilation and those for whom religious and class interests overrode ethnolinguistic ones. At the same time, the use of the state to further these varied interests, and the use of ethnic ideologies to further class and religious interests, became established practices; these were to become increasingly important as, after Confederation, francophones became increasingly integrated into the economic and political processes of the Canadian state.

In the following section, I will explore the economic processes which drew francophones increasingly into the English-dominated economy, in a process which undermined francophone institutions but sharpened ethnic stratification. As with any such process, the internal migrations of the post-Confederation period called the nature of the boundary between French and English into question, forcing some to cross it, others to call for its elimination, and still others to reinforce it, in so many attempts to further individual interests through collective mobilization and to further collective interests through individual action.

2.3. Internal migration (1867–1960)

For many in Canada, the draining off to the south of francophone farmers was a source of consternation. For the Catholic Church, it meant loss of direct control over a substantial group of people. For the British, it meant the loss of a source of labour. The result was a major campaign to recruit French-speakers from Quebec (as well as eastern Ontario, Acadia and even New England) to colonize northern Ontario. Through the last half of the nineteenth century, and indeed well into the first part of the twentieth, emigration from Quebec was redirected, as French-speakers, guided by the Church, established agricultural settlements up the Ottawa river and across northern Ontario, participating also in the new zones of exploitation of lumber and minerals, and, after 1880, in the construction of the Trans-Canada railway. While French emigrants to New England eventually assimilated, those within Canada remained socially, and, to some extent geographically, distant from English-speakers, establishing their own cooperatives and credit unions, as well as their own schools (Juteau-Lee 1982: 171). This was also true of the francophone agricultural colonization in the West.

Mining formed the basis of urbanization in northern Ontario. Sudbury, Timmins, Cobalt, Haileybury, Kirkland Lake, Porcupine, all are towns built around the extraction, and in some cases the processing, of minerals: nickel, silver, gold. The mines attracted immigrants from Europe, as well as francophones and anglophones from other parts of Canada, and eventually the local French colonizers also began to participate, sometimes combining mining with farming or work in the lumber industry, but often moving into the towns. In many cases they were able to reconstitute community ties. However, they also came into greater contact with workers of other origins (but with whom they often shared a religion), and the boundary began to be more permeable. This permeability is in part reflected in the rate of intermarriage, which increased in the post-War period and is quite common now (in 1981 it was close to 40 percent; Bernard 1988: 169).

The mines and lumber formed the basis for many of the industries located in urban areas of southern Ontario and Quebec; others were based on manufacturing, but still required locally-produced raw materials in many cases. The urban industries of the south began attracting increasing numbers of francophones from rural areas across Ontario, Quebec and the Maritimes, beginning in the late 1800s and continuing through to the present. A good deal of Ottawa's wealth is based on the lumber industry; however, it is important to recognize the role of the government as an employer and generator of jobs in support sectors after Ottawa became the capital of the country in 1867. In some cases, francophones were actually targeted for recruitment. This was the case in Welland, where the francophone community dates to the recruitment in 1918 of a group of weavers from Montmorency (Quebec) for a newly opened branch of a cotton mill (Beniak et al. 1985; Lapointe et al. 1987; Choquette 1987). The Toronto francophone community dates to the arrival of francophone workers (mainly fron Quebec and Acadia) who came to find jobs in Toronto's manufacturing industries in the 1880s (Maxwell 1977).

It was generally more difficult to reconstitute community ties in the move to the industrial centres of the south than it was in the move from rural to semi-rural or urban centres in the north. In part, the difficulty was linked to the nature of the immigration: only in rare cases, such as that of Welland, did several (or many) families emigrate together, and find themselves numerous and cohesive enough to establish some basic institutions which might serve as reception agencies for future arrivals. Class interests tended to prevail over ethnic ones, and residence patterns were more related to class and to place of employment than to language or religion. The heightened salience of class over other interests was accentuated after the Second World War, as more francophones entered the middle class and the private sector.

As of the 1950s, then, across Canada, francophones generally found themselves concentrated at the lower end of a hierarchy of occupations, along with many recent immigrants. (The indigenous population, by this time, was generally marginalized, its primary means of livelihood destroyed). While still concentrated in Quebec and the Atlantic region, important settlements had been established across the country, especially in Ontario, but also in Manitoba and

Table 1. Francophone assimilation in Canada, 1931–1991.

Year	French ethnic origin	French mother tongue	French spoken at home
1931	2,927,990	2,832,298	
1941	3,483,038	3,354,753	
1951	4,309,326	4,066,529	
1961	5,540,346	5,123,151	
1971	6,180,120	5,793,650	5,546,025
1981	6,984,215	6,249,100	5,923,010
1986	6,985,945	6,354,845	6,015,680
1991	6,146,600	6,505,565	6,211,234

Source: Lachapelle and Henripin 1980: 336; Statistics Canada

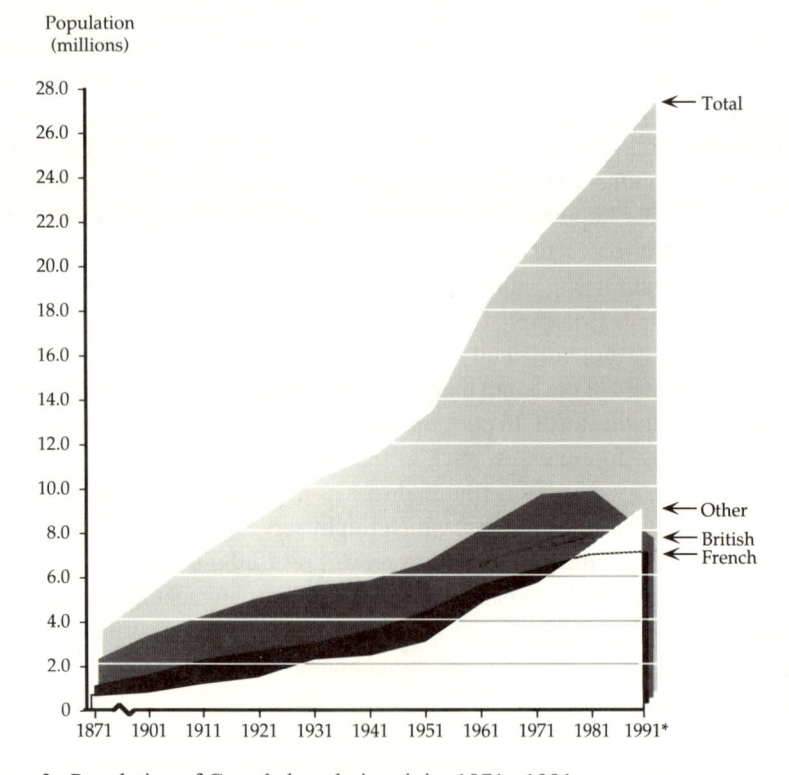

Figure 2. Population of Canada by ethnic origin, 1871–1991.
Source: Lachapelle and Henripin 1980: 336; Statistics Canada
* The 1991 census results for ethnic origin are not strictly comparable to prior years' figures, due to changes in admissible categories, compilation methods and an increase in the number of people reporting "Canadian" as ethnic origin.

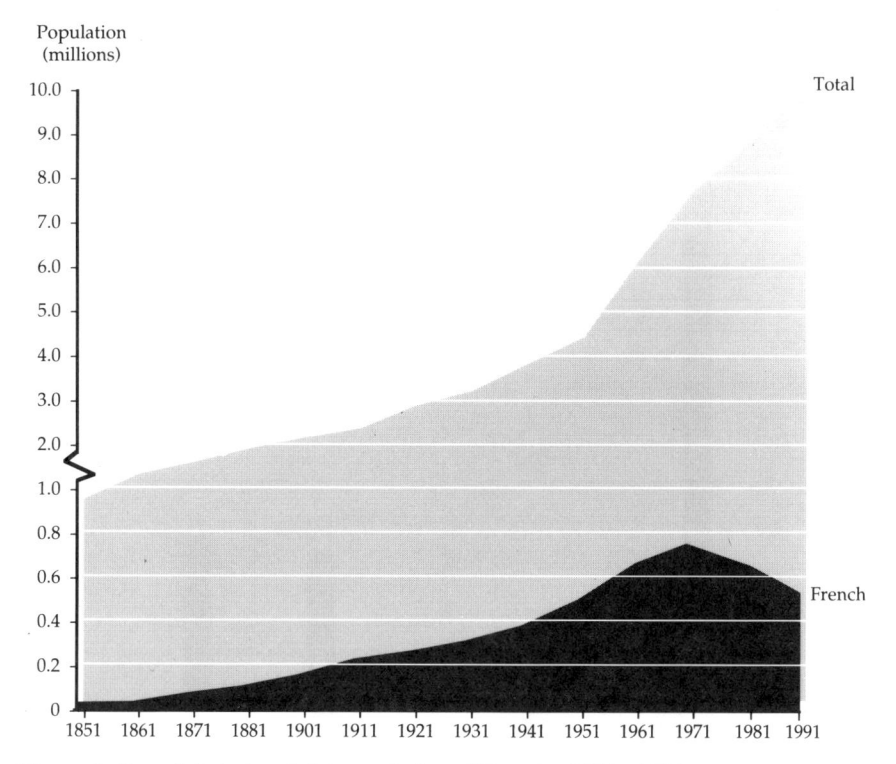

Figure 3. French (ethnic origin) population of Ontario, 1851–1991.
Source: Bernard 1988: 171; Statistics Canada

Alberta, and, to a lesser extent, Saskatchewan, British Columbia, the Yukon and the Northwest Territories.

It is probably best to think of the various forms of economic activity which francophones engaged in as being superimposed one on the other, rather than as a set of successive ways of life each of which eclipsed the last. In addition, individuals often moved back and forth between their region of origin and their region of immigration, and kept family ties with the place they frequently still considered home. Thus if proportionately fewer francophones engaged in farming, fishing and the lumber industry in the 1950s than in the 1850s, nonetheless this way of life had scarcely vanished. In some cases, participation in subsistence farming and in the lumber industry supplemented family incomes now derived mainly from mining. This combination was, of course, more difficult to sustain in the industrial areas of the south. Nonetheless, as a whole, francophones tended to be concentrated at the lower ends of the occupational scale in the primary sector (mainly agriculture, forestry and mining) and the

2   The French in Canada: A historical overview

Population
(millions)

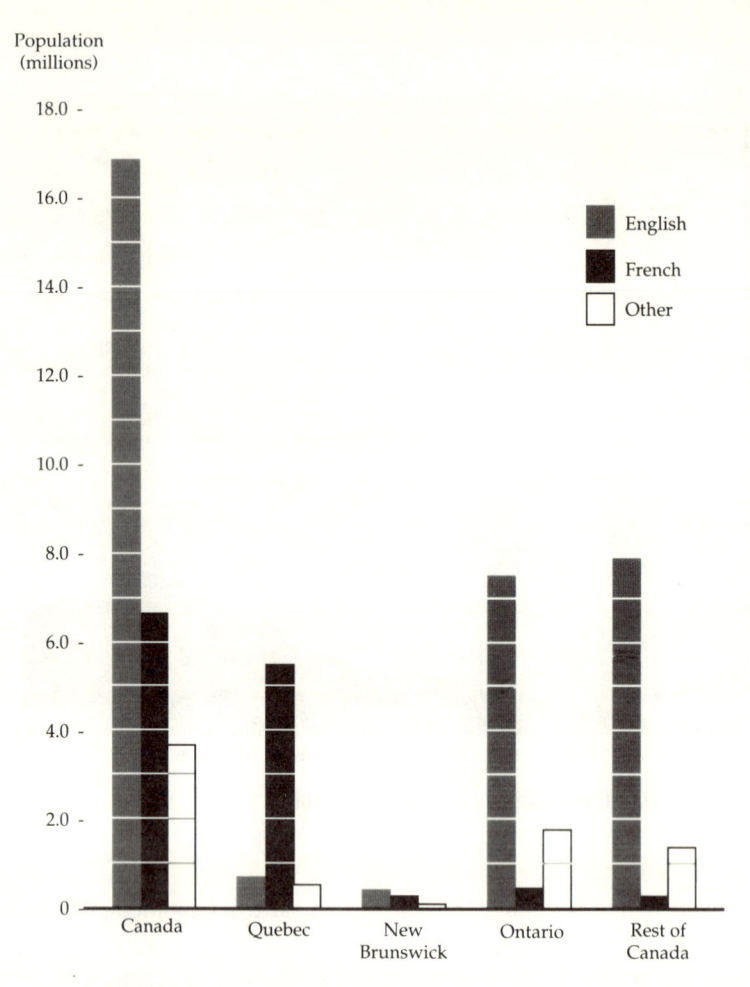

Figure 4. Population of Canada and regions by mother tongue, 1991.
Source: Statistics Canada

secondary sector (industry and construction). Some, mainly women, began to penetrate the growing service sector, and women also entered the teaching and nursing professions (Coulombe 1985). At the same time, the old francophone élite (mainly the clergy, doctors and lawyers) persisted, as did the merchant class. In addition, they were joined by some new members of the bourgeoisie who had entered anglophone-controlled businesses, or who had found jobs as civil servants in the ever-expanding federal government.

By 1960, the French population in Canada, and specifically in Ontario, had survived, but had also undergone some major transformations. The most obvious

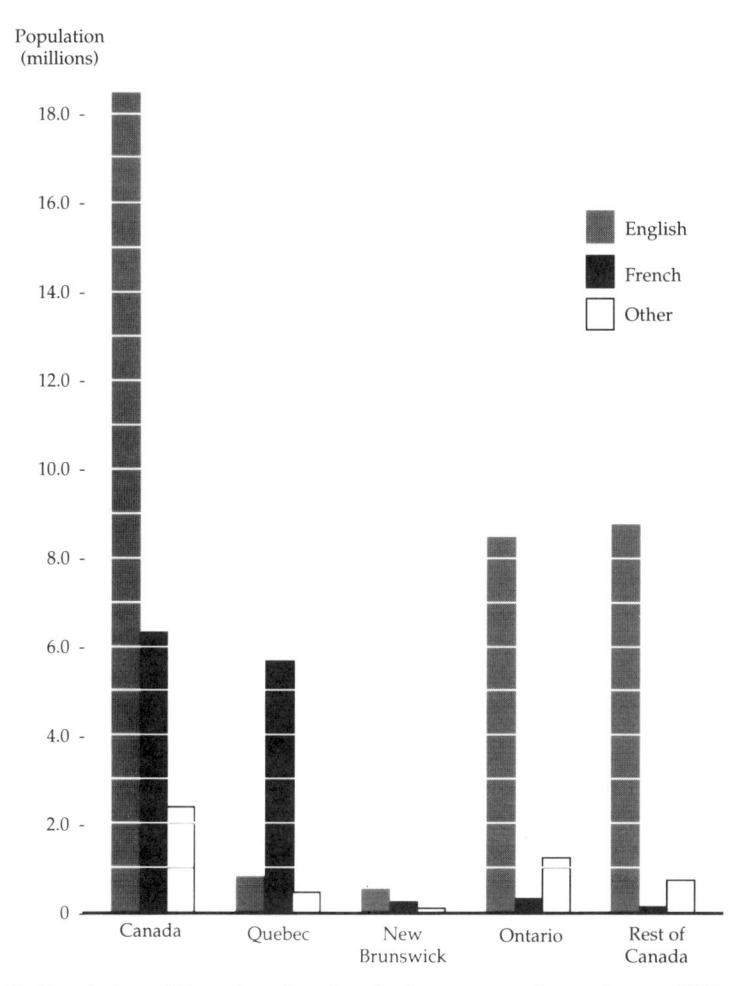

Figure 5. Population of Canada and regions by language spoken at home, 1991.
Source: Statistics Canada

one is demographic: a majority in 1763, francophones constituted a dwindling minority by 1960. The figures and tables here provide some population statistics for Canada and Ontario for the latter part of the nineteenth and for the twentieth centuries.[9] Generally, the difference between the numbers of people who claim French ethnicity, the numbers for whom French is their first language and the numbers who still use French at home is considered an index of assimilation.

In many areas, especially outside Quebec and among the middle class, assimilation had begun to make inroads. The population was increasingly urban, and

2 The French in Canada: A historical overview

Table 2. Francophone assimilation in Ontario, 1931–1991.

Year	Total population	French ethnic origin	French mother tongue	French spoken at home
1931	3,341,683	299,732	236,386	
1941	3,787,665	373,990	289,146	
1951	4,597,542	477,677	341,502	
1961	6,236,092	647,941	425,302	
1971	7,703,106	737,360	482,045	352,465
1981	8,625,107	652,900	475,605	307,290
1986	9,001,170	531,575	485,310	340,545
1991	10,084,885	527,580	464,040	300,085

Source: Bernard 1988: 171; Statistics Canada

increasingly unable to maintain some of its major institutions. It was still, as always, involved in producing wealth for anglophones; however, the new conditions under which this was done drew francophones into greater and greater contact with other groups and tied them ever closer to national and international economic processes.

While it is clear that ethnic categories were central to the social division of labour in Canadian society, as well as to political mobilization, it is less clear how boundary processes actually functioned. At one level, participation in separate social institutions, notably religious ones (but also schools, hospitals, and other institutions), formed part of the separation in the distribution of material and symbolic resources. There was, however, contact across the boundary which must also have served to define it, especially as francophones became increasingly integrated into anglophone-controlled industries and social institutions; this is where language (as well as other forms of communicative behaviour) must have played an important role. The following section is an exploration of the role of language choice and bilingualism in the definition of the ethnic boundary under conditions of social and economic change.

2.4. Ethnic stratification and patterns of bilingualism

Clearly, ethnic stratification contributed directly to the persistence of French despite occasional English attempts at fostering assimilation. Most francophones were able to live out their lives without encountering English-speakers. Those who did so were in many ways in niches which consisted, at least in part, in the management of French-English relations: the clergy and professional élite who managed relations with English governors, and small businessmen and foremen who managed relations between francophone labour and anglophone management in mines, sawmills and factories.

Little is known about patterns of bilingualism in the seventeenth and eighteenth centuries, nor even much about the nineteenth and early twentieth centuries. Certainly, lack of contact among groups was an important element of ethnic relations. Still, it is important to discern the relationship between those without contact and those who lived, daily, on the boundary.

Barth (1969) has argued that there are several ways in which dominant groups can use language to maintain an ethnic boundary, and hence their dominant position. One way is to impose the dominant group's language on subordinate groups; however, one effect of such a strategy is to facilitate incorporation or assimilation, which may or may not always be in the best interests of the dominant group. Many English-speakers in Canada have, in fact, argued this position, and continue to do so, and it has also been, at various points, a component of government policy. It is currently a central element of Quebec government policy, in its attempt to consolidate francophone dominance within Quebec. The exclusive use of English or French in face-to-face interaction, occasionally documented in fiction, or, for example, in the reports of school inspectors (Welch 1988; Gaffield 1987; Choquette 1977), has existed through most of Canada's history, and can be seen as an interplay of strategies of domination and resistance.

A second strategy consists of preventing a subordinate group from gaining access to one's language, thereby retaining privileged access to situations in which the resources under the control of the dominant group are distributed. In Canada, anyone who wants to participate in decision-making at the highest levels of the business sector, for example, had to, and in many cases still has to, speak English. In the large company in which I did my fieldwork in Montreal in the late 1970s, for example, major decisions were made in closed meetings in which English was used, or more importantly perhaps, around the lunch table among anglophones. There are two ways in which this privileged access to language can be maintained. One is for members of the dominant group to become bilingual, refusing to use their own language with members of the subordinate group. The other is for the dominant group to rely on bilingual brokers to manage interactions with the subordinate group, brokers who may be recruited from within their own ranks, from the ranks of a subordinate group, or from a third group altogether.

Elements of all these strategies can be discerned in the limited information available. There is some evidence of limited French spoken by anglophone businessmen, or by housewives who employed francophone women and girls as domestic help. In the company in which I did my fieldwork, most anglophone managers could put together a few words of ungrammatical French; their wives could probably buy food or discuss cooking and housecleaning with their domestic workers in French, but little else. This use of French was (and is) limited, both in its grammatical and lexical scope and in its range of uses. Indeed, the very lack of fluency on the part of these anglophones is a mark of how limited the contact is, how circumscribed by unequal power relations. Lack of fluency can also be seen as a way to mark differences, that is, as a way to avoid being taken for a member of a stigmatized group. Certainly, although within Quebec anglophones are becoming increasingly bilingual, it is still a source of astonishment to francophones to come across an anglophone who speaks fluent Canadian French.

Brokers have also played an important role in the management of ethnic relations. These brokers were drawn from the ranks of francophones and other groups, although they also included members of the English-speaking working class and some English-speaking small businesspeople (Hughes 1943: 82–83).

One demographic study, conducted by Stanley Lieberson in the early 1960s, provides a point of reference (Lieberson 1965, 1970). Lieberson's survey of the distribution of bilingualism in Montreal at that time revealed that the city was inhabited at that time by about 65 percent francophones and 22 percent anglophones, along with about 13 percent speakers of other languages (see also Baillargeon – Benjamin 1980). This population could, however, be described as being made up of four major groups in terms of patterns of language use.

Speakers of languages other than English or French tended to learn English as a second language, although some also learned French. Anglophones tended to be monolingual ("kitchen French" notwithstanding); so did francophone women, most of whom were not in the wage-labour workforce, francophone children under the age of 18, and older francophone males. Francophone males between the ages of 18 and about 55, on the other hand, were mainly bilingual. Lieberson surmised that this was due to the fact that, among francophones, this group and only this group came into regular contact with anglophones as a result of being employed in anglophone-owned factories. While presumably once they retired they did not entirely forget English, they no longer had any occasion to use it, and in any case their proficiency was probably limited due to the conditions of acquisition and use. Interestingly, Cartwright (1982) found a similar pattern among francophones in Northern Ontario in the 1970s: the highest rates of French unilingualism were among children under the age of 14 and adults over the age of 65.[10]

My own ethnography of a Montreal company in the 1970s indicated that the greatest degree of bilingualism among employees of the generation Lieberson would have been examining existed among the foremen and superintendents who were responsible for the articulation between (monolingual) anglophone management and (monolingual) francophone labour (Heller 1982a; Heller et al. 1982). Foremen and superintendents, while usually promoted from the francophone factory floor, also included members of the English-speaking (mainly Irish) working class. By the time of my arrival in 1978, it was much too late for me to reconstruct the conditions of their acquisition of English and the parameters of their use of English and French; the old set of relations had already changed. Still, it was clear that part of the process of boundary maintenance had to do not only with who had access to which languages and under what conditions they might be used, but also with how well each language was mastered. The persistence of non-native-like qualities in the second language was clearly an important way in which it might be possible to be bilingual and yet not threaten the basis of the ethnic boundary: to speak the other language "too well" could be seen as making claims on the roles traditionally reserved for members of that ethnic group, or as inappropriately distancing oneself from one's own.

The role of immigrants as brokers has rarely been explored, although it has been noted that certain groups, such as Jews in the first part of the twentieth century and Italians since the 1950s, have a rate of bilingualism in French and English higher than that of anglophones. Immigrants may have acted as brokers within the working class, or as economic intermediaries, for example, as salespeople. At any rate, Lieberson (1970:93) indicates that in Quebec during the period 1921–1961, there was a gap of approximately 10 percent between the proportion of speakers of other languages who learned French and that of speakers of English, as well as a gap of 40 percent-50 percent between the proportion of immigrants who learned English and the proportion of francophones who did so.

While partial and not wholly satisfactory, the picture that emerges is one in which a strategy of unilingual anglophone domination met not only with francophone resistance, but also could not overcome the economic and institutional barriers which the British themselves had been instrumental in creating. In addition, too great an opening to English could threaten, not the domination of English, but rather the domination of anglophones. Nonetheless, the boundary had to be negotiated, although not at the expense of any loosening of anglophone control. Anglophones and francophones managed these various contradictions through a combination of two strategies.

The first was the use of brokers, drawn from the ranks of class strata (francophone, anglophone and other) at the interface of anglophone management and francophone labour, and at the highest levels among the élite (although it would be surprising if the forms of language in question were similar in these two zones of contact). The second was limited bilingualism among other members of the population, confined to specific situations of interaction and (one is tempted to say calculatedly) involving non-native-like command of the second language. On either side of the boundary, the most important form of linguistic capital was defined in terms of a monolingual norm defined by élites (hence, for example, the constant preoccupation of the francophone élite with the quality of French spoken in Canada). Bilingualism may have been necessary, but it was nothing to be proud of.

After the Conquest, then, francophones remained major contributors to the production of wealth owned and controlled by the English Protestant élite, whether that wealth was in the form of food, furs, lumber, minerals or manufactured goods. Their own élite, including the French Catholic clergy, played an important role in maintaining these relations of power. Finally, these relations were undoubtedly reflected in and constructed through the distribution of access to linguistic capital in the form of proficiency in French and English, and the particular conventions of their use, both in terms of language choice and in terms of deployment of a wider or narrower range of more or less native-like forms within each language. This particular form of border patrol was part of the persistent ethnic stratification which, while it put most French-speakers at an economic disadvantage, also contributed to the maintenance of ethnic boundaries and hence to the survival of French language and culture.

These were the conditions which prevailed just at the point where francophones were becoming not only more integrated into the Canadian economy, but also more aware of the political power available to them. The events of the 1960s, the mobilization of francophones, as a nation, to use control of the apparatus of the state within Quebec to break through the barriers of ethnic stratification, were to have a profound impact on the value of French and English, and in particular, of bilingualism, in the management of relations of inequality and the opening up of life chances in Canadian society. These processes have differentially affected francophones, anglophones and speakers of other languages, inside Quebec and beyond the frontiers of the new nation-state. However, in order to understand those different experiences of Québécois nationalism, it is essential to grasp how the process unfolded first, within Quebec itself.

2.5. The ethnic mobilization of the 1960s

French Canadian nationalism has a long history, but it has taken a variety of forms, and has found a variety of champions. It was for a long time associated with the French Catholic Church and its "mission" in the New World. In the terms of this mission, the French felt that they were designated as playing a central role; they considered themselves, in a sense, as the privileged standard-bearers of the faith. The various manifestations of French Canadian nationalism which we have seen across the nineteenth and twentieth centuries can also be understood as resistance to English pressure to assimilate, or, at the very least, to act as good subjects of the British Empire (for example, by fighting wars as part of the British forces). Finally, it must be understood as a response to the increasing strength of the English industrialists, which both broke down the traditional basis of organization of French Canadian society and cemented the role of the French as subordinate producers within an English-owned system.

Since the 1960s, however, French Canadian nationalism has taken a new form. First, the role of the Church has been considerably weakened, in part by the entry of francophones into urban industrial environments to which the Church was slow to adapt, in part because of a struggle between Church and State for control of social institutions. Second, as part of this struggle, ethnic mobilization has focussed on existing state apparatuses, in particular on the provincial government of Quebec. The old form of pan-Canadian French mobilization has not disappeared, but finds itself in a difficult struggle with the most successful francophone mobilization to date, the one that has used the Quebec state apparatus to permit francophones to gain access to sources of wealth directly and as francophones, that is, without having to assimilate.

Two general processes have contributed to this new form of nationalism and to its relative success as a strategy of ethnic mobilization. The first has to do with the increase in the economic strength of Ontario, and in particular of Toronto (now Canada's financial centre), at the expense of Quebec and Montreal. The second has to do with the expansion of the role of the state, manifested in particular in the growth of civil service bureaucracies at both the federal and provincial levels.

Clift and Arnopoulos (1979) have argued that the shift of the centre of financial decision-making from Montreal to Toronto was linked to the loss of importance of Montreal's geographic location. Montreal's wealth was based on its strategic position in the fur trade; at the confluence of the St. Lawrence and Ottawa rivers, it controlled the passage of goods from inland out across the Atlantic. It was able to continue to use this position to advantage in the lumber industry, and in the export of minerals and wheat, for which it served as rail terminus after the 1880s. Nonetheless, the changing material basis of wealth (from furs to lumber, wheat and minerals) and changes in the mode of transport already weakened Montreal's position. The improvement of shipping on the Great Lakes and the construction of canals from the Lakes to the Hudson and other American rivers shunted a lot of business to the south, and increased the importance of Toronto's location.

After the Second World War, the growth of industry in southern Ontario solidified Toronto's importance. In addition, Toronto financiers were able to gain control of some key areas for the extraction of primary resources, notably the Abitibi-Temiscamingue area straddling the Quebec-Ontario border south of James Bay.

As a result, several adaptations occurred. First, many companies expanded their operations in Ontario at the expense of operations in Quebec; indeed, many shifted their head offices from Montreal to Toronto. Montreal's English-speaking financial community began, around the 1960s, to find that their expertise was needed in Ontario, and that in any case economic opportunities there were greater than they were in Quebec. This led to a sort of vacuum at the management level of private enterprise in the Montreal offices. At the same time, the Montreal offices came to control not the national or international markets where English was most widely spoken, but the regional market of Quebec, dominated by French-speakers. This *succursalisation* 'branchification' (Heller 1989a; Lacroix – Vaillancourt 1981) of private enterprise has become one of the greatest dilemmas of the Quebec private sector, at the same time that it opened opportunities to francophones of which they had previously only dreamed.

While this process of reorganization of the English-speaking Canadian private sector was occurring, profound changes in the francophone community were simultaneously contributing to the redefinition of ethnic relations in Quebec, and ultimately across Canada. Central to these changes was a struggle for control of social institutions between the Catholic Church and the emerging apparatus of the Quebec provincial government.

The Second World War and concomitant industrialization played a role in this struggle. First, they solidified the importance of urban centres as a source of income for individuals and a source of wealth for the community. The move to the city probably broke apart many of the ties between the people and the Church and undermined community ties in general; certainly, it drew the French into national and global networks much more directly than had previously been the case. In addition, through the creation of a new tax base, it was the State, as well as private enterprise, which benefitted from the wealth produced through industry; the State came into a resource base such as it had never had before. By 1960, the Quebec government had managed to consolidate a political and economic power base. The sheer numbers of francophones within Quebec made them available as a forceful political bloc within Quebec and in Canada; in addition, Canadian provinces have a fairly broad scope of action (education, notably, is a provincial jurisdiction), and can make important unilateral decisions. At the same time, especially outside Quebec, these same social processes contributed to increasing francophone assimilation (after 1961, the rate of assimilation could reach 50 percent in areas where francophones formed small minorities of about 5 percent of the local population; Lachapelle 1990). This spectre also served as a rallying point for collective mobilization.

Interestingly, until very recently, the English élite of Quebec had never participated greatly in provincial politics, preferring the arena of Ottawa, probably because until the 1960s there was little real power in Quebec, and also because anglophone interests were certainly national (or international) rather than strictly regional. Of course, anglophones also formed a small minority within the Quebec population. In the early 1960s, then, the provincial government, made up largely of members of the French-speaking élite, voted into power by the French-speaking majority, found itself able to envision a programme of change. It had often been said that the high birth rate of French-Canadians constituted a form of revenge against the English for having conquered Canada; this *revanche du berceau* [revenge of the cradle] became a basis for using political avenues in order to achieve social change. The Quiet Revolution was about to begin.

2.5.1. La Révolution tranquille and its aftermath in Quebec

The term "*La Révolution tranquille*" [the Quiet Revolution] was coined in the mid 1960s to describe the massive non-violent social change which Quebec was undertaking. In the 1950s, Quebec intellectuals, largely drawn from the professional class (and including among them Pierre Trudeau, the future Prime Minister of Canada), were arguing for the necessity for Quebec to modernize: to develop its industrial base, vest greater powers in the state than in the Church, democratize access to education. Beginning in the early 1960s, under a new provincial government, Quebec embarked on just this course. The government, in taking over the major social institutions of Quebec life (notably education and medicine), created fundamentally different conditions of life and also, in so doing, grew into a major bureaucracy. It established a system of socialized medicine, and took control of most medical institutions earlier and to a greater degree than did other provinces. It democratized access to education, standardized it and established public funding through high school. It would later establish the CEGEPs, the *Collèges d'enseignement général et professionnel*, where high school graduates could seek publicly-funded university preparatory or vocational training. Eventually, it also took over a great deal of control of the university system, establishing a province-wide community-oriented "state" university, and binding the existing universities more tightly to the state.

Many of the newly educated found jobs in the recently expanded civil service. But the civil service could not continue to absorb all the members of what was, in essence, an expanded middle class (Clift and Arnopoulos 1979). It is not surprising that the 1960s should have seen the expression of frustration of francophones who, having been subordinate producers in an English-controlled system for so long, were now finding their attempts at moving out of that position hampered by obstacles to access to major forms of wealth in the private sector. Instead, these frustrations led to a collective taking of stock of ethnic relations in Canada. Under the conditions of the 1960s, many francophones opted for a strategy of collective mobilization in order to accomplish their social, economic and political goals. Some individuals did attempt strategies of assimilation; these were occasionally successful, but not always, and the cost was always high. Once a large number of people invested in a strategy of mobilization, of course, assimilation became extremely dangerous, since it threatened the very basis of a collective strategy.

In response to the stirrings of nationalism in Quebec, both the federal and provincial governments undertook reviews of ethnic relations in Canada (Government of Canada 1967–1969; Gouvernement du Québec 1972). The results were not pretty. On the most salient measures of success, namely educational achievement, occupational distribution and income, the French were very low on the scale. In 1961, the only groups lower on the income scale were Italians and Native groups (Lacroix – Vaillancourt 1981). Within Quebec, intellectuals and artists contributed to the collective *prise de conscience*, and culture became a central arena for the construction of a Québécois identity (cf. Handler 1988). On the eve of Canada's centennial celebrations in 1967, French-English tensions were running high, and some people were wondering whom the party was really for.

The basis for mobilization was the numbers of French-speakers who could vote as a bloc in two arenas, the federal and the provincial. At the federal level, French-speakers, especially in Quebec, controlled a large number of seats in the House of Commons. At the provincial level, of course, French-speakers controlled the entire state apparatus. As a result, French-speakers held an important weapon in the federal arena beyond their control of parliamentary seats: they could take themselves out of Confederation altogether, removing the wealth and the market of Quebec from the national network. Many of the political events of the last 25 years can be seen as a tension between francophones' attempts to gain access to social mobility inside and outside Confederation. The question is simply which path to advancement is likely to be most effective, and opinions are divided on that subject. As will be seen, the consequences of this tension for francophones outside Quebec are enormous.

By the late 1960s and early 1970s, then, francophones had begun a process of collective mobilization which aimed at procuring entry for francophones, as francophones, into the existing arenas of power in Canada. It is significant that the aim of mobilization so clearly has been to integrate francophones into national and global networks, that is, to gain entry into an existing economic and symbolic marketplace, and not to construct an alternative one (Bourdieu 1977b; Woolard 1985). Having already entered this world, at the bottom of the scale, francophones are moving to maximize their position, that is, to move upwards within that marketplace, as francophones, without having to pay the costs, and run the risks, of assimilation. In any case, it is not clear what a viable alternative basis for the creation and control of wealth might be, and so, perhaps, mobility in the system in which they were already involved seemed a more evident path. This can be contrasted with the dilemma currently faced by many Native groups, who must choose between participation in a system dominated by Whites, and rejection of that system in favour of former (or at least radically different) ways of life (Heimbecker and Potvin, personal communication; Pauls 1984; Yuzdepski 1983; Gardner 1986; Regnier 1987).

The federal government, whose power depended on Quebec remaining within Canada, had for several years been embarked on a nation-building path (reflected, for example, in the adoption during the 1960s of a national anthem and a new flag which did away with the old symbols of British imperialism; Handler 1988; Breton 1984). In the mid 1960s, it established a Royal Commission on Bilingualism and Biculturalism (sometimes jokingly referred to in English as the Bi and Bi Commission), through which the notion of two founding nations (the French and the English) was developed and modified through reference to the place of those nations in a multicultural society.[11] The federal policy of bilingualism has had many consequences, among them the creation within the federal civil service of bilingual positions, and a recruitment policy designed to increase the numbers of francophones there. Mobilization thus, at least initially, facilitated francophone entry into the federal arena: if Canada was to keep Quebec within Confederation, it had to provide opportunities for francophones outside Quebec, and most especially, within the federal government. Francophones had to be made to feel that they had a stake in Confederation.

Access to the private sector was more difficult. Previous changes had provided the francophones with the qualifications to make them candidates for positions at the management levels of companies and financial institutions, and, as Clift and Arnopoulos (1979) point out, there were increasing numbers of places at those levels in the Montreal offices, places vacated by westward-moving anglophones. Nonetheless, francophone access to the private sector, although not impossible, did prove difficult, no doubt for a number of reasons. In part this may have been because the language of the private sector, embedded as it still was in national and international networks, remained English, and not all otherwise qualified candidates spoke English well enough, or in the right way, to participate. Further, control of hiring undoubtedly remained in the hands of anglophones. In any case, these factors contradicted the purpose of the mobilization, that is, to permit francophones a full range of social mobility without having to rely on knowledge of English or of the anglophones' way of life.

In addition, the provincial government of Quebec did not intervene directly in this area for many years; instead, its action remained limited to the domains which were traditionally under the control of the provinces. The laws passed in the late 1960s and early 1970s focussed on the language of education and on language planning. The rationale was that if the quality of French could be improved, francophones would take more pride in their language, and if more children could be schooled in French, more people would end up naturally using French beyond school age. Legislation regarding francophones has always focussed on language and not on ethnicity; the ethnicity of francophones does not rest on the kinds of ascribed characteristics (such as sex and race) which usually form the basis of affirmative action programs. However, the focus on language raises complicated questions of evaluation, which no piece of legislation has been able to address. This was particularly problematic for Quebec's 1974 law regulating access to English-language schools on the basis of proficiency in English; it proved next to impossible to evaluate that proficiency in a way which interested parties felt was equitable. In addition, focussing on the language of education had no effect on the value of French and English, which had its source elsewhere, in the areas of the private and public sectors where wealth was actually produced.

Eventually, the government of Quebec acted directly: in 1977 it enacted Bill 101, the Charter of the French Language. Among its many provisions, it decreed that only French be considered the language of work, which meant that all internal and external communications, both oral and written, had to be in French only, and that only knowledge of French could be used as a criterion of hiring, although certain exemptions could be granted if a convincing case was made. This legislation had the effect of helping francophones over the hurdles, and management levels of private enterprise became increasingly francophone.[12] The old anglophone recruitment networks have been replaced by new francophone ones. In the brewery, a school- and family-based network was replaced by a system of recruitment drawing on francophones with technical qualifications emerging from recently-established training programmes in CEGEPs and universities. The shift was accomplished primarily through the hiring of new, francophone (and themselves credentialled, technically qualified) staff in the personnel department.

Once this was accomplished, of course, the new francophone managers quickly encountered some of the basic paradoxes of their position. First, they had wanted access to national and international networks as francophones. Their ability to achieve this was in part due to their ability to mobilize collectively as a political and as an economic force, but this was also bound up with the regionalization of the Quebec economy. The scope of action of the new business people was therefore not what it might have been had Montreal still been the financial centre of the country. In order to gain access to that larger network, it was still necessary to learn to speak English, and it was still anglophones who made the decisions at that level. In many cases, the upward mobility of francophones within specific companies and institutions in fact required leaving Quebec altogether (at least temporarily).

For some individuals this has meant, ironically, a renewed threat of assimilation. Others have managed to carve out a specific brokerage niche for themselves: in some cases, they spend a few years learning the ropes and English in head offices or other branches outside Quebec, whereupon they return to Quebec and positions of authority in upper management levels where the articulation between the Quebec and national or international economies occurs. In other cases, the move outside Quebec becomes permanent, but the role remains one of brokerage between an English-dominant head office and its Quebec partners or clients. While the threat of assimilation for the adults in these cases is diminished, given the heavy investment in French, it is still present for their children, growing up removed from the centre of francophone power in Quebec.

Two additional paradoxes have emerged from the success of francophone mobilization in Quebec, both having to do with the identification of ethnic mobilization with control of the apparatus of the provincial government, that is, with the notion of the nation-state. The first has to do with the place of non-francophones within Quebec, and the second with the role of francophones outside Quebec.

Collective mobilization within Quebec was always predicated on the social inequality suffered by francophones identified as a distinct culture. In this way, by appealing to common traditions and common values, mobilization cut across class lines within the francophone community, enabling working-class francophones to see mobilization as potentially at least as much in their interests as it clearly was in the interests of the new middle class. The success of the mobilization has had several effects in this regard. First, it is not clear to what extent the francophone working class has in fact benefitted from the mobilization, nor what might happen should such class divisions become more visible than they currently are. Second, many of the common values and traditions appealed to were directly linked to the way of life of French-speakers under conditions of subordination, and thus are different from, and may even conflict with, those which are emerging out of the new forms of life. However, most importantly, ethnic mobilization for control of the state has run headlong into the problem of belonging, *l'appartenance*, based on citizenship or residence rather than ethnicity (Breton 1984).

The dilemma which francophones in Quebec are facing is largely one of the legitimization of their control of the state, the legitimization of Quebec as the only authority capable of representing francophone interests and the regulation of access to the state as a source of power. Since the discourse of legitimization has been based on the notion that only in Quebec can francophones, whose interests are defined as distinct based not only on historical inequalities but also on a notion of historically-based cultural commonalities (Handler 1988), look after their own interests, it is important not to lose sight of the relative lack of power that francophones continue to have within Canada. In other words, francophones within Quebec must continue to see themselves as dominated in the federal context in order to legitimize their dominance within the provincial context. Further, claims to francophone rights outside Quebec must be forfeited.

In order to solidify francophone dominance within Quebec, the 1977 Charter of the French Language not only decrees French to be the language of work, but also makes French the only official language of the province, limits access of residents to education in English, and requires French to be the only language of public signs (in 1988, Bill 178 specified that this pertains to outside signs; inside businesses with under 50 employees, signs may include other languages, in less prominent characters than the French). There are clearly symbolic aspects to some of this legislation; in addition, in practical, material terms, the law had the effect that all residents of Quebec, no matter what their mother tongue or place of birth, would participate to a much greater extent than before in the social institutions of the francophone majority.

For example, only parents who themselves were educated in English in Quebec (or elsewhere in Canada if they were residents of Quebec in 1977), or (at least one of) whose children already attended English-language schools in Quebec, have the right to send their children to English-language schools. Since most immigrants in the past entered English-language schools, and assimilated or integrated into the anglophone community, this represents a radical shift in orientation. It has also been particularly difficult for French-language schools to adjust, long-accustomed as they have been to a relatively homogeneous student body.[13]

The process of incorporation of non-francophones has acquired increasing importance as the birth rate among francophones has fallen. In a period of about 30 years, Quebec went from having the highest birth rate in North America to one of the lowest (Berthelot 1990: 78; Caldwell – Fournier 1987). According to the Ottawa newspaper *Le Droit*, outside Quebec the birth rate among francophones dropped from 4.314 per 1000 women in 1960 to 1.49 per 1000 women in 1990 (*Le Droit*, 6 June 1990). Immigration has correspondingly increased. Quebec now finds itself faced with the claims to full participation in Quebec society and Quebec social institutions not only of Quebec's anglophones, but also of immigrants of many origins, some of whom already speak some variety of French, but many of whom do not. Indeed Quebec desperately needs these other groups.

However, the presence of immigrants poses a problem. If such residents and citizens are to count fully as Québécois, what of the common heritage, the *patrimoine*, which these groups do not share and which has been the basis for francophone mobilization and the source of legitimacy for their control? The democratic and state-building processes which francophones were able to use to their advantage are now undermining the very basis of their mobilization as a homogeneous group. At the same time, how can francophones maintain an attitude of dominance towards immigrants, or even more so, the native population, when they have been fighting the ill effects of structures of domination themselves?

The second set of paradoxes resulting from the successful mobilization of Québécois francophones has to do with the relationship between francophones inside Quebec and francophones outside Quebec. As indicated earlier, the threat of Quebec's separation from Canada produced at the federal level a commitment to national bilingualism: if it were possible to live in French (or English) anywhere in Canada, a major justification for separation would disappear. At the same time, francophones outside Quebec, who had long been engaged in the same struggle that the Québécois seemed to be winning, became more vocal in claiming their rights.

2.5.2. The impact of Quebec nationalism on francophones outside Quebec

For the francophone communities outside Quebec, however, events in Quebec were something of a double-edged sword. On the one hand, successful Québécois mobilization was causing federal and other provincial governments to wake up and take notice of the inequalities pervading ethnic relations, and Québécois mobilization had the effect of facilitating the mobilization of francophones outside Quebec. On the other hand, it became increasingly difficult for francophone nationalism outside Quebec to appeal to a pan-Canadian sense of nationhood. As a result, francophones outside Quebec have split in their reactions to this situation.

Some continue to think of themselves as French Canadians, and to link their survival to the survival of Canada. For example, consider the call which emanated from the *Centre francophone* of Sault Ste. Marie after the municipal council had adopted a resolution enshrining English as the city's only official language. The following is the suggested text of a letter to be sent to the municipal council:

> *Faisons le Canada!* Canada unite! *Par respect pour les droits des minorités et pour renforcer l'harmonie et l'égalité entre les deux peuples fondateurs, je demande par la présente au Conseil de ville de Sault Ste-Marie de révoquer la déclaration d'unilinguisme du lundi, 29 janvier 1990.*
>
> Let us build Canada! Canada unite! Out of respect for minority rights and to support harmony and equality between the two founding peoples, I hereby request that the municipal council of Sault-Ste-Marie revoke its declaration of unilingualism of Monday, January 29th, 1990.[14]

Others have long since begun abandoning a pan-Canadian sense of nationhood, and articulated their newly forming identities as the Québécois had done, around existing provincial lines. French-Canadians became Franco-Ontarians, Franco-Manitobans, Fransaskois, and so on (Bernard 1988; Lee – Lapointe 1979). In Ontario, some francophones have sought to strengthen the ethnic (as opposed to territorial) component of this identity (and possibly thereby distance themselves from the English-dominated "Ontario") through the use of the terms *Ontarie* and *Ontarois* (Bernard 1988; Juteau-Lee 1980; Lee – Lapointe 1979; Vallières 1982). Each group has begun to construct its own identity through the use of history, folklore and the arts. But this development underscores the facts that the separate history and unfavourable demographics of the other provinces forced francophones outside Quebec to bargain with an anglophone-dominated state apparatus for their rights; unlike the Québécois, nowhere did they have the numbers or other resource base necessary to take control.

However, these two strategies underlie a central dilemma which Québécois nationalism poses for francophones outside Quebec. This dilemma is well illustrated by the different positions taken by the *Fédération des francophones hors Québec* (an umbrella group for francophone organizations outside Quebec, since 1991 known as the *Fédération des communautés francophones et acadienne du Canada*) with respect to the federal government's 1989 Meech Lake constitutional accord. The FFHQ initially opposed the federal government's offer to recognize Quebec as a "distinct society". If Quebec is considered a distinct society it is because it embodies the distinctiveness of francophones; if Quebec lays claim to that status, francophones outside Quebec cannot expect any province but Quebec to look after their interests. For the FFHQ, this would mean, in effect, agreeing to waive the legitimacy of their struggle for recognition in their home provinces. However, the FFHQ later changed its position, since, in the evolution of the debate on the Meech Lake Accord, Quebec began to argue that to oppose the accord was to oppose francophone rights and francophone control of Quebec; it was, furthermore, to "reject" the legitimate place of francophones in Canadian society. The FFHQ not only could not be seen to take that position, but also recognized that the strength of francophone minorities outside Quebec was intimately tied to the strength of Quebec as a political entity.[15]

Worse still, the power of Quebec is predicated on its claim to being the only legitimate representative of francophone interests: the worse things are for francophones outside Quebec, the stronger Quebec's claim to a separate identity. Indeed, this has led to a number of difficult moments in recent events. In 1989, Franco-Albertans went to court to obtain rights to education in their own language; the government of Quebec refused to support their cause, since to do so would provide a precedent for other provincial governments to support anglophone, indigenous and immigrant language rights in education within Quebec. In 1990, when many Ontario municipalities declared themselves unilingual English in a form of backlash at recent extensions of French-language services at the provincial level, many Québécois pointed to this as evidence that it is not possible to live in French outside Quebec, and so the French identity of Quebec must be strengthened, rather than seizing the opportunity to support the rights of francophones within those Ontario municipalities to services in their language.[16]

Francophone power outside Quebec is intimately linked to the strength of Quebec. However, the strength of Quebec is built in large measure on a logic which precludes the continued existence of linguistic minorities with full rights; in particular, it precludes the enlargement and strengthening of the rights of francophone minorities outside Quebec.

In the following section, I will examine more closely what the emergence of Quebec nationalism and the successful mobilization of Quebec francophones has meant for the francophone minority of Ontario. A brief sketch of the history of francophone rights in Ontario, which tended to be articulated through the domain of education, will provide the background for a more detailed examination of the ways in which Franco-Ontarians have mobilized in order to use the apparatus of the Ontario provincial government for the achievement of their own social and economic goals. Finally, I will discuss the consequences of that process for the construction of Franco-Ontarian identity.

2.6. The French-language minority in Ontario

In the 1960s, in some cases independently, and in some cases in response to pressure and encouragement from the federal government and from newly mobilized francophone communities outside Quebec, several provincial governments moved to increase the possibilities their own francophones had for living in French. Each province has its own history and has developed its own dynamic, which I will not discuss at length here. Suffice it to say that francophones outside Quebec enjoy highly variable sets of rights and institutions. At one extreme, there is the Atlantic province of New Brunswick which has the highest proportion of francophones to the total population outside Quebec. In 1969 it declared itself officially bilingual (it remains to this day the only officially bilingual province in the country). New Brunswick also has two parallel school systems, one English and one French. At the other, there are provinces like Alberta, where a member of the provincial legislative assembly was reprimanded for having spoken in French during the course of parliamentary proceedings, and where, until 1990, francophones had to fight on a community-by-community basis for the establishment of French-language schools.[17]

In Ontario, while the government has always been reluctant to move towards official bilingualism, since the late 1960s it has slowly granted increasing rights to the Franco-Ontarian community. Up until the 1960s the Ontario government adopted a variety of stances vis-à-vis the francophone population. For the greater part of the nineteenth century the communities were left more or less alone, sometimes in the explicit hope that assimilation would simply occur. Towards the end of the nineteenth century, however, direct attempts were made to limit francophone rights, notably by limiting French-language instruction.

In 1885, English instruction became obligatory. In 1890, it was no longer permissible to use any language other than English unless the students understood no English. Francophones protected their schools by moving from the public to the separate (Catholic) school system, and by insisting that their children understood no English. Throughout this period Irish and French battled for control of the Church in Ontario; in the end, in order to control "their" religious institutions, the Irish allied with the English Protestants against the French (Choquette 1977). In 1913, the government passed the now infamous Regulation 17, which imposed such impossible conditions on bilingual schools that it blocked their operation. This only served to mobilize the francophone population, and to re-awaken their sense of identity and community. It also contributed to the growth of lay leadership among Franco-Ontarians (Choquette 1977). The schools continued to operate in a semi-clandestine fashion; in 1927 the regulation was neutralized, although it was not finally repealed until 1944 (Choquette 1977, 1987; Mougeon and Heller 1986; Welch 1988).

In the period between 1927 and 1968, French-language education existed in a kind of legal limbo. As part of the Catholic system, schools could only be publicly funded through Grade 10 (Catholic schools had lost the right to public funding for the last three years of high school in 1909). In a few communities, the Church operated *collèges classiques*, private institutions covering the equivalent of the end of high school, for the education of the élite. Anybody else who wanted to pursue education any further had to do so in English. Not surprisingly, the education level of francophones of that generation remained low. Education was, however, an important arena of community mobilization, as it is to this day. The *Association canadienne-française d'éducation de l'Ontario* (ACFEO), an important lay lobbying group, had already formed in 1910, during the difficult period which culminated in the passage of Regulation 17. Serving as an arena for the development of lay leadership, it laid the groundwork for political mobilization. In 1939, a francophone teachers' association, the *Association des enseignants franco-ontariens* (AEFO), was formed, followed in 1944 by a francophone trustees' association, the *Association française des conseillers scolaires de l'Ontario* (AFCSO). Both are important community organizations today. In addition, in 1965, as part of the creation of a network of community colleges of arts and technology, the Ontario government provided for a bilingual campus in Ottawa.

The mobilization of francophones in the 1960s had a direct effect on the degree of support Franco-Ontarians began to receive from their government. The Premier of Ontario embarked on a campaign to prove to Quebec that it was worth staying in Canada, and did this in part by improving francophone rights in his own province. In 1968, the Ontario government agreed to publicly fund French-language education through high school, that is, to the end of Grade 13 (or about age 18), making French one of the province's official languages in the area of education. This had, of course, the effect of drawing francophones closer into the sphere of state control, and loosening the hold of the Church on Franco-Ontarian communities. It also drew francophones into closer contact with anglophones, since the schools in question were to be established within existing (and in almost all cases English-dominated) boards of education. In most cases, francophones were willing to go this route in order to obtain improved educational programs. However, there was one drawback. English-language Catholic schools were already funded by the government through Grade 10, and so it would be possible for French-language schools to remain in the Catholic system until that point as well. However, the government was only prepared to fund French-language education in Grades 11 through

13 through the public system, as it was already doing for English-language schools.

Francophones were thus faced with the choice of having to continue to fund the last three years of high school themselves, as English Catholics did, or switching to the public system at the high school (Grades 9 through 13) level. Switching to the public system meant creating much wider access to high school, but it also meant losing a certain measure of control. This caused great debate and dissension in most communities, but eventually most Catholic *collèges* closed down, and new public high schools opened. However, for individuals, this frequently created a dilemma. While it was possible to send one's child to a Catholic French-language elementary school, it was necessary to choose between language and religion at the high school level. Not all families chose to remain in the French-language schools.

The shift from private *collèges* to public high schools was not always accomplished easily, and could be particularly problematic in areas where no French-language high school had previously existed: the English-dominated school boards which were suddenly responsible for the creation of French-language high schools did not always react graciously, and in some areas francophones had to fight hard for their rights (cf., e.g., Sylvestre 1980; Juteau-Lee 1982; Arnopoulos 1982).

In some communities, however, these schools were bilingual (the so-called *écoles mixtes*) rather than entirely French. While in principle this might have meant a full range of programs in each language, in practice there have often been fewer courses offered in French than in English. In any case, students are mostly free to choose, and enrollment in (and hence perceived demand for) courses with French as the language of instruction tends to decline (Churchill et al. 1985). The reasons for this are complex, but are clearly related to the perceived value of English and of certification from an English-language educational institution. As well, there is a sentiment among many francophones that the highest value resides in bilingualism, which can best be achieved through participation in domains of both languages. For this reason, many politicized Franco-Ontarians oppose bilingual schools, calling them "*foyers d'assimilation*". Frequently, this division falls along class lines, with the upper-middle and middle classes (as well as the intellectuals) supporting French-only schools, and the lower classes the *écoles mixtes*; this has led to bitter fights within some Franco-Ontarian communities (cf., e.g., Lapointe et al. 1987 concerning such debates in Welland).

These debates, in one form or another, occurred in many areas. For example, in Toronto in the early 1960s there was still only one elementary school (established in 1887), attached to the parish of Sacré-Coeur. This school had been French and then English; in 1928 it became bilingual. However, its major clientele was always working class. By the early 1960s there was a growing French-speaking middle class in Toronto, comprised mainly of Quebec and European businesspeople and intellectuals (Maxwell 1977). These families lobbied for, and obtained, a school closer to their class interests; Ste-Madeleine was opened in 1966. With much difficulty, a *collège* was also opened; it experienced several moves and changes of administration in its ten-year (1959-1969) history. In 1968, after much discussion, and some dissension, the decision was made to take advantage of the Robarts government's offer. The *collège* was closed down, and in 1969 the École secondaire Étienne-Brûlé was opened, named for the young French explorer who had been the first white person to set foot in what is now Ontario, and who, in fact, explored the Humber river, which now forms the western boundary of the City of Toronto. The school still exists, and is now part of the recently created French-language public board of metropolitan Toronto.

In the subsequent fifteen years, the government acted only slowly to bolster the rights of francophones. The Education Act of 1974 specified rights of access to French-language education; in particular, it guaranteed provision of services only "where numbers warrant". In the following years, rights in education were consolidated, and new schools were opened in areas where they had not previously existed. This was notably the case in Toronto, where three Catholic elementary, two public elementary schools and, eventually a public high-school level "module" (a French-language instructional unit housed within an English-language school) were opened over the course of the decade. In the late 1970s, francophone trustees won the right to establish *Comités consultatifs de langue française* in boards where they were a minority. These CCLFs, composed of elected francophone community representatives as well as representatives of the (usually mainly anglophone) school trustees, were permitted to advise the board at large on matters pertaining to French-language schools, although they exerted no direct control over them.

Bilingual programs with access to earmarked government funds were extended to four more community colleges (in Welland, North Bay, Sudbury, Timmins and Cornwall) and to three universities which had independently begun bilingual programs (the University of Ottawa had been providing programmes in French and English since the middle of the nineteenth century; Glendon College of York University, in Toronto, and Laurentian University, in Sudbury, were, however, not established until the 1960s). In 1972, the government established the position of Assistant Deputy Minister for Franco-Ontarian education within the Ministry of Education. In 1980, it established an advisory committee on Franco-Ontarian education (the *Conseil de l'éducation franco-ontarienne*, or CEFO). The role of both the Assistant Deputy Minister and of the CEFO was, however, largely limited to giving the government advice in the area of Franco-Ontarian education.

Outside the area of education, there was even less change in provincial legislation and provincial services. In 1974, the province established an advisory committee, the *Conseil des affaires franco-ontariennes*, or CAFO, whose job was to advise the government in all areas of francophone affairs save that of education. From 1977 to 1985, it reported to the government coordinator of French-language services (a position created in 1977). In 1985, the CAFO was disbanded, and replaced by the *Office des Affaires francophones*, under the aegis of a cabinet minister granted the sub-portfolio of "Francophone Affairs".

The Franco-Ontarian community began organizing itself to respond to this new basis for the development of their community, to learn how to engage their new interlocutor, the anglophone state, and to define for themselves a new identity and new sets of goals, building on and also responding to events in Quebec. As in Quebec, artists, notably rock and folk musicians and playwrights, engaged in the task of constructing this new Franco-Ontarian identity (Arnopoulos 1982). In 1968, the major francophone lobbying group, the *Association canadienne-francaise d'education de l'Ontario* dropped the word "*éducation*" from its title, thereby symbolically extending the scope of its interests and concerns (Jackson 1988: 121).

While the overall level of education achieved by Franco-Ontarians did rise during the 1970s, it remained lower than the Ontario average (Churchill et al. 1985; ACFO 1985). In addition, the assimilation rate continued to be high (Castonguay 1977; Bernard 1988)[18] and Franco-Ontarians tended to remain concentrated in lower-paying jobs in sectors of the economy which were becoming increasingly marginal (Juteau-Lee 1982; ACFO 1985; Mougeon – Heller 1986). The new Franco-Ontarian élite, bolstered by increasing numbers of teachers and civil servants (Juteau-Lee 1982; Welch 1988: 304–305), continued to mobilize to address these persistent problems. Their strategy, however, has remained largely the same: lobby the government to increase French-language services, particularly in the area of education.

In the course of the 1980s, several political events had an impact on the Franco-Ontarian community and in particular on its educational system. Notable among them was the repatriation, in 1982, of the Canadian Constitution, also known as the Charter of Rights and Freedoms (see section 2.0.). Among the Charter's many provisions, Article 23 defines who may and who may not send their children to minority-language schools (English-language schools in Quebec and French-language schools outside of Quebec). Article 23 states that parents who are:

(1) Canadian citizens
   (a) whose first language learned and still understood is that of the English or French linguistic minority population of the province in which they reside, or
   (b) who have received their primary school instruction in Canada in English or French and reside in a province where the language in which they received that instruction is the language of the English or French linguistic minority population of the province, have the right to have their children receive primary and secondary school instruction in that language in that province.
(2) Citizens of Canada of whom any child has received or is receiving primary or secondary school instruction in English or French in Canada, have the right to have all their children receive primary and secondary school instruction in the same language.
(3) The right of citizens of Canada under subsections (1) and (2) to have their children receive primary and secondary school instruction in the language of the English or French linguistic minority population of a province
   (a) applies wherever in the province the number of children of citizens who have such a right is sufficient to warrant the provision to them out of public funds of minority language instruction; and
   (b) includes, where the number of those children so warrants, the right to have them receive that instruction in minority language educational facilities provided out of public funds.

The Charter of Rights and Freedoms has had an impact on Franco-Ontarians in a number of ways. I have already discussed the tensions surrounding the Meech Lake and Charlottetown Accords, designed to permit Quebec to sign the Charter while feeling that its rights are protected. Second, as will be seen in more detail in Chapter 4, Article 23 has had a particular impact on Franco-Ontarian education. During the course of the 1970s, Franco-Ontarian schools had often been obliged to accept children whose proficiency in French was less than complete. In some communities, there was pressure to establish admissions committees to screen applicants. Since Ontario was a signatory to the Charter it is bound to some extent by Article 23. As a result, admissions committees can now only deliberate cases which fall outside the rights defined by the Charter.

Finally, the wording of Article 23 has been taken as the basis of a court challenge with the goal of obtaining greater francophone control of French-language minority education. In 1984, the *Association canadienne française de l'Ontario* took the province to court, arguing that the French version of section

3(b), which contains the phrase "*établissements d'enseignement de la minorité linguistique*" ("minority language educational facilities" in the English version) had to be taken to mean schools controlled by the linguistic minority. It was manifestly not the case, outside of a few boards in eastern Ontario where francophones actually formed a local majority, that francophones were able to control their schools: they voted for trustees along with everyone else, and only in some communities had access to *Comités consultatifs de langue française*, which, as mentioned above, had no decision-making power or budgetary control. The case was won, and in 1986, Bill 75, guaranteeing minority control over their own schools, was enacted by the new Liberal government which had come to power in Ontario in 1985.[19]

In 1984, as one of its last acts, the Conservative government agreed to publicly fund the separate school system through to the end of high school. This move was probably intended as a form of conciliation to anglophone and immigrant Catholics; indeed, the arrival of hundreds of thousands of Italian, Portuguese and East European Catholics through the 1960s, 1970s and 1980s had massively reinforced the Church and the separate school system. The government said nothing about what this might mean for francophones, and it is entirely possible that this issue was given little thought.

However, within the Franco-Ontarian community this move reopened the debates of the 1960s: should French-language high schools be Catholic or not (cf. Frenette – Gauthier 1990)? Communities reacted in a variety of ways. In some, such as Timmins, the public French-language high school was simply transferred to the separate board; in others, such as Iroquois Falls, the same move was eventually accomplished, but not without debate. In still others, the public high school remained open, although in some areas Catholic high schools were also created. This was the case, for example, in Sudbury and Toronto.

As will be seen in Chapter 4, the possibility of establishing French-language schools in either Catholic (separate) or public systems has led to some interesting changes. In some communities, notably Sudbury, Timmins, Thunder Bay and Sault Ste. Marie, some francophone parents have become frustrated with the French-language schools within the Catholic board. They claim that the boards permitted the admission of too many children who speak little or no French outside school, and that this has had a negative effect on their children, both in terms of the threat of assimilation and in terms of their children's access to knowledge through the medium of the French language. They thus lobbied the public board for the creation of French-language schools where they would not have to live with the consequences of having admitted non-francophones before the Charter of Rights and Freedoms came into effect, and where the linguistic criteria of admission for those who do not have rights according to the Charter would be more stringent.

In Sudbury and Timmins these efforts have been successful. In Sault Ste. Marie and Thunder Bay they unleashed a strong negative reaction not only at the board level but also at the level of the municipal government, which then moved to make English the only official language of the city. Sault Ste. Marie's move (the irony of its French name has not been lost on commentators) occasioned similar initiatives elsewhere in Ontario, and indeed became a cause of national debate on the state of French-English relations. Many argued that the "national malaise" had not been so deep since the mid 1960s.

The English backlash has not really been primarily directed at the schools issue. Clearly a complex event, it is tied up with Quebec nationalism, recent negotiations over the extent to which the federal government will recognize Quebec as a "distinct society", and, indeed, most of the events and processes of the last 25 years of negotiations over French-English relations and the role of the state: the federal policies of bilingualism and biculturalism, Quebec's Charter of the French Language, its 1980 failed referendum on sovereignty-association, its recent legislation on the language of public signs and, more immediately, Ontario's Law on French-Language Services. The debates concerning the "English only" movement will be discussed further in Chapter 3: the texts of the municipal resolutions, and subsequent comment on them, reveal widely divergent visions of the relationship between language, equality and the state.

In 1986, the provincial government passed legislation guaranteeing provincial services in French in designated areas of the province. To be a designated area, a region must include 5,000 francophones or francophones must constitute 10 percent of its population. In practice, Bill 8 (as it is commonly known, although, of course, it ceased to be a Bill once it was enacted into law; the official title is "An Act to provide for French-Language Services in the Government of Ontario"), which came into effect in 1989, covers more than three-quarters of the territory of the province. It directly affects only provincial government ministries and related agencies (and, of course, those who deal with them). It guarantees only that clients may receive services; the working language of the provincial government remains English.

The impact of Bill 8 on the Franco-Ontarian community, beyond involving it in renewed tensions with a threatened anglophone population, is largely to bind it further to the state. Indeed, Bill 8 has opened up employment opportunities within the provincial civil service, and many of the best and the brightest among Franco-Ontarians have done a tour of duty there. The structure of implementation includes support for the minister responsible (through the *Office des Affaires francophones*), the (now defunct) *Commission des services en français* and positions for French-Language Coordinators within each ministry. The advisory function ensured by such committees as the CAFO and the CEFO has thus been absorbed directly into the government bureaucracy. The CEFO was disbanded in 1990. In place of these bodies, the government established yet another committee, with representatives from a variety of fields within the Franco-Ontarian community. However, this new committee and, in most instances, the francophone bureaucrats have only limited control over francophone affairs, and still retain an advisory function which limits their scope of action.

Over the course of the last twenty years, Franco-Ontarians have become more and more closely involved with the provincial government. Their class structure has become diversified, and so has the range of populations from which they draw, as more and more immigrants who have French as a first or second language arrive on the scene. On the one hand, strengthening group identity has resulted in progress, in terms of increased access to resources like education and jobs. On the other hand, the results of that mobilization have drawn francophones farther and farther into mainstream life, and rendered the quality of their everyday experience less and less distinct from that of so many others who share their way of life.

In these respects, Franco-Ontarians share the experience of the Québécois, and indeed, the course of events in Ontario has not only been profoundly influenced by Quebec, but also emerges from many of the same sources. Nonetheless, there is a crucial difference, in that Franco-Ontarians cannot hope to take control of the state in the way that the Québécois have done; instead, they have chosen to use the state to the best of their ability in order to set up parallel institutions. In addition, Franco-Ontarians must resolve the contradiction inherent in Quebec nationalism, which simultaneously provides support for and undermines the legitimacy of the presence of French outside Quebec. The way in which they do so will have an impact on the possibilities for Franco-Ontarians to develop, as francophones, over the course of the years to come.

2.7. Franco-Ontarians in the 1990s

In the 1980s, Franco-Ontarians concentrated their efforts on the use of the courts and of government to achieve greater control over their institutions, using Franco-Ontarian education at the primary and secondary levels as their battleground. That battle largely won, they successfully lobbied the government for the creation of a French-language community college in the Ottawa area, which opened in 1990. Current efforts are directed towards the establishment of additional French-language community colleges in northern and southern Ontario, a Franco-Ontarian university, and the expansion of programs at all levels beyond the traditional humanities and social sciences, to include natural sciences and technology.

All these efforts are directed at the same time towards greater institutional autonomy and towards the integration of francophones into provincial, national and international networks, which has to be balanced against the maintenance of ethnic boundaries on the basis of which this integration was achieved. In recent position papers the *Conseil de l'éducation franco-ontarienne* (CEFO 1989) and the *Association canadienne-française de l'Ontario* (ACFO 1989) articulate this double objective. The CEFO argues that:

> (...) [d']une part, [la collectivité franco-ontarienne] veut conserver ses traditions et, d'autre part, elle veut s'ouvrir au monde moderne et aux valeurs universelles. [... on the one hand, the Franco-Ontarian community wishes to retain its traditions and, on the other, it wishes to open up to the modern world and to universal values.] (CEFO 1989 (1): 3)

The ACFO argues that education, and in particular the university, is central to Franco-Ontarian aspirations. Indeed, it argues, the possibility for the Franco-Ontarian community to fulfill *"(...) ses besoins dans le nouvel ordre d'une économie mondiale à laquelle elle veut participer pleinement"* [... its needs in a world economy in which it wishes to participate fully] rest on its ability to control its educational institutions and (in part in so doing) to maintain its sense of identity (ACFO 1989:1):

> Il faut enraciner le système d'éducation post-secondaire dans un cadre culturel français, déterminé, rattaché avant tout à la vie quotidienne des Franco-Ontariens. [It is necessary to root the post-secondary educational system in a definite French cultural framework which is attached above all to the daily life of Franco-Ontarians.] (ACFO 1988: 6)

Because of the goals and context of mobilization, Franco-Ontarians must manage three forms of opposing forces or tensions. The first is the tension between Quebec and Canada, between knowing that their fate is dependent on the strength of Quebec and the realization that Quebec's strength rests in part in its ability to identify francophones exclusively with its territory and its state apparatus.

The second tension is one that is shared by francophones in Quebec: the tension between the maintenance of a sense of identity and full participation in global economic networks. Central to the argument of Franco-Ontarian activists is the notion that full access cannot be achieved unless Franco-Ontarians are able to maintain a separate sense of identity and control a set of institutions which will allow them to define the best means to their ends. Their goals are not different from those of other groups; however, they argue, they must follow their own path to those goals.

To the extent that Franco-Ontarians are successful in this, they must manage a third tension, one already manifested more openly in Quebec: the regulation of access to the valued resources that they themselves control. In part, this has to do with the management of relations of inequality between francophones of Canadian origin and more recent arrivals, as well as across class lines (Bernard 1988). Franco-Ontarian integration into the economic and political networks of the province, the country and beyond brings them into closer contact with others who share Franco-Ontarians' evaluation of the worth of Franco-Ontarian resources, notably of their language. In the following chapter, I will explore the shifting value of French and English as valued resources and how their use in regulating access to other symbolic, as well as material resources, underlies the current dynamic of French-English relations in Canada, and, in particular in Ontario.

Chapter 3
Language in the ideology and politics of ethnic mobilization

3.0. The contested terrain of language

On January 29, 1990, the council of the Corporation of the City of Sault Ste. Marie passed the following motion:

> Whereas the City of Sault Ste. Marie is composed of many different ethnic groups, languages and cultures;
> And whereas the City of Sault Ste. Marie has always shown respect for each of these cultures by providing preferential treatment for none;
> And whereas the City of Sault Ste. Marie has throughout its history had one common working language for all of its written and oral communications, which is English;
> And whereas the preferred common language of commerce, business, trade, science and normal everyday activities is English;
> Now therefore be it resolved that the Corporation of the City of Sault Ste. Marie in the interests of maintaining goodwill, harmony and sound and responsible fiscal management continue as it has in the past to accept the use of English as the official language of communication with its citizens and all levels of government, thereby demonstrating the concept of equality for each ethnic, cultural and language group in its jurisdiction.
> And further resolved in accordance with the provisions of the Municipal Act of Ontario Part VII and more specifically Section 104a of said Act the Council of the Corporation of the City of Sault Ste. Marie declares English to be the official language of the said Corporation.

This resolution triggered the latest in Canada's waves of linguistic crises. It was, of course, not an isolated event, but rather part of a process which had been developing for many years. It did, however, become a focus for a heated, emotionally-charged debate over the value of French and English and their role in the everyday lives of ordinary Canadians. If the story of the Sault Ste. Marie resolution is worth telling, it is because it reveals many aspects of the ways in which language serves as a battleground for the definition and advancement of specific ethnic and class interests.[20] Perhaps most importantly, it reveals ways in which those interests are pursued through the development of discourses which are, superficially at least, about something else: national unity and cultural difference, simple economics and rich heritages, tolerant neutrality and racist bigotry.

The Sault Ste. Marie resolution was one of a series of such declarations of English monolingualism which Ontario municipalities had been debating since some time in the 1980s. Most of these city council motions had been passed in small municipalities of central and eastern Ontario, generally in areas with little or no francophone population. For the most part, they had been instigated by local members of the Association for the Preservation of English in Canada (APEC), a right-wing language rights group founded in Toronto in the late 1970s. (APEC's central argument is that official bilingualism creates the conditions for a francophone takeover of Canada.) For many months, local small-town English-only resolutions received little attention; while usually reported in the press, they were frequently dismissed as the actions of right-wing fringe groups in peripheral regions. By early 1990, indeed, only about 35 of Ontario's 839 municipalities had passed such resolutions, and some had explicitly passed opposite resolutions supporting bilingualism (after 1990 the movement, such as it was, lost steam).

The Sault Ste. Marie resolution, like so many of the others, was initiated by a local APEC-affiliated group, the SAPELR (Sault Ste. Marie Association for the Preservation of English-Language Rights). Unlike the others, it immediately received national attention. For the first time, such a resolution had been passed in a large urban area of some importance to the provincial economy. In addition, the Sault has a relatively large francophone population, one that is fairly well organized, and possesses institutions and networks of its own; some of its members had, indeed, been lobbying recently for increased services and a more extensive and integrated institutional base. It began to look as though English-rights activists were gaining more power than most people had thought possible.

In discussions of the resolution and its motivations, three events have been mentioned. These three events, as symbolic points of repair, indicate the ways in which the Sault Ste. Marie City Council, as well as the many commentators on the Council's activities, think about what French and English represent in their lives. The discourse which calls into play and constructs these three key events is designed to legitimate actions which have language as their focus, that is, which take language as a terrain on which to struggle for the advancement of certain ideas, and hence of certain interests.

The first event is the request in 1989 by a small number of francophone parents to have a French-language school established in the public school board (this request has so far been denied). French-language schools had long existed in the Catholic school board in the Sault, but a group of parents increasingly felt that too many English-speaking children were enrolled there, and that it was difficult for their children to preserve their language under those circumstances.

3.0 The contested terrain of language

The establishment and recognition of francophones' educational rights through the Ontario court decisions of the mid 1980s emboldened these parents (like other parent groups elsewhere in the province) to seek educational services which corresponded more closely to their idea of what French-language education should be about: an educational system which would serve the interests of those who identify themselves as francophones, and not avenues of access to French for people who do not count themselves as francophones. In addition, at about the same time, the francophone community of the Sault began lobbying for the establishment of a community centre; indeed, the idea was to open the school alongside the community centre, in order to provide a stronger institutional base for the community and to tie the school more tightly to other community activities and members.

A second event was the implementation in November 1989 of Bill 8, the Ontario government law guaranteeing provincial government services in French in designated areas of the province. While the law says nothing about municipal services, Sault Ste. Marie and other city councils have argued that the logical next step will be to impose precisely that level of service without adequate financing.

These same people were concerned, as was Council, that the province was contemplating extending the obligations set out in the French Language Services Act to include municipal services within designated areas (including Sault Ste. Marie). While it is true that the *present* wording of the legislation does not make such services mandatory, there are several factors which have caused municipalities real concern about what the next steps might be.

The text of the resolution itself establishes a way of discussing these two events. The references to showing "respect for [different ethnic groups, languages and cultures] by providing preferential treatment for none" and to "goodwill and harmony" can be seen as ways of addressing the specific requests of francophone parents for educational and cultural services. "Goodwill and harmony" and "the respect of cultures" depend on equal treatment for all. The best way to achieve this, it is argued, is to use one language, English. English is thereby presented as a neutral language, favouring no one group.

A letter sent by the mayor of Sault Ste. Marie to the City Council on February 19, 1990, uses similar language:

> The resolution was no doubt, in part, an expression of frustration by not only Council, but many in the community who were concerned because of some demands in the last few years for what appeared to be special status schools and a cultural center (...) The resolution acknowledges that the English language has been accepted by all, regardless of ethnic background, as the common language by which we do all our business in this City. The resolution attempts to avoid divisiveness by building on our similarities (...)

The second theme is addressed in the resolution through references to "sound and responsible fiscal management". The Mayor's letter elaborates at some length on this theme:

> (...) the resolution makes a statement about our ability to finance the business of the City Corporation being conducted in more than the one language which language has satisfactorily served all of us over the years. There is no question that the resolution is in response to the French Language Services Act and our fear that the Province might just take the next step that it is being encouraged to take. Our fear is that the extra service will be one that practically speaking is not required in our city and fiscally speaking is not affordable, regardless of which level of government is paying, given other priorities which have been the subject of "tight budgets".

The Mayor and the City Council make the argument that their resolution is a question of fiscal responsibility: providing services in two languages costs more than providing them in one. Indeed, it costs too much.

Finally, the 1989–1990 wave of municipal declarations of English unilingualism in Ontario (of which Sault Ste. Marie's was only the most visible) was also frequently placed in the context of Quebec's language legislation, and particularly of its controversial law mandating unilingual French signs on the exteriors of private enterprises. The argument advanced is one of provincial parity: either all provinces (including Quebec) should make special provisions for their linguistic minorities, or none should. If Quebec can legitimately seek French monolingualism, then Ontario should be free to establish itself as an English monolingual province.

The Sault City Council's resolution was met with applause from some corners and accusations from others. The applause was presented on most of the same terms as those offered as justifications of the resolution. The following example, perhaps extreme but nonetheless telling, is from a letter to the editor of *Sault This Week*, published March 14, 1990.[21] The writer's first premise is that the City Council affirms "equality for all languages and cultures, with English as the common official language. Citizens of all races believe it is good economics and common sense." Indeed, the writer argues, this position is so reasonable and natural that it is shared by "ordinary" francophones:

> Ordinary French Canadians, who don't mind having one official language and one nation are put in a bad position. To francophone groups, they are "ashamed of their language", while, on the other hand, an angry and frustrated majority might think they are part of the problem.

Francophones' demands are presented as the position of a small group:

> Ottawa has developed a new group of "Francophones-First", who are dividing French-Canadians and demanding special status and rights. These people label any opposition as anti-french bigotry. I think it is very important to identify this elite francophone power group who demand everything on the basis of their racial priority.

3.0 The contested terrain of language 83

The writer contrasts a reasonable and fair position, held by the majority of "ordinary" people, which argues that equality for all is achieved through the dominance of one language, with a position presented as based on the interests of a few, paradoxically accusing the majority of bigotry while making an essentially racialist, "special" case.

To make matters worse, the elected representatives of the people are imposing on the majority the will of the minority, in this writer's view:

> Now in Ontario, politicians and editors are saying Bill 8, The French Language Services Act, will not cost municipalities a penny, somebody else will pay for it. Who are they kidding? Governments have no money except from taxes, so the people of all municipalities will pay for Bill 8, and bilingualism and french only schools, and Sudbury Laurention campus on the French Riviera,[22] and Francophone Summits, and pay... and pay... and pay... how much federal and provincial money, status and rights can francophones use, before becoming a power none dare challenge?

The message is clear: all taxpayers are expected to fund activities and institutions which will have the effect in the long run of increasing the power of francophones at the expense of other groups.

The central argument of this discourse, shared by the City Council of Sault Ste. Marie, and by public statements by members of the Association for the Preservation of English in Canada (APEC), is that social equality among ethnolinguistic groups can only be achieved through the use of one language. English is presented as neutral, as providing equal opportunities for all. The fact that English is the native language of one of Canada's ethnolinguistic groups is not considered a relevant point. During a televised debate in March 1990 on *The Journal*, a "newsmagazine" show which until 1992 followed the nightly Canadian Broadcasting Corporation news, Ron Leitch, the president of APEC, argued that to accord French-language rights to francophones was to accord special rights to one group. Don Boudria, a federal member of Parliament representing a bilingual region of eastern Ontario, pointed out to him that instead, APEC's position accorded special rights to one group, anglophones. Mr. Leitch's response was "Well, Mr. Boudria, I can't talk to you, because you're out in left field without a mitt!"

The accusations levelled against the Sault Ste. Marie City Council, and Council's response to them, equally reveal differing ideologies concerning language and equality in the Canadian state. The accusations principally took two forms: the City Council was described as bigoted, even racist, and/or was taken to task for threatening Canadian national unity. In order to counter these accusations, on February 19, 1990, the City Council passed a second resolution:

> Whereas the council of the City of Sault Ste. Marie by resolution dated January 29th, 1990 declared English to be the official language of the said Corporation;

And whereas several persons, organizations and some in the media have read the resolution to be or intended to be a declaration against French Canadians;

And whereas the City of Sault Ste. Marie is very proud of the fact that French Canadians played an important part in the growth and development of our City and our Country from the very earliest days;

And whereas the French Canadian culture continues to form an important part of the multicultural makeup of Sault Ste. Marie of which we are all so very proud and the celebration of which is heartily encouraged;

Now therefore be it resolved that the Council of the City of Sault Ste. Marie very proudly recognizes the important role which French Canadians have played in the growth and development of our community and our country over the past four centuries; and further the continuing contribution which French Canadians make to the social, economic and cultural well-being of Sault Ste. Marie and Canada, a contribution appreciated by all of this City and Country;

And further that the French Canadians of Sault Ste. Marie be heartily encouraged to continue in the celebration of their important history, ancestry and culture as an integral part of this community's proud multicultural fabric.

This second resolution, however, did not calm the troubled waters of the Sault, nor of the rest of the country, increasingly taken up in the debate. Some local commentary well expresses the continued concerns, and helps explain why the second text did nothing to alleviate people's anger and fears. An article published in *The Sault Star* on February 22, 1990, describes the reaction of the local *Centre francophone*:

"The resolution does not address the reality of our two languages in Canada, in Ontario and in the Sault Ste. Marie area," states the release. "It suggests that the French-Canadian community 'celebrate' its culture in a folkloric manner as with any other ethnic group, thereby failing to recognize the value and the presence of the French language in our community as one of the official languages of Canada (…) We urge council to recognize that minority rights are being threatened by the English-language rights groups and to realize that the French language is not and never should be considered as an ethnic group since French is one of the official languages of our country.

The francophone argument rests on a key assumption of the Canadian federal policy of bilingualism and multiculturalism, that while all groups should enjoy a measure of freedom to maintain differences, native peoples, anglophones and francophones have historically-entrenched rights of a different order. For francophones, English cannot be a neutral language; it is, instead, the language of the other founding group, the language of the dominant group, a language clearly associated with the interests of a specific group of people against whom mobilized francophones have been struggling for generations. By the same token, they themselves reject the notion that their interests can be taken as equivalent to the interests of any other non-English-speaking group in Canada; to be treated on the same level as immigrant groups is to reinforce the power of anglophones and to diminish their own life chances.

3.0 The contested terrain of language

While some anglophones take the position illustrated by the motions of the Sault Ste. Marie City Council, for many others the recognition of francophone rights, and the acceptance of the legitimacy of federal language policies, has become an article of faith. The ideology of this group is expressed in many different ways. One fundamental concern is the preservation of national unity: better to invest in the acquisition of French than to have Quebec separate and the country fall apart. At the same time, this concern can be taken as a realistic appraisal of the political and economic power of francophones within Canada: better to invest in learning French in order to have access to economic and political power in a bilingual Canada, than to undermine the economic and political strength of the federation through a monolingualism which menaces the federation's very existence.

This position is expressed well by Doug Millroy, a columnist for *The Sault Star*. In his column of February 24, 1990, he takes on the question of the relationship between language and national unity:

> (...) As for the controversy caused by the English-only resolutions passed by so many communities in Ontario in recent months, I take heart in the number in recent weeks that reaffirmed their support for the official bilingual and bicultural nature of our country. It shows that many major areas are still committed to the concept of a country envisaged by the two founding peoples so many years ago. I believe over the years that this concept will be strengthened, as the children of the French language and French immersion programs increase in numbers, flowing into the work force able to meet the requirements of any job that is advertised as bilingual, thus easing the minds of those whose greatest fear has been that their children wouldn't be able to compete. In these children, who are mastering what was common in Quebec but what most anglophones of past generations would not even consider attempting, lies the greatest hope for this country. I truly believe that they will meet the test and the Dominion will continue to reach from sea to sea.

In this column, Millroy associates the goal of national unity with the existence of bilingual individuals who will fill jobs which require proficiency in both French and English. The link is not made explicit, but presumably Millroy's notion is that in order for a bilingual country to function, certain kinds of jobs will entail the use of both languages. The individuals who will be able to fill those positions, Millroy indicates, are currently being trained in "French language and French immersion programs".

Indeed, the phenomenon of French immersion is the clearest expression of the kind of position Millroy takes. French immersion programmes are programmes in English-language schools in which French is not only taught as a subject, but it is also used as a medium of instruction. The basic idea, best expressed in various publications on communicative language learning theory within the field of applied linguistics (cf. notably Canale – Swain 1980), is that it is possible to develop proficiency in both one's mother tongue and a second language by using both in a wide variety of communicative situations, with appropriate pedagogical support. The emphasis is thus placed on language use over language instruction, and is reflected in the use of French in as wide a variety as possible of communicative situations within the school.

Since 1965, when anglophone parents in the Montreal suburb of St. Lambert first successfully lobbied for an improvement in French-language instruction for their children (Lambert – Tucker 1972), French immersion programmes have spread across the country and enrollment has increased every year. In 1990–1991, 255,052 children outside Quebec (or almost 7 percent of the total school population outside Quebec), and 30,800 children in Quebec (or about 31 percent of the English-language school population in Quebec) were enrolled in French immersion programmes (Canadian Parents for French (CPF) 1992).[23]

At the same time, it is important to note that certain groups are overrepresented in this population. While the extent of overrepresentation seems to be decreasing, especially in large urban centres such as Toronto (Hart et al. 1988), it remains nonetheless true that the French immersion population is mainly Canadian-born, English mother tongue, white and middle class. Olson and Burns (1983; cf. also Olson 1983) have argued that French immersion helps middle-class anglophones maintain their class position at the expense of other groups. At the same time, it is clear that middle-class anglophones, especially those living along the language border in Quebec, Ontario and New Brunswick, would be the first to feel the effects of the political and economic mobilization of francophones, since their class position had in the past been based on a certain set of relations with francophones which had been radically transformed by the events of the 1960s. While some reacted by moving to monolingual English-speaking parts of Canada, by developing a militant monolingual stance or by retreating into English enclaves, many recognized that the maintenance of their access to jobs in management in the private sector and in administration in the public sector would henceforth depend on their ability to use French (Heller 1990).

Indeed, most research on the French immersion population indicates that, while the Canadian federal ideology of bilingualism is often brought to bear on the issue, most parents and students are principally immediately motivated by economic considerations; as one recent commentator put it, *"Jusqu'à présent, la politique du bilinguisme canadien et les désirs des yuppies torontois sont sur la même longueur d'onde."* [Up to now, the policy of Canadian bilingualism and the desires of Toronto yuppies are on the same wavelength.] *L'Actualité*, 1 May 1990, p. 35). For some, especially for federal politicians, national unity may be the principal goal; indeed, one could hardly expect a federal politician to take any other position, since the meaning and value of the federal government absolutely requires a united country. However, for most ordinary people, national unity is only compelling as an idea to the extent that it is seen as the most effective means to achieving or maintaining valued resources, whether material or symbolic. As a motivation for action, it may, and in this case does, take second place to the immediate consideration of obtaining access to those resources. Parents and students are interested in French immersion because they think it will give them an advantage in competing for bilingual jobs, that is, for the kinds of jobs created by the necessity of holding a bilingual country together. If those jobs turn out not to exist, or if francophone rather than anglophone bilinguals are hired to fill them, then anglophone enthusiasm for bilingualism will no doubt wane.

It is important to emphasize that parents' interest in French stems from an interest in bilingualism, not in assimilation to the francophone population, whether parents opted for enrolling their children in French-language schools (Heller 1987a; see also Chapter 4) or in French immersion programmes within English-language schools or school boards. In many respects, the fact that French immersion exists as a separate programme within English-language schools is a sign of this; in principle, many more anglophone parents could have sent their children to French-language schools than actually chose to do so.[24] Indeed, much early research on French immersion focussed not only on the extent to which the programmes helped students acquire a high level of proficiency in French, but also on the programmes' effect on the development of reading and writing skills in English, as well as on academic achievement in general (Heller 1990; Swain – Lapkin 1981; Lapkin et al. 1983). Parents were not prepared to sacrifice their children's opportunities to develop English-language and academic skills in order for them to learn French; French had to be added to the range of skills and knowledge to which they were already committed.[25]

At the same time, research on the effect of French immersion on attitudes towards or degree of interaction with members of the francophone population shows that little or no change occurs (Genesee 1978; Swain – Lapkin 1981). Students retain mildly favourable attitudes towards francophones, but rarely interact with them, even in areas (such as Montreal) where francophones in fact form a numerical majority. It is not known what happens to immersion students once they leave school; that is, it is not clear whether or to what extent they use French in their working life, or interact with francophones (in French or in English).[26]

Finally, while it is clear that French immersion students acquire a greater degree of proficiency in French than do their counterparts in regular ("core") French programmes, it is also clear that the dream of perfect bilingualism has not been realized. Instead, students reach a plateau at which their receptive skills outweigh their productive skills (Harley 1984). Interestingly, most discussion of this phenomenon and what to do about it has focussed on pedagogical problems and techniques (see, for example, Swain 1985; Lyster 1987). Rarely have analysts focussed on the social and political reasons underlying immersion students' inability to use French in a more native-like way, reasons which are probably associated with the instrumental nature of students' motivations and with the economic interests which are at the base of the existence of the programmes, and which are manifested in the characteristics of the programmes themselves (notably in the emphasis on learning within the school milieu and on pedagogical techniques, and in the difficulty of establishing relations with francophones through school or outside school; see however Heller 1990; Chevalier 1990). In other words, the plateau effect is seen to stem more from imperfections in pedagogical technique than from the social significance of differing forms of verbal performance in French and English. I would argue, however, that, whatever the pedagogical impediments, it is socially difficult for immersion students to sound like native speakers of French: to do so would be at the same time to stake a claim to the rights (and to be subject to the obligations) of members of the francophone ethnolinguistic group.

Nonetheless, as Millroy's article indicates, immersion students are popularly perceived to be serious contenders for bilingual positions, and, in a general way, to be well-placed to benefit from whatever advantages might flow from bilingualism. Perhaps not surprisingly, this fact has met with some expressions of concern on the part of francophones.

Part of the mobilization strategy of the 1960s entailed a re-definition of conventions of interethnic language choice: whereas for many years it was assumed that the language of French-English interaction (and the default language of public communication between strangers) should be English, increasingly politicized francophones began imposing the use of French in these interactions (Heller 1982b). The use of a language in any form of interaction was taken to be symbolic of (and in many ways was actually constitutive of) the dominance of that language in the wider social context. In order for that strategy to be successful without actually impeding communication, of course, it was necessary for anglophones to learn French. However, once that began to be the case, francophones began to wonder about the full range of the consequences for them of anglophone bilingualism.

Among other things, while francophones generally feel positive about anglophones' willingness to share the burden of bilingualism, it is less clear to them that anglophones also share the burden of being a dominated minority. At the same time, anglophones clearly do share the advantages of bilingualism, an advantage which, in the past, was one of the few privileges of being francophone.

For francophones, then, the immersion phenomenon and the anglophone bilingualism which it represents, has come to symbolize yet another strategy of anglophone domination.

There is little systematic research in this area, but some indices will serve to illustrate my point. First, within the limits of immersion research, less and less attention has been paid to the impact of immersion on French-English relations in Canada (an aspect of immersion which was widely discussed and which featured prominently in the rationale for the programmes in the early days). On the other hand, the impact both of immersion and of the presence of anglophones in French-language schools (especially outside Quebec) has been the object of attention, specifically within the francophone research community.[27]

During the 1980s (and still today) much attention was devoted to the impact of anglophone students on the use of French and on the maintenance of French-language proficiency as well as of francophone ethnocultural identity of francophone students, as well as on their academic achievement (Desjarlais et al. 1980; Churchill et al. 1985; Mougeon – Heller 1986; Mougeon 1987; Heller 1987a; see also Chapter 4). Towards the end of the 1980s, francophones also began paying attention to the impact of immersion on the francophone community. For example, the Conseil de l'éducation franco-ontarienne, the advisory body to the Ontario Ministry of Education, commissioned a study on that subject (Bordeleau et al. 1988), and in 1989 a Franco-Ontarian academic journal, the *Revue du Nouvel-Ontario* released a special issue entitled *"L'immersion et les Franco-Ontariens"* (Cazabon 1987). Both reflect the ambivalence felt by francophones in the face of growing anglophone bilingualism, but more heavily stress the threat to francophone autonomy and possibilities for social and economic advancement which that bilingualism represents.

That feeling of threat, the concern that bilingualism is simply another strategy of dominance is perhaps more clearly reflected in the commentary of a francophone high school student. Several years ago, I was hanging around after a Grade 13 French class with the teacher and several students. Somehow the conversation turned to bilingualism and its economic advantages. One girl said that she was sure that her bilingualism would be an asset on the job market, but that she was concerned about the competition she was likely to face from bilingual anglophones. If anglophones are doing the hiring, she reasoned, surely they will be more inclined to hire one of their own, even if the francophone candidates were more fluently bilingual. As a result, anglophones would once again have the advantage; *"Les anglophones nous ont tout pris"*, she said, *"maintenant ils veulent nous prendre notre langue."* [The anglophones have taken everything from us, now they want to take our language away from us]. By learning French, anglophones are appropriating the one valuable thing francophones have left, and using it to advance themselves at the expense of the dominated minority.

The same kinds of concerns seem to be operating elsewhere. An anglophone civil servant of my acquaintance, who occupies a bilingual position, recently expressed to me her frustration at not being able to use French in her job. She complained that francophones refuse to speak French to her, on the grounds that it is not their job to help her maintain her proficiency in French. Clearly, while the anglophone feels that she is operating in good faith, the francophones regard her as a threat to their exclusive control of the one form of knowledge which gives them any degree of power in their workplace, namely, the knowledge of French. To allow anglophones extended access to and use of that language is to hand back to them the power for which francophones have been struggling so hard and for so long.

At the same time that francophones must struggle for control of French, they also increasingly express concern over their access to English. Historically, if anybody was bilingual in Canada, it was certain sub-groups of francophones, and if there was a problem for them in the relationship between language and social mobility it was how to become socially mobile without also becoming anglophone. One consequence of the successful mobilization of francophones, however, has been the increasing possibility for them to rise to upper levels of management in private enterprise and in administration as monolingual francophones. However, at those levels English is still essential, as the language of business and wider communication not only nationally but also internationally.

Some monolingual francophones now feel concerned that their chances of social mobility will again be compromised (see Chapter 2, section 2.5.1.). There are a number of different ways in which this concern has been addressed, but perhaps the most revealing has been an attempt on the part of some francophone parents in Montreal to convince their children's school board to extend English-language instruction (notably by beginning instruction in Grade 1 instead of Grade 4, or by using it as a language of instruction in one or two subject areas). This has triggered great debate and controversy, as some francophones argue that French is now solidly enough entrenched, at least within Quebec, to permit consideration of the extended learning and use of English without that constituting a threat to French, and others argue that the survival of French in North America requires continual protection and vigilance (cf. Lightbown 1988; Bibeau 1982).

This debate, which is occurring largely within Quebec, parallels that outside Quebec, between francophone parents who prefer bilingual education and those for whom *les écoles bilingues* represent the surest and quickest path to assimilation. Underlying the debate is a disagreement both over the value or necessity of bilingualism (must it be essential for francophones to use English in order to gain access to certain forms of social, economic and political resources?), as well as, among those who welcome or at least accept bilingualism, over the best way for francophones to achieve it and to use it to attain their own social, economic and political goals.

In turn, this debate parallels, at least in some respects, the debate within the anglophone community over whether or not bilingualism is a desirable goal, either at the collective or at the individual level. The major difference, of course, is that among anglophones who welcome or accept bilingualism, very few doubt that it will be possible to use bilingualism to advance individual interests, to fulfill individual aspirations, and even fewer examine the consequences of bilingualism for the collective identity and future of anglophones as a group.

While these debates revolve only around French and English and francophones and anglophones, similar concerns are expressed with respect to the relationship between these languages and others spoken in Canada (see also Chapter 4). Most notably, current Canadian policy places French and English on the same level, but distinguishes between them and the languages of the native population or of immigrants. Most francophones argue that this distinction is necessary to the preservation of francophone rights, since to do otherwise would be to reinforce the power of anglophones: if all languages are considered equal, it is argued, English will inevitably come to dominate (cf. Berthelot 1990). The francophone claim to special status is, of course, based on historical circumstances, specifically, on their role in the colonization of Canada (recognized in much of the legislation concerning the political organization of the colony, and later of the country) and on their exploitation as a conquered people. Immigrant groups argue that current considerations outweigh historical ones, that is, that the struggle against inequality is relevant to all ethnic groups in Canada in the same way; for them, the claim of francophones (or anglophones) to special status discriminates against other groups.

Of course, the federal policy of bilingualism, a strategic response to the specific historical circumstances of the 1960s, has also clearly opened the door to the consideration of the rights of other groups, for precisely these reasons. While the Royal Commission of the 1960s began with a mandate to study the situation of bilingualism and biculturalism in Canada, it rapidly shifted its mandate to include multiculturalism. This compromise, which permits the recognition both of the specific rights of francophones as a distinct and special group and of the general rights of all ethnolinguistic groups, has laid the groundwork for debates which continue to this day.

In addition, of course, the situation of native groups remains highly problematic, as discussions continue within and among native communities, and between native communities and various levels of government, over the possibility of native autonomy. The clash between francophone mobilization and the rights of native groups was clearly expressed in the aftermath of Bill 101. While native groups could understand the rationale behind the promotion of French-language rights in Quebec, especially as they concerned the obligations of anglophones and immigrants to use French, they disputed the right of the Quebec government to impose such obligations on native peoples. As a result of their arguments, their special status within Quebec was recognized; nonetheless, the fact that they were obliged to dispute the law's application to them is an indication of how little attention has been paid to their situation, and of how little power they have.

The tension between the ideology of pluralism, the right to be different within a broad national framework without losing rights, and the recognition of different statuses for different categories of groups, has yet to be resolved, nor, for that matter, has the tension between the ideology of pluralism and the ideology of homogeneous nationhood. In Canada, these ideologies are debated through the domain of language, and language becomes itself a contested terrain in a number of ways.

First, groups, and individuals within groups, debate their vision of society through debates which centre on policies of monolingualism, bilingualism or multilingualism. At the same time, those policies are seen to be related to the various possibilities of cultural pluralism, although the relationship between language and culture is not necessarily seen as being one-to-one. Nonetheless, what is done with language is seen as having an effect on culture. Groups exist which argue for English monolingualism across Canada, or alternatively English monolingualism outside Quebec, and groups exist which argue for French monolingualism within Quebec. Groups exist which argue for bilingualism across the country, or alternatively bilingualism outside Quebec. In all these cases, language may or may not be seen as equivalent to culture: for some, learning a language means some form of cultural assimilation or integration, while for others it is a pragmatic strategy which permits different groups to live together while not necessarily having any consequences for their ability to maintain their culture. On the other hand, each of these positions has clear consequences for the responsibility of the state in fostering cultural assimilation or cultural pluralism. Groups also exist which argue for bilingualism and multiculturalism; others argue for nation-wide pluralism.

Second, different ethnolinguistic groups may compete for access to the same linguistic resources. Sometimes, or more accurately for some members of different groups, at different historical moments, under specific social circumstances, these may be the resources of one language within a framework of monolingualism, or the resources of two or more languages within frameworks of bilingualism or multilingualism. Third, within and across groups, members may dispute the legitimacy and value of specific forms or varieties within each language at play in the repertoire of individuals or the speech economy of communities.

In the remaining sections of this chapter, I will discuss the various ways in which language is a contested terrain in Canada from two points of view. The first looks at language as a form of capital, that is, as a resource which is valued in its own right, because it operates symbolically to regulate access to and the distribution of material resources or other symbolic resources. By looking at French and English as valuable resources, it will be possible to examine the social, economic and political underpinnings of the debates over language and nationhood which have periodically marked our history and which have recently seen a resurgence.

The second point of view looks at language as an ethnic emblem, that is, as a badge of ethnic identity which serves to regulate the nature of ethnic boundaries. As such, language serves as a means of regulating access to participation in ethnic networks, and hence, again, to the resources which an ethnic group controls. It also serves as a terrain on which to define what it means to be a member of an ethnic group, in terms of the rights and obligations of the members, in terms of the nature of paths not only to material wealth and power but also to symbolic sources of prestige, and in terms of the very nature of what constitutes wealth, power and prestige.

In both these cases, it will be necessary to examine how ethnolinguistic boundaries overlap or reinforce other forms of social organization. The social position of individuals, as anglophones or francophones, as men or women, as Catholics or Protestants or members of other religious groups, and as members of different occupational groups, is intimately bound up with the nature of the knowledge they gain about the world as well as of the opportunities of which they may more or less easily avail themselves. Most importantly for my purposes, it is linked to a set of relations to language, in terms of the kinds of language or languages individuals are likely to learn and in terms of what that represents in the form of access to valued resources. As a result, different strategies of social mobility, and specifically the use of language (language choice, language learning, language policy) as part of those strategies, are likely to be more or less attractive or seem more or less feasible. An individual's experience of language, and the felt consequences of that experience for that person's life chances and quality of life, are not simply a product of his or her ethnic identity, but are part of a set of strategic responses to life conditions in which social considerations other than strictly ethnic ones also play a role.

In particular, I will look at the way language has been used as a means of ethnic mobilization which represents the definition and achievement of not only ethnic, but also class (and to some extent gender) interests. More precisely, language has become the basis of an ethnic mobilization which mainly serves the class interests of certain members of the anglophone and francophone ethnic groups. This has consequences not only for the ways in which the value of language as linguistic capital is defined or in which its significance as an ethnic emblem is constructed, but also for the ways in which language is used to gain access to different forms of power. In turn, this process leads to the possibility (and, as we have seen, often the realization) of consensus or conflict across ethnolinguistic and class lines.

The ethnic nationalist mobilization of francophones in Canada has in part been accomplished through and in part been reflected in an increase in the value of specific forms of Canadian French. In addition, it has shifted the focus of identity from an ethnicity independent of political boundaries to one in which ethnic affiliation is at least possible to claim on the basis of language and residence, both of which are relatively easy to achieve. Finally, since it has been relatively successful, it has radically changed relations of power both among ethnolinguistic groups and also within them, especially within the francophone group. Not only are francophones and anglophones competing for power in ways quite different from what had been possible for the francophone mobilization of the 1960s, but francophones now find themselves caught up in internal relations of inequality which before had corresponded with, rather than overlapped with, ethnolinguistic boundaries. These relations of inequality concern not only economic relations, but also include relations with members of immigrant and native minorities. These processes themselves call into question both the nature of what it means to be francophone and the moral basis of mobilization.

3.1. French and English as linguistic capital

For most of Canada's colonial and post-colonial history, French and English operated in separate realms. While most francophones and anglophones might have agreed that the value of English and French had to be calculated with respect to each other, there were still possibilities for social advancement within each group which existed independently of the other language. If French was stigmatized with respect to English, and valueless in the situations English-speakers controlled, it nonetheless had both symbolic and material value in the situations controlled by French-speakers. Education, access to the liberal professions or the clergy, moral and practical help from the Church or from neighbours, all could be achieved without English.

The social and political changes of the post-War period, culminating in the francophone mobilization of the 1960s and 1970s, changed that scenario. Middle-class francophones and middle-class anglophones are now competing for the same resources, both in the political and economic arenas. In Bourdieu's terms, while in the past, francophones and anglophones operated in symbolic marketplaces which only overlapped, now that their economic networks and political activities centre around the same set of resources, their symbolic marketplaces are also increasingly integrated.

A central issue in this process is, of course, the value of French and English. These languages have value insofar as they permit their speakers to achieve the economic, political and social resources which they desire. A major consequence of mobilization, of course, has been to permit francophones to control access to two forms of resource which are generally considered valuable in Canadian society. One form is economic: new, francophone-controlled companies, and, through the Quebec government, the primary resources and primary resource exploitation within the boundaries of Quebec. The second form is political, in the shape of the power francophones wield as a voting bloc within Canada. Of course, that power only exists as long as Quebec is part of the federation, and only matters as long as other Canadians see keeping Quebec within the federation as being in their economic and political interest. In the meantime, both the economic and political forms of power which francophones now hold are meaningful within the same general network and marketplace as that which lies in the hands of anglophones.

Since francophones and anglophones are, for all practical purposes, now in the same marketplace, one set of concerns has to do with their ability to operate freely in that marketplace as monolingual francophones or monolingual anglophones, or whether instead it is better to try to construct two separate, albeit connected, sub-markets, to try to construct two completely different, alternative markets, or, finally, to try to operate as a bilingual market. In each of these cases, French and English remain valuable; however, the value and type of bilingualism which results from each may be different.

The debates surrounding the Sault Ste. Marie City Council motions illustrate the changing value of French and English and the ways in which they operate as capital in different ways for different people. At this level, what is at issue is the extent to which any language other than English can be said to have value in public exchanges, especially in situations which make a difference to people's lives (such as obtaining services or information from the municipal government). In these terms, the representation of English as neutral is, of course, false: it remains a form of capital to which some members of society have easier and more complete access than others. As a result, anglophones, as an ethnic group, have an advantage over other groups. Since it is the capital which they already possess which is the one to be the basis of exchange in public life, they have no effort to make to acquire forms of capital which they do not already possess. Also, to the extent to which it is anglophones who are in a position to decide not only which language but also which forms of language are to be the most valuable (the most persuasive, the most prestigious), they are also in a position of privilege: in a word, they are the ones who set the rules of the game, the standards by which their own and other people's performances are to be judged.

At this level, then, francophones argue that they have an equal right to set the rules of the game. The debate internal to the francophone community here is whether it is necessary (or possible) to set the rules of the game within a separate market. If so, the question remains whether that market should revolve around similar or different material and symbolic resources; until now, discussion has only touched on the former. If not, the question remains of how francophones can retain access to the bilingualism which becomes valuable in such an integrated market, and, beyond that, to what extent they can use their historically privileged access to bilingualism to advance themselves socially and economically. Of course, even if a separate market were to emerge, there would likely be a role for bilingual brokers.

Many anglophones see the same kinds of value in bilingualism: a value stemming from the necessity of including French within economic and political exchanges, since francophones hold power in those arenas now to an extent and in ways which are relatively new, and a value stemming from the need for bilingual brokers to forge a link between monolingual anglophone and monolingual francophone zones of an integrated marketplace. These are the middle-class anglophones who aim at jobs at management levels of private enterprise, where the Quebec market and Quebec producers are important, or at jobs in administration in a public service which, at the federal level and increasingly at the provincial level, requires the use of French.

In certain domains of life, then, the ability to speak both French and English does make a difference to the kinds of resources to which one can gain access. This makes a difference, of course, mainly to those people who can actually aspire to those positions. The contested terrain of language is defined mainly in middle-class terms. Anglophones who find their class position threatened by competition from francophones react either by rejecting the value of French or by embracing it; working class anglophones are largely peripheral to these concerns, and so, it is not surprising, for example, to find them largely absent from French immersion programmes. Francophones who can aspire to these positions also have a choice: they can also embrace bilingualism, or they can seek increasingly autonomous domains in which French is the only form of capital required. For working-class francophones, the situation is different. Some may embrace francophone nationalism in the hope that it represents greater chances for social mobility than continued anglophone dominance, as well as a way of expressing resistance to that dominance; for others, especially those outside Quebec, the need to survive bolsters the value of English in their lives, and undermines that of French.

The major difference between francophones and anglophones of the middle class who opt for a strategy of achieving bilingualism lies in the gap between the capital they possess and the capital they need to acquire, as well as in the opportunities presented to them to acquire it. Moreover, that gap lies within relations of power between francophones and anglophones which, at base, remain asymmetrical: despite francophone gains, anglophones still have more power in Canada than do francophones. For anglophones to learn French entails, then, a reliance on formal methods, such as schooling. Breaking through the ethnic barrier is difficult, not only because anglophones remain fundamentally interested in retaining their identity as anglophones, but also because of resistance they encounter from francophones who are unwilling to enter into such close competition with anglophones for the same resources. For francophones to learn English is still less problematic than the other direction; English, as Canada's dominant language, is accessible in a wide variety of domains, everywhere outside the few areas of Quebec, Ontario and New Brunswick where the circumstances of some individual's lives (notably of those not in the work force) protects them from exposure to English. The problem instead, in most contact zones, is retaining French, that is, in reinforcing the attraction of the resources francophones do control and hence the value of the language through which access to them is controlled.

For francophones there are an additional set of concerns about linguistic capital which stem from the nature and development of francophone mobilization. In the past, the form of French which both francophones and anglophones considered prestigious was the European standard, for reasons having everything to do with France's role in the world, and nothing to do with the lost corner of its former empire. In order for Quebec nationalism to appear legitimate, it was important, among other things, to redefine the nature of the variety of French which was to be associated with power and prestige. Indeed, artists and intellectuals have contributed greatly to the symbolic validation of local varieties of French, simply by writing plays and songs in the (previously only spoken) vernacular, or by producing dictionaries of Québécois French and undertaking scientific studies of the vernacular. Over the years, the almost diglossic relationship of the vernacular to the European standard has been reshaped into a continuum, with some varieties corresponding to either regional or class-based distinctions, and available for exploitation in a range of differentially-valued communicative situations. One result has been the development of the linguistic dimension of new structures of class-based inequality within the francophone community, which corresponds to the nature of differentially-valued varieties of Canadian French associated with the élite, the middle class and the working class.

At the same time, the importance of adopting a Canadian variety as a legitimate standard, as a means of legitimating Canadian francophone nationalism, has thrown up a barrier between francophones who master that variety (or something close to it) and those, mainly immigrants but also anglophones who learned French at school, who master some other variety of French. The relationship here, however, remains ambiguous, since Canadian varieties have come to represent both the old basis of mobilization against the dominance not only of English but also of European French, and also the new power of francophones in Canada.

The contested terrain of language can thus be seen in terms of shifts in the value of languages and of linguistic varieties, which are accompanied by shifts in the position of groups with respect to those varieties. Those who master them are in a position of advantage; those who do not master them must decide whether to reject the new system of values or to make the effort to acquire the forms of capital newly rendered valuable. Either strategy has consequences both for the economic and political resources to which individuals and groups may have access, and also for different forms of prestige. These strategies also have consequences for the meaning of ethnic identity and for the ability of individuals to perform adequately as members of ethnic groups.

3.2. French and English as ethnic emblems

As the dominant language in Canada, English never functioned, at least not until recently, as an emblem of ethnic identity. If English-speakers associated themselves with some superordinate category, it was usually within the terms of the British Empire, or subsequently the British Commonwealth, and only recently with Canada as a sovereign political unit. However, as Breton (1984) has pointed out, the construction of Canadian identity (through such symbolic acts as the creation of a flag and the national anthem, or the adoption of metric weights and measures in contradistinction to the British and American systems, or through more direct means such as the repatriation and amendment of the constitution) emerged precisely from the processes of francophone ethnic mobilization of the 1960s, and hence has been associated more with the construction of a bilingual identity than with the hegemony of English.

English has long been the language of assimilation; the cultural boundaries of the English-speaking population in Canada have been highly permeable. If individuals of British descent have associated the English language with a distinct identity of their own, they have done so in ways that are more reminiscent of the imperial order than with any form of latent or nascent ethnic mobilization. In addition, that identity has usually been associated with religion as much as with language; the best example is that of the Orange Lodge, a male voluntary association which functions to protect the interests of Protestant English-speakers.

The challenge to the hegemony of English which was produced by the francophone mobilization of the 1960s and onwards has, however, had the effect of triggering a questioning of the identities associated with the English language. Many anglophones, of course, continue to see themselves as representative of the dominant order (and hence neutral, or lacking specific identity); if francophone mobilization has had an effect here, it has been to mobilize a defense of this stance, represented most dramatically by the Association for the Preservation of English in Canada. Others have opted for the construction of a bilingual identity, associated with participation in and advancement through the federal political unit as a sovereign entity. In addition, some have come to recognize that access to political and economic power, as well as to social status, is in fact regulated through ethnolinguistically defined networks; in other words, the challenge to English hegemony has made visible, for some, the underlying mechanisms of that hegemony. Finally, especially among the anglophones most centrally subject to the power of francophones, the English-speaking minority of Quebec, the competing power of French has led to the emergence of anglophone identity, cross-cutting and overarching status lines generated by forms of difference within the English-speaking population.

The association of language with ethnicity is thus historically relatively recent, and emerges from the mobilization of francophones in the 1960s. Hitherto, language was thought of as one aspect of social difference between groups who thought of themselves as races, as representatives of an imperial order or as nations. Religion was at least as salient as language as an emblem of identity, and with the arrival of the Irish and other non-francophone Catholics, became a sometimes competing, sometimes reinforcing, source of affiliation. Most importantly, identities cut across political units; French-Canadian and English-Canadian nationalism embraced all francophone or anglophone inhabitants of Canada and looked outwards also to groups with whom identity was shared within a larger (at least originally imperial) world order. By adopting a strategy of mobilization focussed on legitimating control of Quebec on the basis of cultural distinctiveness, francophones placed language at the centre of the construction of ethnic identity, not only for francophones, but for all other linguistic groups in Canada.

There are a number of reasons why language should have emerged as the most salient dimension of ethnic mobilization among francophones. Certainly, it was the one characteristic which francophones shared exclusively, given the ever-increasing number of non-francophone Catholics in Canada, and functioned effectively to mobilize adequate numbers of individuals within the boundaries of Quebec. Second, the Church and the State had been set up in many ways as opposing powers; to mobilize on the basis of religion was either to propose a Catholic take-over of the state apparatus, or to propose a new form of political control through the Church within the bounds of the Canadian state. However, the purpose of mobilization was precisely to enter into the modern, secular world of the centralized state; the Church had not succeeded in providing francophones with access to valuable resources, and had lessening credibility as an ideological force to be reckoned with. It did not, at the time, seem possible, or even desirable, to have both; certainly the Church did not quickly show itself to be open to the forces of change. Finally, a focus on language is consonant with the prevalent ideology of the modern democratic state; it is possible for anyone to learn a language without being forced, necessarily, to adopt a culture, and learning a language is achievable in a way that changing, say, colour or sex, is not.

It is this latter dimension, however, which is at the heart of the dilemma posed by the use of language as an emblem of ethnicity in the context of francophone ethnic nationalist mobilization in Quebec. On the one hand, French is supposed to symbolize the distinctiveness of Quebec francophone society, to embody its particular values which reflect a common past (and thereby lays the basis of a common future). It is meant to impart the sense of belonging which binds individuals to the group, and to legitimate francophones' claim on the territory of Quebec. It is also used very explicitly as a criterion of inclusion and exclusion in subtle everyday ways as well as in the broad legislative means the government has at its disposal (for example, in setting admissions criteria for immigration or evaluative criteria for hiring processes).

On the other hand, the use of language as a basis for mobilization, in particular the way it has been used in Quebec, has consequences for the definition of ethnic identity once mobilization is successful enough to attract any outsiders. By requiring non-francophones to use French in the workplace, and by requiring immigrants to learn French and to send their children to French-language schools, the francophone population of Quebec permanently alters its composition and the very nature of what it means to be French.

This dilemma is at the heart of debates in Quebec about such issues as immigration policy and the language of the school. On the one hand, Quebec has invested heavily in the invention of a French-Canadian national tradition based on the historical experiences of francophones in Canada and in the construction of a common culture based on the experiences and culture of francophones established in Quebec for several hundred years. The importance accorded to the construction of this common culture is reflected in the development of a government bureaucracy for linguistic and cultural matters, and in an emphasis on cultural forms which stress the synchronic and diachronic independence from English and anglophones of francophone cultural life, whether in the areas of folklore or language, music or art, drama or film (Handler 1988). Artists and intellectuals, notably university faculty and students in linguistics, folklore, history, political science, sociology and anthropology, have contributed to the development of a theory of Quebec society as distinct and culturally bounded, emerging thus out of a rural, agricultural and community-oriented life. There is an internal dilemma here which requires resolution, namely the fact that the construction of Québécois identity based on a rural and agricultural past is negated by the purpose of the construction of that identity, namely, to provide the basis for the emergence of new Québécois able to participate fully in national and international commercial, technical and scientific domains. Nonetheless, with all its contradictions, this theory is at the basis of the legitimation of recent and current political mobilization and strategies for the achievement and maintenance of political control within Quebec.

On the other hand, Quebec does not have the basis for population maintenance which allows it to retain the numbers it needs for its political base, and in any case, it possesses already a significant number of non-francophone residents. The political necessity to include these groups, rendered morally necessary by the logic of democratic mobilization, poses a problem for the maintenance of the image of Quebec society painted by the culture and language industry. This problem is the subject of much discussion, in the media and within the social institutions most directly affected by these processes, notably in education. For some, the only solution is to practice a policy of assimilation, justified by the need of a minority to defend itself. For others, such a policy is unjustifiable given that it is precisely against assimilation that francophone mobilization is aimed. As a result, it is either necessary to develop a new identity which admits the contribution of members whose background and historical experience have been different, or else to somehow recognize this contribution without undermining the cultural values and practices which francophones hold to be central to their notion of themselves. The consequences of successful mobilization involve sharing power, and now francophones find themselves wondering how to do that while still retaining that notion of themselves which was necessary for mobilization in the past, and, many will argue, necessary for a constant mobilization which addresses the unchanged minority status of francophones in Canada, indeed, in North America as a whole and in the world.

Significantly, though ethnicity has been central to the struggle for power in Canada, the term itself has been avoided in any official discourse, and generates unease among many people, whatever their background. The major reason for this is that the term has come to signify powerlessness: nations may lay claim to the control of states, but ethnic groups are necessarily a minority who can never claim exclusive control of any political unit. Just as anglophones have never been accustomed to thinking of themselves as an ethnic group as a result of their position of dominance, so any group which aspires to that kind of power must distance itself from any perception of ethnic status. A specific dimension of this problem is that francophones' claim to power is based on distinguishing themselves from other groups; if ethnic processes apply to all linguistic groups, then all have equally weak or strong claims to political sovereignty. At the same time, the federal government cannot be seen either to support too strongly nor to undermine the claims to power of different groups. The federal terminology of bilingualism and multiculturalism, and the Quebec terminology of interculturalism and distinct societies, transform ethnic processes into a discourse of nation and state, and render legitimate struggles for power within the discourse of democracy.

Nonetheless, the struggle for power in Canada remains an ethnic one. The fundamental question is whether groups can use language to gain and regulate access to valued resources, and to set the criteria by which access shall be regulated. In this particular case, the question revolves around the distribution of one set of resources among ethnic groups (rather than the establishment of parallel or competing sets of resources), each of which seeks to retain privileged access to those resources on its own terms. Language functions not only as an emblem of identity, but as a means in and of itself to define group boundaries and to regulate access to the resources which the group controls. As such, it becomes itself a valued resource, a form of symbolic capital worth fighting to preserve or to acquire.

3.3. Consequences of mobilization: Blurred boundaries and new hierarchies

Francophone nationalist mobilization, built on the concept that francophones cannot move out of a position of domination without national self-determination legitimized through a concept of cultural distinctiveness, has had consequences for the value of French and English in Canada, for the ways in which francophones think about themselves in relation to other groups, and for what it means to be francophone. In particular, these effects flow from the fact that francophones have been able to compete relatively successfully for economic and political resources as francophones. However, the nature of their mobilization has placed them in a paradoxical position.

I have discussed above the dilemma posed by the need to include as Québécois, or in some cases simply as francophones, people who do not share the same social and cultural history as do those who are at the centre of mobilization processes in Quebec (and elsewhere in Canada, for that matter; cf. Chapter 4). Not only does this pose a problem in terms of the definition of what it means to be French, it also raises the thorny issue of how francophones can gain access to power without reproducing the very structures of domination against which they themselves have been struggling for so long. This same issue emerges in any consideration of social stratification within francophone society. As long as all group members are convinced that ethnic mobilization represents the best strategy for social and economic advancement, such a mobilization process can be maintained; if social mobility is blocked within francophone society, however, those who are excluded can, if they are able, be expected to search for new avenues. Until now, mobilization has in fact produced excellent results, as the managerial class grows and levels of education among francophones rise. The question remains as to what will provide the most fruitful path to the increased expansion of the power of that group, and as to what strategies they can find to remove obstacles to social mobility for those who have benefitted less from mobilization.

Second, the new power of francophones has attracted anglophones, who are learning French in an effort to retain their status in Canadian society. The very people who have traditionally held power through English monolingualism are now finding ways to retain power through bilingualism. This dilemma is particularly frustrating for francophones, and not only because it represents particularly stiff competition for the resources everyone covets. In addition, economically successful francophones must face the fact that the object of their mobilization, namely integration as francophones into national and international markets, still requires the use of English, since that market functions largely in that language. Francophones (like most other non-English speaking groups in similar positions around the world) cannot fully participate in it without a command of a language which happens to represent the structures of domination against which they have been fighting for many years. Not only that, but the bilingualism which had been theirs almost exclusively when it was a hallmark of domination, is now harder and harder for them to come by, while in the meantime anglophones pursue it ever more assiduously.

Third, the new power of francophones, and in particular the Quebec nationalist form that it has taken, poses specific paradoxical problems for francophones outside Quebec. To the extent that anglophones see their future as best assured by a country which includes Quebec, francophones outside Quebec are strengthened; it is therefore in their best interests to support Quebec. But Quebec is arguing a territorial line, which, if carried to its logical conclusion, effectively denies the legitimacy of francophone rights anywhere else in Canada. One product of this dilemma has been the distancing of francophones outside Quebec from that province, and the emergence of new quasi-national identities which coincide with provincial boundaries.

The anglophone minority within Quebec faces a related dilemma: in order to be taken seriously as a minority requiring protection, anglophones in Quebec must also recognize the minority status of francophones and their need to protect their own rights. The anglophone minority in Quebec is also part of the Canadian anglophone majority, and once was the dominant group in Quebec, despite its numbers; the francophone majority in Quebec is also a dominated minority, both numerically in the Canadian context, and historically in terms of power within Quebec.

Quebec's territorial argument also engages the monolingual and frequently extreme position of those anglophones who reject the Trudeauian vision of a bilingual Canada. As the two discourses develop, they reinforce each other: Quebec argues that francophones cannot be protected anywhere where they do not have real and exclusive political power, and hence Quebec should be recognized as the legitimate representative of francophones, while anglophones outside Quebec argue that if Quebec wants to be the sole legitimate defensor of francophones, there is no need for francophone rights to be protected elsewhere.

For immigrants and native groups the dispute between anglophones and francophones can sometimes seem to be a dispute between élites over control of the country, a country to which they stake equally legitimate claims, but from which they often feel excluded. While francophone mobilization had the effect of breaking English hegemony and hence opened the door to the possibility (indeed the necessity) of discussing a pluralist society, it also entails a discourse which relegates other groups to separate categories. This sets up a paradox:

francophone mobilization has been legitimized on the basis of being counter-hegemonic, but its success has carried with it the development of new forms of hegemony.

While most of the resources at stake lie in the ways wealth is produced, education has been central to the development of the discourse of mobilization and the debates over the contradictions it has both revealed and constructed. Education has become important not only because it is there that the knowledge and certification for participation in the world of work are distributed (and also often produced), but also because it is a central institution for the allocation of linguistic resources themselves.

In the chapters that follow, I will further explore the symbolic and material issues touched on here in a general way by examining how they manifest themselves in the specific circumstances of French-language minority education in Ontario. Many of the issues experienced in Quebec, and elsewhere in Canada, are revealed here: the problem of competition among francophones and anglophones for access to bilingualism, the problem of the domination of francophones by anglophones, the problem of the opening up of francophone society to immigrants, the problem of the lack of consensus among francophones regarding individual assimilation or collective mobilization strategies of social mobility.

However, precisely because this is the view from the other side, as it were, it provides a particularly trenchant means of examining the consequences for Canada of movement between policies of bilingualism and policies of territoriality. In Franco-Ontarian education, it is possible to see where the limits of a policy of bilingualism may lie, but it is also possible to see what the specific consequences of territoriality might be for those who find themselves caught on the wrong side of the border.

Chapter 4
The school system as border patrol

4.0. The school as ethnic institution

The Franco-Ontarian school functions as a sort of border patrol, regulating access to membership in the group and to the resources the group controls. It is the major social institution of the Franco-Ontarian community; participation in the school is a commitment to the community, and it entails subscribing to the protection and promotion of Franco-Ontarian interests. Symbolically, this commitment is signalled through the use of the language of instruction of those schools, that is, through speaking and writing in French. At the same time, the school is one of the most important domains where children can learn that language. The schools thus function to distribute symbolic resources, perhaps the most important of which is the language which itself is the key to participation in the school-related activities where resources are distributed.

The school's regulating function operates on two levels: as a system, and in the everyday life of schools. The ideology and practice of Franco-Ontarian education in the everyday life of schools will be taken up in Chapter 5. In this chapter, I want to examine how the Franco-Ontarian education system functions to regulate access to the group. By "system", I refer to the various aspects and manifestations of educational institutional processes. These include institutions which are involved in decision-making about Franco-Ontarian education, institutions involved in the provision of educational services, and institutions involved in supplying the providers of educational services.

Educational decision-making at the broadest level rests on legislation. Education is primarily under the jurisdiction of the provinces in Canada; in the case of Ontario, it is regulated according to the provisions of the Education Act of 1974. Institutions involved in decision-making processes (beyond the legislature and the courts) include government agencies, notably the ministries of Education (for the pre-school, primary and secondary levels) and of Colleges and Universities (for post-secondary education) and para-governmental agencies, such as the *Conseil de l'éducation franco-ontarienne*, an advisory committee which existed until 1990, or the *Conseil des affaires francophones*, a new advisory committee established in 1991. It includes elected groups, notably school trustees. Professional organizations, representing Franco-Ontarian teachers, superintendents, librarians, *animatrices et animateurs culturels*, and others, are also involved, although less directly than the administrative levels of the school board hierarchy (directors of education, superintendants, school principals). Parent-teacher associations (known either as *Associations parents-instituteurs* or *Associations parents-enseignants*, API or APE) play a role, mainly in influencing policy at the school or school-board level.

The provision of educational services at the primary and secondary levels operates through publicly-funded schools within school boards whose jurisdictions are legally defined. Teaching and administration, as well as curriculum development and implementation, rest, of course, in the hands of professional educators, who must legally possess the appropriate qualifications in order to ply their trade. In most cases, this means holding a teaching certificate, although in some instances (for example, for *animatrices et animateurs culturels* responsible for extra-curricular cultural programmes) other qualifications, such as an undergraduate degree, suffice. Two schools of education, one at Laurentian University in Sudbury and one at the University of Ottawa, produce teachers qualified to practice in Franco-Ontarian schools. Educators from other provinces or countries are required to obtain official recognition of their degrees. Agents of the Ministry of Education must be similarly qualified, and, in practice, are almost always drawn from the ranks of the teaching profession.[28]

At the post-secondary level, the situation is somewhat different. There are French-language programmes among both community colleges and universities, and educators at that level generally possess either an undergraduate (in the case of the community colleges) or a graduate degree (in the case of the universities) in the appropriate disciplines. The government has greater control over the community colleges than it does over the universities, who jealously guard their autonomy, although both depend heavily on government financing. As is the case with the Ministry of Education, the Ministry of Colleges and Universities has agents responsible for working with the college and university officials responsible for French-language programmes.

Franco-Ontarian educational institutions also draw on resources from outside the school, college or university systems. These include (government-funded, government-subsidized or university) agencies or private firms. They produce teaching materials, conduct research, provide extra-curricular activities, produce policy-oriented position papers, or provide basic services such as school meals or transportation.

The regulating function of the Franco-Ontarian educational system can be addressed by examining who is allowed to participate in it. This participation, includes, of course, the institutional functions described above, perhaps the most important of which for my purposes has to do with who makes decisions about

Franco-Ontarian education. In addition, of course, it is necessary to address the question of who is allowed to attend Franco-Ontarian schools, that is, of the processes of selection which operate at the level of admissions criteria. Finally, it is necessary to address the question of selection processes within the school.

Processes of deciding who controls Franco-Ontarian schools and who is allowed to participate in the system have a major impact on the nature of what it means to be Franco-Ontarian. First, these processes affect the extent to which the interests of specific groups are served by participation in the Franco-Ontarian educational system. Second, as a result, they affect the nature of what are defined as educational goals, hence what counts as Franco-Ontarian education. Third, they affect the extent to which Franco-Ontarians, or those groups who have constructed themselves as Franco-Ontarians, can accomplish their goal or goals. As I have argued (see Chapter 2, section 2.7), currently these goals are in fact double: attaining access to global resources while (and in many ways through) retaining a sense of Franco-Ontarian identity.[29]

The major strategy for achieving this goal has been to use the apparatus of the state to model the educational system in ways which facilitate Franco-Ontarian access to "universally" valued forms of knowledge and types of certification, as well as the construction of specifically Franco-Ontarian resources. In large part, this has meant struggling for francophone control of French-language education within the state system. Since embarking upon that course, it has become important for those with an interest in Franco-Ontarian education to define who counts as a francophone in terms that are intelligible within the state's educational bureaucracy. The urgency of such clarification is heightened because of increasing competition (at least within the middle classes) over the valued resource which the French language has become in Canada.

However, as I argue, developing francophone control and concomitant efforts to specify criteria of inclusion and exclusion have led frequently to conflict among groups with opposing interests. Notably, middle-class francophones find themselves in conflict with middle-class anglophones over the extent to which Franco-Ontarian schools can, or should, serve the interests of both groups. Newly-formed contradictions arise as well, not least of which is the contradiction between processes of formation of ties of solidarity among francophones as an oppressed group and processes whereby inequality may be produced within the francophone community itself. It becomes increasingly difficult to rally all components of the population to the Franco-Ontarian cause of fighting common oppression when certain groups within that population themselves feel oppressed by others; this is notably the case of immigrant groups who feel shut out of the educational process by the locally-established population. It also extends in many cases to class conflicts; the working class frequently sees its chances for social mobility as residing in bilingualism, especially as it is reflected in concomitant educational certification, hence it argues for access to instruction in both French and English within their schools. However, the middle class has heavily invested in the development of monolingual institutions, and hence desires instruction in French only (Welch 1988; Lapointe et al. 1987).

Two stories will illustrate the issues I want to take up. In early 1984, the French-language advisory committee of a nearby school board approached our Centre with a request. There was a bitter dispute raging between factions of parents whose children attended the two French-language schools administered by the board. One group claimed that the school had admitted too many students whose command of French was weak, and whose parents spoke no French at all. As a result, they said, all the students were speaking English, and even meetings of the *Association parents-instituteurs* were conducted entirely or partly in English. They depended on the school to provide their children and themselves with a wholly francophone milieu in order to help them retain their language and their identity, but instead the school was turning into a *foyer d'assimilation*, and even their children's academic achievement was suffering.

Their opponents argued for the right of non-francophones to be present at the school; they pointed to the central role non-francophones had played in convincing the board to open the school in the first place, and they argued that in a truly democratic and bilingual Canada everyone should have the right to choose their children's language of instruction. Some added that the presence of both French and English in school affairs was beneficial to the children: the best way to achieve bilingualism was to integrate both languages into the institutions of the community and the daily lives of its members, not separate them out into different domains. They disputed the effects of the presence of non-francophone children on the linguistic and academic development of the children. The board wanted us to conduct a study of the schools, feeling that an academic study might provide them with a way of handling the increasingly explosive situation on their hands.[30]

The second incident concerns the problems of immigrant parents. In late 1986, I walked into my classroom to find some of my students in heated debate. At the centre of the discussion were a teacher in a French-language high school in another public board, and the parent who had just been elected president of that board's French-language advisory committee. There had apparently been something of a coup the previous night. The former advisory committee, which had consisted entirely of francophones of Canadian extraction (that is, whose families had been in Canada for generations), had been confident of re-election. Instead, they were swept out of office and replaced by a slate consisting entirely of francophones who had recently immigrated to Canada from other parts of the world: Lebanon, Haiti, Morocco and elsewhere. The teacher expressed his surprise and his concern; echoing the sentiments of members of the former committee, he claimed not to understand what was behind the mobilization of this new group, and hence found their tactics inappropriate. He also wondered where the old guard would fit in now in the schools which they had so long thought of as theirs. The new president explained that the new office-holders had been feeling disenfranchised; frustrated at what appeared to them to be a lack of understanding and awareness on the part of the old committee, they felt they had no choice but to make sure that they could represent themselves.

Both of these stories are about rights of access, and they illustrate the two opposing sides of the problem. In the first case, a group of parents felt threatened by what they perceived as an attempt to use their school on the part of anglophones, the most dominant linguistic group in Ontario. They feared that the dominant group would use the school to gain access to French, and in so doing would destroy any effective possibility for actually preserving "authentic" French for the Franco-Ontarian children enrolled there. The dominant group would change the nature of the value of the linguistic resource distributed there, taking what had been a symbolic emblem of ethnic identity, and turning it into a mere technical means of communication. This would strip from francophones their major means of constituting ethnic identity, and prevent them from maintaining privileged access to bilingualism. Indeed, some parents preferred to withdraw from the school altogether, even enrolling their children in English-language schools, rather than see this happen.

In the second case, francophones were forced to face the social differences within their group; it was not enough that francophones had won control of the committee if they were unable to see that, in this specific case, social change had created a new form of social difference among francophones, and that that social difference was threatening to become a basis for social inequality. More broadly, this case points to the general problem of social difference and social inequality within the boundary, which cannot be wiped away in the interests of collective mobilization against domination from outside. Of course, this problem becomes more and more evident as francophone mobilization succeeds.

These two stories further illustrate how these problems are manifested in specific ways due to an historical conjunction of processes. The specific ways in which Franco-Ontarian education has become part of the state system, and the ways Franco-Ontarians have attempted to exert control within that system, lay the groundwork for struggles over access to French which emerge out of the relative success of francophone mobilization. These struggles involve a number of groups who identify themselves more or less closely with the Franco-Ontarian cause; they include members of the dominant English-speaking middle class as well as immigrants from a wide variety of backgrounds.

In this chapter I will describe the legal context of governance of and access to Franco-Ontarian education; this is essentially a description of the ways in which francophones have moved over the past twenty years to take control over the elementary, secondary and post-secondary French-language education system within the legal and bureaucratic context of the state. It is also an account of how the federal and provincial governments' goals in the area of ethnolinguistic rights constrain Franco-Ontarians' courses of action. Finally, this account will highlight the ways in which these processes have brought to the fore two issues which are at the heart of current difficulties in clarifying the criteria of inclusion and exclusion which should permit the school system to fulfill its role as border patrol.

The first issue is the problem of students who arrive at school speaking little or no French (it is variously referred to as the issue of the *non parlants* or of *refrancisation*). This problem has practical dimensions insofar as teachers are not trained to teach in what becomes, for all practical purposes, a second-language context. Teachers find it especially difficult to function where a wide range of proficiency in French is represented in one classroom. But the problem has symbolic dimensions too, since it negates the basis of the claim for the legitimacy of the schools, namely that they are there to provide a special form of instruction for a distinct group of people, and in so doing, will contribute in turn to the maintenance of that distinctiveness.

The problem is, moreover, central to the debate about the best ways to achieve bilingualism, and about who may have privileged access to it. Is the primary goal of the school to advance the cause of students who already speak French, and to guarantee their privileged access to this form of linguistic capital, or is it to distribute French as widely as possible in order to provide a broader basis for the language's survival? Which of those goals is most readily attainable given the material and social conditions in which the schools exist?

The second problem has become known as the issue of *multiculturalisme*; this refers to the presence in Franco-Ontarian schools of students of an increasingly wide variety of ethnocultural backgrounds. Their presence calls into question the basis of group solidarity, what it means to be Franco-Ontarian. In so doing, it underscores some ways in which inequalities within Franco-Ontarian society may have been relegated to the background in the common struggle for rights and resources.

Taken together, these issues represent central processes of boundary formation and change. The way they get resolved will have a large impact on the meaning of what it means to be Franco-Ontarian. It will also have an impact on the way in which French is distributed, and hence on the ability of members of different ethnolinguistic groups to gain or retain access to bilingualism.

4.1. *La gestion:* Who sets the rules of the game?

The history of control of Franco-Ontarian education has been marked by a basic shift over the course of the last hundred years or so, from control situated primarily in the hands of the Catholic Church to control situated primarily in the hands of the provincial government of Ontario (Welch 1988; also cf. Chapter 2). This shift has had many effects, of course, among them to make it possible for members of the lay élite to position themselves as spokespeople for the community (Choquette 1977). This élite was drawn originally from the ranks of the professional classes, and its members were generally active in Church affairs. This élite still exists; however, in the 1960s, as government began to play a wider role, as education became more widespread and as Franco-Ontarian institutions began to proliferate in the wake of political mobilization, new élites began to emerge, drawn from the ranks of educators, government bureaucrats, artists and other intellectuals, and businesspeople (Welch 1988). It is these groups who have been fighting for control of Franco-Ontarian education. In some instances, the old and new élites are in conflict with each other, the first stressing the importance of the relationship between language, religion and community, the second the importance of universal values and technical skills and qualifications, although both groups share a sense of the importance of Franco-Ontarian identity (Welch 1988; Frenette – Gauthier 1990). At a broader level, both groups are engaged in negotiations with the state over the extent to which they may exercise exclusive control over Franco-Ontarian schools and post-secondary institutions within a state-run educational system.

This is the fundamental issue underlying the problem of *la gestion* (or governance): to what extent is it possible to use the educational system of the Ontario government to achieve the Franco-Ontarian community's (increasingly universalistic) economic and social goals, through the development of a strong ethnolinguistic (and hence necessarily particularistic) community? As Franco-Ontarian education has become more and more bound up in state processes and bureaucracies, the issue has become more and more salient. Until now, the élites, who have vested interests in control of Franco-Ontarian education, have maintained that it is possible to answer the question positively, and have developed strategies to increase their control of the French-language school system within the constraints of the legal and political systems which bind all citizens of the province. This section is an account of that struggle, as it affected first the elementary and secondary, and then post-secondary, levels of the educational system.

1968 is generally considered the date as of which Franco-Ontarian schools firmly became integrated into the provincial system, by virtue of the Ontario government's declaration of its commitment to public funding of French-language schools from kindergarten through to the end of high school,[31] and its affirmation of French as an official language of education (cf. Chapter 2). At the same time, the many small boards which had existed across the province were consolidated; as a result, French-language schools found themselves, for the most part, in school boards dominated by anglophones.

The shift in general was problematic, causing tension between the supporters of Catholic education and those who were prepared to make the compromise the government was offering. In addition, there was tension over the nature of the schools to be established, including discussion of the desirability of offering some form of moral education and the extent to which English should be used as a language of instruction. The religious issue tended to divide both the old and the new élites and the middle and working classes; the language issue corresponded principally to a class division (Frenette – Gauthier 1990; Lapointe ct al. 1987; Welch 1988; cf. also Chapters 2 and 3). While some communities opted in the end for bilingual schools, most eventually obtained French-language public high schools; frequently courses in values education were offered, and, in many respects, the public schools differed little from Catholic ones.

However, for a large part of the 1970s the supporters of French-language education also had to invest energy in mobilizing support simply to create schools in areas where they did not exist, since the new legislation often encountered resistance from the anglophone majority. The struggle in the Penetanguishene area, while particularly bitter, nonetheless provides a good example of the issues.

In the late 1960s and early 1970s, the Simcoe County Board of Education had added a few courses with French as the language of instruction to its otherwise English-language programme. These courses served not only the francophones of the region, but also the anglophones who would otherwise have lobbied for immersion programmes. In the late 1970s, the board's *Comité consultatif de langue française* (or CCLF) began lobbying for a homogeneous, distinct, French-language school. Many anglophones opposed this move, since the quasi-bilingual programme served their interests, and they feared that the establishment of a separate French-language school would prevent their children from having access to any form of French-language instruction. Others simply opposed the exercise of minority rights in such a fashion. Many francophones also preferred to maintain a "bilingual" programme in the English-language high school. Certainly the school board did what it could to avoid having to establish a French-language school.

Several years of bitter struggle followed, involving boycotts and the establishment during a 10-month period of an illegal French-language high school. By 1982, a school, l'École secondaire Le Caron, had been established, although its physical plant was inadequate and it was unable to offer a full range of courses. As we shall see below, this state of affairs eventually led to a lawsuit which was to have a profound effect on Franco-Ontarian education across the province. (See Sylvestre 1980 and Marchildon 1990 for more detailed accounts of the Penetanguishene struggle.)

Additional features of the new conditions under which French-language schools were to be established created difficulties both for elementary and secondary schools. The Education Act of 1974 specified that French-language educational services were to be provided only "where numbers warranted". Other regulations concerning levels of enrollment, which applied to English schools, were also applied to French ones. These regulations included the number of students required to open a school (generally 300), and the number required to obtain special services (such as an on-site librarian, speech therapist or psychoeducational consultant). In many communities, especially in southern Ontario where the francophone population was rarely concentrated within specific neighbourhoods or even regions, it was difficult to amass enough students in one place, first to justify opening a school, and second to obtain the kinds of services that were available in the local English-language schools. In response to this problem, in some areas, parents sought free bussing, to permit a dispersed population to come together in one school (it is now possible for students in southern Ontario to spend two or three hours a day on the school bus). As we shall see below, one other result of this difficulty was the admission to French-language schools of students who spoke little or no French.

By 1980, schools and services had largely been consolidated (although problems persisted in many areas). Parents and other members of the Franco-Ontarian community were then able to turn to the nagging problem of decision-making. As a minority in most boards, francophone parents had little control over the election of trustees. Even where they were able to influence such elections, their trustees were often a minority on the board. Otherwise, francophone input to board decision-making was indirect, through the minority-language advisory committees (CCLFs).

French-language advisory committees generally simply institutionalized the problem of the necessity of going to members of the majority in order to obtain resources for the schools. In 1984–1985, for example, CCLF members, school administrators and teachers in one board complained to me about the difficulty of obtaining the services of a speech therapist and of a librarian, or even of obtaining adequate, up-to-date teaching materials, since every request had to be processed either through an anglophone-dominated board of trustees or an anglophone-dominated board bureaucracy (and sometimes both); the majority, it was felt, had little understanding of the needs of the French-language schools, and were constantly preoccupied with the needs of the vast majority of English-language schools which dominated the board. The CCLFs were of limited usefulness since they were, after all, only advisory committees, and had next to no real power.

In addition, in some areas, such as Toronto, parents of different backgrounds and representing different interests began struggling for control of the local committee. Two forms of struggle emerged: conflict between parents who opposed the presence in the schools of large numbers of non-francophone students and those who saw no, or little, problem with that phenomenon, and struggle between francophones who had long been established in Canada and those who were more recently arrived. Both these issues will be taken up in detail in the following section.

In general, however, many people became increasingly frustrated with the limits imposed on the development of Franco-Ontarian education by the current administrative arrangements. These included parents whose children were enrolled in French-language schools, francophone trustees and CCLF members, and organized spokespeople of the Franco-Ontarian community. The courts became essential instruments in their attempts to sort these problems out. In 1983, two lawsuits were brought before the Ontario courts which were to have a profound effect on the basic conditions of provision of French-language services and on the control of French-language schools.

Both lawsuits were based on provisions of Article 23 of the Canadian Charter of Rights and Freedoms, the federal constitution which had been repatriated and amended in 1982 (see Chapter 2). Among other things, Article 23 was designed to protect rights to minority-language education across Canada, that is, to English-language education in Quebec, and to French-language education outside Quebec. As indicated in Chapter 2, it also defined the nature of the population having rights to minority-language education. Once the Charter was signed (although not by Quebec), the federal government issued a challenge: you have a constitution now, it said, use it (Marchildon, personal communication).

The two lawsuits which were a response to this challenge were coordinated and mutually supportive. The first was filed by Jacques Marchand, a parent from Penetanguishene, on behalf of a large group of parents with children enrolled in the École secondaire Le Caron.[32] When the Marchand family moved back to

Penetanguishene from the Windsor area in 1983, the community was caught up in the latest episode of the long struggle for the establishment of adequate French-language educational services which had marked the community for a decade.

Specifically, students at Le Caron wished to have access to courses in wood- and metal-working, at the time impossible since the school board had set up the school without the appropriate workshops and equipment. The board argued that Le Caron students were not numerous enough to warrant the construction of workshops; they could use the workshops in the local English-language high school, even though it meant returning to the English-language milieu they had fought so hard to get away from, and in addition required using the space at the convenience of the English-language school. Further, to do so required travelling half an hour into town. Marchand and others felt that the francophone students were being discriminated against, and that, contrary to the Charter of Rights and Freedoms, the "where numbers warrant" constraint prevented francophone students from receiving educational services equivalent to those offered to anglophones. In taking the matter to court, Marchand, backed by the *Association canadienne-française de l'Ontario*, argued that minority-language education should be a matter of equity, not equality. When the case was finally resolved in 1986, the courts found in favour of Marchand, effectively rendering void the limitation of numbers in the provision of minority language educational services.

At the same time, in 1983, the ACFO instituted its own proceedings against the government. Their lawsuit was also based on Article 23 of the Charter of Rights and Freedoms. The ACFO focussed on the wording of section 3(b), which refers in the French version to the "*établissements d'enseignement de la minorité linguistique* [educational facilities *of* the linguistic minority (my emphasis)]". The English-language text reads "minority language educational facilities", but both French and English versions have the force of law. The ACFO read the French text to mean, more or less, "educational facilities belonging to the linguistic minority", and so, on the basis of this reading of the wording of the French text, the ACFO argued that francophones had the right to direct control of French-language educational institutions. In 1985, the Ontario Court of Appeal found in its favour.

The resulting 1986 legislation (Bill 75), which came into effect in late 1988, made provision for that control. Specifically, it provided for the creation of two autonomous French-language boards, one in Ottawa and one in Toronto, and for the establishment of minority-language sections (*Conseils d'éducation de langue française*, or CELFs) within other boards.[33] Those boards and sections are controlled by trustees elected directly by those having rights of access to

4.1 *La gestion:* Who sets the rules of the game?   117

minority-language education (again, as defined by Article 23). Boards may buy the services of other boards to provide French-language services for students if they feel they cannot provide them themselves.

Article 23 has thus become the basis for decisions regarding rights of access to Franco-Ontarian education; that fact has not been without problematic consequences of its own, due principally to the ways in which rights of access to minority-language education are defined.[34] First, Article 23 protects the rights of access of parents who already have children enrolled in those schools, and those children will themselves have those same rights when they become adults. This group thus includes parents who would not have such rights according to the other criteria specified in the article, because they themselves were not educated in French and because French is not their first language.

Second, it excludes some parents whom, many feel, should be included. In early 1990, the Ministry of Education released a consultation document which proposed, among other things, a broadening of the Article 23 definition. Specifically, it aimed to include French-speaking immigrants by extending rights of access to permanent residents of Canada (and not only to Canadian citizens), to those who, of Canada's two official languages, learned French first, and to those who (or whose children) attended a French-language elementary school anywhere in the world.[35]

Finally, the use of Article 23 has not completely clarified the issue of access: schools may not refuse access to parents who have the identified rights, but it is not clear whether they may accept parents who do not. Certainly, many schools continue to accept not only the children of parents whose rights would be established under the proposed changes, but also those of others who would still fall outside the limits; those children are generally screened by admissions committees, who usually are most concerned with the children's ability to speak French.

Currently, then, it would appear that the long struggle for Franco-Ontarian control of Franco-Ontarian education, within the state-run education system, has largely been won. The consequences of this process are still largely unclear, since Franco-Ontarians have been controlling their schools only since December of 1988. Certainly a number of technical problems remain to be worked out, and the relationship between the public and Catholic sectors is still problematic.

Furthermore, most areas of the province are convinced of the necessity of full-fledged boards, rather than the current format of French-language sections alongside (usually more numerous) English-language sections of regionally-defined school boards. Several areas of the province have been lobbying for homogeneous French-language boards along the lines of those which already exist in Toronto and Ottawa; one such request has already been granted. This trend, however, will test the limits of the strategy adopted by the community over twenty years ago. Now that francophones have largely obtained the control they sought, will they, in fact, be able to use the system both to bolster and to redefine what it means to be Franco-Ontarian? Will it be possible to adopt universal values and acquire skills necessary to entry into the global economy, and still be something different, still be, in some sense, Franco-Ontarian?

Of course, anything the Franco-Ontarian community accomplishes at the level of elementary and secondary education can be neutralized if similar changes do not occur at the post-secondary level. If fundamental changes have occurred at the elementary and secondary school systems, the same has not been true of the community colleges and universities. As a result, just as it has lobbied for, and obtained, increasing control over French-language elementary and high schools (albeit within the general state apparatus), so is the Franco-Ontarian élite now lobbying for increased autonomy in the area of post-secondary education. Beginning in 1968, French-language courses or programmes were established on six campuses of the provincial community college system (which offer two-year programmes leading to certificates in technical, service and semi-professional fields). Currently, among Ontario's sixteen universities, four are designated as bilingual by the provincial government (University of Ottawa, with its affiliated theology faculty, Université St-Paul; Laurentian University, with its affiliated theology faculty, the Université de Sudbury; the Collège universitaire de Hearst, also affiliated with Laurentian; and the Collège Glendon, which is part of York University).

While some components of these institutions have been offering French-language programmes for many years (in Ottawa's case, over a century), by the 1980s it had become clear that the range of programmes available in French community colleges and universities in Ontario was severely limited compared to that which was offered in English (Churchill et al. 1985). In particular, it was evident that the programmes which were available were concentrated in the humanities and the social sciences, the traditional occupational domains of the francophone élite. Very few francophones thus ever became qualified in those fields, and at the high school level, it was difficult to find qualified and enthusiastic teachers who could provide role models and convince students that there might be a future for them in science. No wonder, it was argued, that so few francophones pursued studies in the areas of science and technology; no wonder that already in high school students began dropping those courses (Churchill et al. 1985). However, as far as the new élite is concerned, it is crucial that francophones learn to make their way into the areas of science and technology; that is where the modern world is being made, and francophones must have a role to play there if they are to succeed as individuals and as a group.

4.1 *La gestion:* Who sets the rules of the game?

In bilingual institutions francophones suffered from the endemic problem of competing with anglophones for scarce resources, if not having actually to request those resources from anglophones who controlled them. Student organizations and Franco-Ontarian lobbying groups, in particular, began to argue that it was time for francophones to take matters into their own hands: it would never be possible to change their situation within the current structures.

In 1990, the first autonomous, entirely French-language community college opened in the Ottawa area. Plans are currently being developed for similar campuses in the north and the south. It is worth quoting from a recent newspaper article on planning for the southern college, since it expresses well the vision of Franco-Ontarian education which is being pursued throughout the system. The following is an account of the results of the deliberations of the committee responsible for studying the advisability of different models:

> *Un modèle et un seul a été retenu ... : celui de la création d'un collège de langue française à décentralisation relative pour desservir le Centre/Sud-Ouest de la province. Les organismes francophones se sont alors formés en Collectif pour le Collège de langue française du Centre/Sud-Ouest. Le Collectif a d'ailleurs retenu certains principes de base qui devront être respectés dans la mise sur pied de l'éventuel collège de langue française. Ils sont: l'accessibilité des programmes à tous les francophones de la région; un niveau et une qualité de services équivalents à ceux disponibles dans les institutions anglophones existantes; une gouvernance de l'institution par et pour les francophones; la création d'un milieu linguistique et culturel francophone, tenant compte de la dimension ethnoculturelle présente dans la région; des emplacements physiques distincts; un rayonnement de l'institution au sein de la communauté; une juridiction exclusive des programmes de langue française, tout ceci en vue de garder les jeunes dans la région, d'assurer le recyclage approprié de la main d'oeuvre adulte et de donner une continuité à l'enseignement de langue française des niveaux élémentaire et secondaire.* [Only one model was selected...: that of the creation of a relatively decentralized French-language college to serve the Centre/Southwest of the province. The francophone organizations then formed a Collective for the French-Language College of the Centre/Southwest. Moreover, the Collective selected certain principles to be respected in the eventual establishment of a French-language college. These are: the accessibility of programmes to all francophones of the region; a level and quality of programmes equivalent to those of existing anglophone institutions; governance of the institution by and for francophones; the creation of a francophone linguistic and cultural milieu which takes into account the ethnocultural dimension present in the region; a distinct physical plant; links between the institution and the community; exclusive jurisdiction over French-language programmes, all this with a view to keeping young people in the region, to providing appropriate retraining to the adult workforce and to providing continuity in French-language education from the elementary and secondary [to post-secondary] levels.] (*L'Express de Toronto* 27 February – 5 March 1990, p. 3.)

The process is more complicated at the university level, since universities are more independent of government control than are either the school or the community college system. In 1987, the *Conseil de l'éducation franco-ontarienne* organized a meeting to discuss the future of Franco-Ontarian post-secondary education. A youth organization, *Direction Jeunesse*, and the francophone students' organization of the University of Ottawa, presented position papers and arguments which were among the most radical articulated during the two days of the meeting. Nothing less than a Franco-Ontarian university would permit francophone students to fully develop, as students and as francophones. Since then, similar positions have been endorsed by the ACFO. Other interested parties, notably those already working within existing bilingual universities, have also begun lobbying for a Franco-Ontarian university (for example, through the recently-created *Société des universitaires de langue française de l'Ontario* (or SULFO)).

Within the SULFO, and elsewhere, some take an attentuated stance, arguing for increased francophone control, even autonomy, within existing structures, or, at most, the establishment of a separately controlled network which would bring together existing programmes and faculty. Thus most Franco-Ontarian organizations agree on the necessity of increased francophone control over Franco-Ontarian university education, but there is no consensus as to the most appropriate model to adopt. Nonetheless, major Franco-Ontarian lobbying and advisory groups, notably ACFO and CEFO, have focussed on post-secondary education as a key area to be developed. As with the school and community college systems, it is argued that Franco-Ontarians will never be able to obtain the full range of programmes necessary to facilitate their participation in global processes unless they themselves control the institutions; moreover, the participation they seek is participation as francophones, and only direct control over post-secondary programmes will protect that identity.

Because of the way in which the governance of Franco-Ontarian education has developed (and continues to develop), it remains a key arena for working out some of the fundamental problems of Franco-Ontarian life. First, through asserting control of the governance of educational institutions, francophones are attempting to achieve social mobility within a context defined in universal, mainstream terms. While their section of the system is separate, it operates within the same general parameters set by the provincial government for everybody, and aims at "universal" values. At the same time, francophones stake a claim to a separate system in part on the basis of demonstrated historical inequalities and in part on the basis of social difference. Franco-Ontarian lobbying groups and other organizations, as well as researchers and other politically mobilized individuals, have shown that operating in systems where the dominant group is in direct control works against francophones in terms of the general interests which they share with other members of the population: francophones have a higher than average rate of drop-outs and of illiteracy, for example, and those who do go on to higher education are over-represented in the social sciences and the humanities (Churchill et al. 1985; Carrier 1985; ACFO 1985). Ontario's francophones also have been able to mobilize themselves to correct this on the basis of a sense of social and cultural difference of which their language is now the most important emblem. But if their strategy is successful on its own terms they risk losing both bases for their claim to separate systems; they will look just like everyone else. The problem, unresolved, and largely unposed as yet, is how to use these institutions to create a new basis for the ethnic boundary which will still allow francophones access to the resources they wish to obtain.

In the meantime, a second problem, which *has* been the subject of discussion and debate among Franco-Ontarians, also requires attention. As francophones have established their claim to a separate system under the umbrella of the state, they have had to define who counts as francophone. This is the problem of defining the bases of exclusion and inclusion, of deciding (using the courts or otherwise) who may participate in making decisions about Franco-Ontarian education and who may send their children to those institutions. The problem, which is one, fundamentally, of deciding who is a Franco-Ontarian, has become more acute as more people find Franco-Ontarian schools attractive institutions.

The outcome of that process will have consequences for what it means to be Franco-Ontarian in a number of ways. First, those who participate in making decisions about the schools will have something to say about the kinds of behaviour that will be considered appropriate and valuable for a Franco-Ontarian to be able to display. Hence, they will have something to say about the kinds of knowledge (linguistic and otherwise) distributed in Franco-Ontarian schools. To the extent that only some students will already have access to that knowledge outside school, Franco-Ontarian schools (in the same way as any others) will favour certain forms of social and cultural reproduction, potentially placing some groups at a disadvantage while facilitating school success for others. Finally, the social and economic base of those who eventually find their place there will influence the extent to which Franco-Ontarian schools can offer a place from which to build a collective life from a position of power rather than from one of subordination.

However, this process is only beginning. In the following section, I will explore the ways in which the problem of defining the criteria for choosing the players is currently manifesting itself, by focussing on issues on both sides of the power coin. The issue of *non-parlants* points to the problem of the struggle between francophones, as a subordinate group, and anglophones, as a dominant group, over the increasingly valued resource of the French language. The issue of *le multiculturalisme* points to the problem of shifting boundaries which emerge from the new power which francophones have, in fact, been able to acquire.

4.2. *Les non parlants* and *le ...*
Who is allowed to play?

The consequences of the intersec... ...graphic processes with the governance issues ... re manifested in concrete ways in the school system. Two phenomena stand out: the presence in Franco-Ontarian schools of students who speak little or no French, and the presence in those schools of French-speaking students of a wide variety of ethnocultural backgrounds. These are students who, for different reasons, do not conform to the central image that Franco-Ontarians have of themselves, and who, in many ways, threaten not only the ethnic boundary, but the legitimacy of bases for mobilization which brought Franco-Ontarians their institutions in the first place.

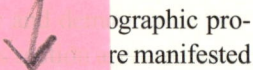

There are several reasons why students who speak little or no French may be present in Franco-Ontarian schools. In many cases, the underlying issue has been the necessity to find enough students to justify opening a school. This is a difficult goal to achieve when the French-speaking population is already small and is often geographically dispersed, all the more so when not all francophones are convinced that a French-language education is in the best interests of their children. But others who come forward to fill the gap do so for a variety of reasons and in a number of ways.

In the most extreme cases they may almost be recruited. One Toronto mother told me that she had never considered a French-language education for her children, since they were an English-speaking family. However, when her oldest child began school, the nearest one was a newly-opened French-language school which needed students; one grandparent had been francophone, and so she sent first one and then her other children there. When she and her family moved out of the community, she had no real intention of enrolling her children in a French-language school in her new neighbourhood. However, the principal of her childrens' old school took the initiative of calling up his counterpart at Ste-Anne, the French-language school closest to the family's new home, and arranged a transfer.

In other cases, non-francophone parents have an expressed interest in ensuring that their children learn French (see Chapter 3). In some instances, this interest has been manifested in enrollment in immersion programmes. However, immersion programmes have not always been available, and in addition, for some, French-language schools were better than immersion, because they

4.2 *Les non parlants* and *le multiculturalisme* 123

offered a better and more authentic language learning experience. For others, there was also an ideological commitment to supporting French-language minority education.

For many of these non-francophone parents, increasing francophone powers of governance are proving unsettling. In Toronto, one high school programme, which attracted many non-francophone parents, is in fact situated within a prestigious English-language high school, and until 1991 the students were free to take a number of courses in the English section, as well as, of course, participating in extracurricular activities. Most of the non-francophone parents and students were pleased with this arrangement. They are associated with one of the highest-status high schools in the city. Further, they are able to take courses in English, which they feel is essential to their preparation for the English-language universities most of them plan to attend. They want their school experience to be bilingual, as corresponds to their vision of what a bilingual country should be like.

When, in December 1988, the new French public school board took over control of this "module" (as such entities have been called), several trustees called for it to be revamped. Specifically, they wanted it moved out of the English school and expanded to provide a full range of programmes in French only. This was necessary, they argued, because the current arrangements made it impossible to create a French atmosphere in the school or to provide a full range of courses in French, and students who considered themselves francophone (the clientèle the board felt had to be their primary concern) felt marginalized and diminished in what was supposed to be their school.

After months of frequently acrimonious dispute, the decision was finally taken to open a new school, entirely French, somewhere else in the downtown area. It is widely expected that a number of non-francophone families will not make the move with the rest of the school when the new institution is opened. Many supporters of the move argue that in the end the school will be the better for it: "*il fallait percer l'abcès*" [we had to pierce the abcess [of endless disputes between groups with opposing interests]]. Other non-francophone parents will, of course, make the move, because they find the arguments in favour of such a move convincing and because they see the possibility of achieving their goal of bilingualism within such a structure. But the terms of the discourse will have changed, and those who argue that francophones need a separate space will have established themselves as the dominant voice.

Two other groups of parents send their children to French-language schools despite limited proficiency in French on the part of their children. The first are parents who are of French origin, and who may speak French themselves, but whose children do not. If the children do not yet speak French, it is usually either because one parent does not speak French and English has become the *lingua franca* of the home, or because the parents have themselves switched to English despite being both of French origin. They nonetheless attach a certain importance to French, comprised of varying proportions of an awakening to the value that French has acquired since they were children, a recognition that they wish to pass on what is, after all, their language to their children, and a desire to return themselves to the community they had left.

The second group consists of parents whose language is generally other than French or English, but who wish their children to speak French. In some cases, the parents may have been educated in French or have learned it as a second language, either in their country of origin or in a francophone country. For some, French as a second language is traditional for their class in their country of origin; others may actually have lived in a francophone region (usually France or Quebec) before coming to Ontario. Numerous Polish, Iranian, Somali and Vietnamese parents whose children are now in Ontario's French-language schools fit that description.

In addition, even where both parents speak French at home, living in a minority situation can have its effect on the ability of the children to speak French. Where there is no French neighbourhood, no French daycare or baby-sitting facilities, no French pre-school activities organized by the community, it is often difficult to ensure that a child will learn French the same way that he or she would in an environment where French was more widely used.

To a greater or lesser degree, then, the problem of children whose proficiency in French is limited is present in most of Ontario. Some school boards attempted to set up admissions committees, usually made up of the school principal, the teacher of the class in which the prospective student would be enrolled, and one or two other teachers from the same school. When the Charter of Rights and Freedoms came into effect, this became a less legally viable solution except for those cases where the parents did not have rights of access. In any case, the committees were (and are) frequently problematic (Heller 1989b): there was not always a consensus among committee members as to what kinds of performances would be considered appropriate or adequate, and some feared that the very arbitrariness of the situation would disadvantage some children, as had the similar screening of children in Quebec after Bill 22 (1974) required students to demonstrate adequate proficiency in English in order to gain permission to attend English-language schools.

Some parents, teachers and principals explained to me what went on in admissions interviews. Frequently, children (often as young as four years old) were asked to name objects in a book or pick out named objects; they were asked to obey simple commands (*Monte sur la chaise, Ferme la porte* [Climb up on the chair, close the door]); they were asked questions about themselves and their home life. In no case was the vocabulary considered esoteric, but some parents felt that the very situation, as a communicative encounter, was strange to the child and sometimes even frightening; they wondered what kind of judgement could really be made on the basis of any performance under such circumstances.

School boards also adopted a variety of programme solutions to this problem (Mougeon et al. 1984; Mougeon – Heller 1986). A survey conducted by one team of researchers (Mougeon et al. 1984) included responses from 42 out of the 55 school boards with French-language schools. These 42 boards accounted for 263 French-language schools; of the 42, 38 reported the presence of English-dominant students, especially in the Northeast, the Centre and the South.

A sub-sample of 29 school boards reported on the programme options they had chosen to address the issue. Where francophones form a strong majority, the problem is less evident, that is, there are fewer students whose command of French is weak, and there are more language learning resources available for those who are present. Hence, the problem is usually not dealt with in an institutionalized way. Where francophones form a weak majority they may not have the clout to get special programmes established, or the problem may be so widespread that all teachers must deal with it in the regular classroom.

Where francophones form about 30 percent-60 percent of the population, however, school boards have tended to establish specific programmes designed to increase the French proficiency of such children to the point where they can be reintegrated into the regular classes. In some boards, there are *classes d'accueil* [welcome classes], in which students are grouped together (usually in a class, sometimes in a school) for one to three years and then reintegrated. In others, students are removed from their classes on an individual or small group basis, and given 30-60 minutes' special instruction, every day or several times a week. These are generally termed *cours de rattrapage* [catch-up classes] or *cours de refrancisation* [refrenchification classes]; the latter term is interesting, since it so clearly implies that the students once spoke French but can no longer do so.

Boards seem, on the whole, satisfied with these programmes. Very little is known about them, however. It is not always clear on what basis children are identified as requiring such support, what forms of knowledge are considered most important for them to master, how decisions are made to reintegrate them into regular classes or what happens to them in the regular classroom once they get there. It is not known how this experience may be different for children who speak little French but for different reasons (that is, whether because they are of non-francophone background, because their parents are assimilated francophones or because English is used as a common language at home between parents of different language backgrounds). But those are questions which go beyond the reasons those children were identified as a problem in the first place: the threat that they presented to the schools' ability to maintain a French-language environment within their walls. Rather, it is in the schools' interests to find a solution, that is, to find a way to keep those students without having their presence perceived as an obstacle to the development of other students.

The solution the school boards have found allows them to admit the students they require in order to operate the kind of schools they want and in order to serve a population they want to serve (and in some cases must serve), while at the same time maintaining French as the dominant language within the school milieu. Finally, it allows them to respond to the concerns of both francophone and non-francophone parents: francophone children are "protected" from the influence of non-francophones for a certain amount of time, until the threat posed by those children is neutralized by their increased command of French; non-francophone children are provided with the language they came to acquire, and are soon enough integrated into the regular class to allow for the interaction in an authentic milieu which was always meant to be part of the package (Mougeon – Heller 1986). Francophones can see that they retain control in this situation, but they can do so without having to give up the students they so badly need to fill their schools. As one commentator put it: "*il faut mettre de l'eau dans notre vin*" [we have to put water in our wine].[36]

But the argument over the proportion of water to wine goes on. Indeed, since the court decisions of the mid-1980s upholding the rights of francophones to equivalent services, and to control over educational institutions, francophones in many areas no longer accept these compromises. As a result, in Sudbury, Timmins, Sault Ste. Marie and Thunder Bay, they have abandoned the elementary schools in the separate school board, and have lobbied the public board to open French-language schools with stricter admissions criteria (see Chapter 3).

The second major issue, that of the increasingly multicultural nature of the student body, is proving less amenable to structural compromise. Certainly, Franco-Ontarians are not alone in grappling with the consequences of immigration. Canada as a whole has always been dependent on immigration in order to function. However, if francophones have been influenced by immigration in the past, it has largely been in the form of competition with immigrants in certain sectors of the economy and in institutions such as the Church, which brings together co-religionists. There were few French-speakers among immigrants of the past (they came instead mainly from the British Isles, northern and then southern Europe, from China, Japan and the Caribbean). While some immigrants learned to speak French because of their social position on the boundary between French and English, rarely did they assimilate to the French-speaking ethnic group.

Further, as Canada has come to increasingly recognize the place of immigrants in Canadian society, francophones have struggled to retain their privileged position as one of the two founding peoples and as speakers of one of Canada's two official languages. Explaining what is for them the intrinsic difference between francophones and immigrants based on francophones' position as a conquered people has become a pressing concern. As indicated earlier (see Chapter 3), the danger perceived by many francophones is that they will be counted as one of many ethnic groups in Canada, on an equal basis with each other, but subordinate to the dominant English-speakers (Breton 1984; Berthelot 1990). They therefore reject the use of the term "multiculturalism", nor do they label themselves as an "ethnic group", for fear of the connotations these terms have acquired.

In the 1960s, the relationship among official language and immigrant groups began to change. First, more francophone immigrants began to arrive. These included those whose first language was French, largely from Europe, but also elsewhere; for example, the late 1960s saw the arrival in Montreal of a fairly large group of French-speaking Moroccan Jews who had fled Morocco after the Six Day War, and Haitians immigrated in several waves from the 1960s on. There have also been, as mentioned earlier, immigrants who speak French because it was a language of schooling or a *lingua franca* in their countries of origin, or who had lived in a French-speaking country before arriving in Canada. This "francophone" immigration was encouraged as an explicit policy by the Quebec government from about the early 1970s, especially as it began to be recognized that the birth rate among francophones was declining drastically. In addition, the provisions of Bill 101 ensured that, after 1977, all immigrants from outside Canada would have to send their children to French-language schools.

Initially, most, though not all, francophone immigrants did indeed go to Quebec. Those who came directly to Ontario were not necessarily aware of a francophone presence there, but once having discovered it, frequently chose to affiliate with it. During a downturn in Quebec's economy in the early 1980s, many immigrants who had initially gone to Quebec moved to the economically stronger urban centres of Ontario. At the same time, much internal migration (including but by no means limited to francophones) was directed to Ontario. In the 1980s, then, the francophone communities of Ontario were welcoming francophones from other parts of Canada, indeed from all over the globe, as well as speakers of languages other than French or English who had learned French somewhere in the course of their lives.

In addition to a diversity of ethnocultural backgrounds, there is also a diversity of class backgrounds and of occupations among Ontario's francophones. Indeed, Bernard (1988) has pointed out that inequalities in income levels and levels of education among francophones are at least as important as those existing between francophones as a whole and other ethnic groups. Thus, there are still francophone unskilled or semi-skilled labourers, but many francophones also fill jobs in the expanding service sector. Finally, since Toronto has become the financial centre of Canada, and since there are now francophones at the management levels of large companies and financial institutions, many of the new arrivals are middle or upper-middle class. Among the latter group, however, there are fewer who establish themselves permanently in Ontario.

I can best illustrate these patterns with the life histories of some of my friends and acquaintances. I met Louise, a high school science teacher, when I was doing field work one winter in a local high school. She had arrived from Quebec the year before with her husband, Marc, and their three children. They moved because Marc had gotten a promotion in the large bank for which he worked, which necessitated a stint in the Toronto head office. After three years in Toronto, Marc received another promotion in the Montreal branch, and the family moved back, probably permanently.

Nadine, on the other hand, had come to Toronto from her native Quebec as a young student, intending to learn English. She enrolled in law school in Toronto, where she met, and eventually married, an anglophone fellow student. She sent her children to French-language schools, but after several years moved them to a bilingual school closer to home.

Nguyen was a Vietnamese high school student whom I interviewed in the course of another study some time in 1985. He and his family had gone to Quebec as refugees a few years earlier. He and his siblings, who spoke no French on arrival in Canada, went to school in French in Quebec. For economic reasons, they moved to Toronto in 1984, as Nguyen was about to begin his last year of high school. Since he spoke no English, it was decided he should attend a French-language school. His parents had been unable to find anything but entry-level service jobs.

Sara was a Grade 7 student in a class in which I was conducting fieldwork in 1986. She and her family had fled Iran when she was still quite young, and had lived in France for several years, where her father worked as an engineer. For economic reasons, they left France for Canada in 1984. Sara had attended school in France, and spoke no English when she arrived in Toronto.

Thus francophones come to Toronto for a variety of reasons. Some are looking for work, some want to learn English, some are transferred, some are political refugees. Not all of them intend to stay, but some of them end up staying

4.2 *Les non parlants* and *le multiculturalisme* 129

even though they never intended to. Some expect to find an English-speaking city where they have no rights as francophones; others do not wish to exercise their rights; still others expect to be able to live at least part of their lives in French, even if they have to struggle to accomplish that. Also, people change the way they feel as their life circumstances change: a job, marriage, children, simply the passage of time, all contribute to changing the meaning of French and English for any individual.

Most of the new arrivals in Ontario have rights of access to French-language education, even if only by virtue of a relatively brief stay in Quebec: Louise and Nadine both sent their children to French-language schools, and Nguyen had no problems enrolling. Only Sara's parents, strictly speaking, could not be said to have the right to send their children to a French-language school, since French is not their first language, and no member of the family was ever educated in French in Canada. However, it is precisely because of families like hers that some educators propose that rights of access be extended to permanent residents of Canada whose first official language is the language of the minority (whatever other languages they may have learned prior to learning French). Indeed, most school principals argue that to turn away a fluent speaker of French, especially when they speak no English, is madness, whatever the constitution says. However, others argue that many of these students do not in fact speak French fluently, and prefer to use the Charter of Rights and Freedoms to exclude them (see Chapter 5 for a fuller discussion of this debate).

Those who were there before the new arrivals sometimes constitute themselves (however fictively; cf. Chapters 2 and 3 and Handler 1988) as *Franco-Ontariens* or *Canadiens-français*; their relatively successful mobilization has been predicated on a constructed sense of shared identity, shared traditions, and shared ways of looking at the world which have grown out of a shared history. To share the valued resource that they have made of French, and to share control of the institutions which regulate access to French, is itself a problem. It is especially problematic when that sharing also entails the full participation in francophone society of people whose background and culture is different. It is feared that the basis of mobilization will be eroded, and that ground won will quickly be lost. Perhaps most importantly, immigration points to the contradiction inherent in francophones' successful mobilization (in the same way as does the presence of anglophones in French-language schools): mobilized as francophones to acquire resources, once those resources are acquired, what is the reason for remaining francophone?

At the same time there is a recognition that this dilemma is a logical consequence of past and current efforts at mobilization and that, in fact, it is important that the francophone population recruit newcomers through immigration, since the birth rate is so low that it alone cannot ensure maintenance of the population. In Quebec, for obvious reasons, the discussion of this matter has been more public than it has been in francophone Ontario. A series of events have kept the question in the public eye there: the shooting of a black youth by a white police officer, race riots in high schools, a controversial television film on immigration to Quebec. The largest school board in Quebec found itself in the midst of an uproar when information about an upcoming parent poll was leaked: the board had planned to ask parents if they thought it would be a good thing for students who were born in Quebec to be separated from those who were not. The board claimed that they had no intention of acting on that information, that it was simply a good measure of parental attitudes towards immigrant students. The public outcry was such that the board was forced to withdraw the question.

Indeed, in Quebec, many anti-racist organizations have sprung up, and anti-racist education is high on the government's agenda. Nonetheless, pluralist education is often placed within the context of the necessity of knowing first who one is before one can accept others (cf., e.g., Berthelot 1990; Lucier 1987). Francophones in Quebec argue that tolerance of others will emerge from francophones' own strong sense of security and identity, which itself depends on their control of the state within Quebec.

> *Notre société oscille encore entre la peur et l'ouverture. Il ne fait pas de doute que l'affirmation de ce que nous sommes a contribué à changer profondément notre perception des Autres. Aujourd'hui, le Québec n'a d'autre choix que de poursuivre dans cette voie, que ce soit à l'intérieur ou à l'extérieur du pacte confédératif. L'histoire de l'immigration est aussi le reflet de notre propre histoire. Un peuple immigrant d'abord, puis rapidement conquis, qui cherche – et qui réussit – à préserver sa langue et sa culture, qui se protège face au conquérant en se refermant sur lui-même. Puis un peuple qui se cherche, qui s'affirme, qui se définit et qui, finalement, exprime sa volonté d'être libre; confiant en son avenir, il manifeste davantage d'ouverture face à l'accueil de l'Autre (...) La reconnaissance du caractère distinct du Québec ne suppose en rien un nationalisme chauvin; il s'agit d'un fait historique, d'une réalité sociale. Cela justifie en principe l'action distincte et autonome du Québec en matière de recrutement et de sélection des nouveaux venus sur son territoire, et fonde, du même souffle, la nature de la société à laquelle ces derniers devront s'intégrer.*
>
> [Our society wavers between fear and openness. There is no doubt that what we are has contributed to profoundly changing our perception of Others. Today, Quebec has no choice but to follow this path, whether within the pact of Confederation or outside it. The history of immigration is also the reflection of our own history. First an immigrant people, then soon conquered, trying – and succeeding – to preserve its language and culture, protecting itself from the conqueror by withdrawing into itself. Then a people searching for itself, affirming itself, defining itself, and finally, expressing its will to be free; confident in its future, it demonstrates greater openness to welcoming the Other (...) The recognition of the distinct character of Quebec in no way implies a chauvinist nationalism; it is a historical

fact, a social reality. This justifies in principle the distinct and autonomous action of Quebec with respect to the recruitment and selection of new arrivals on its territory, and establishes, in the same breath, the nature of the society to which the latter will need to integrate themselves.] (Berthelot 1990: 35 and 65)

The clear implication is that Québécois must know who they are collectively before they can understand what it means to be, say, Haitian or Vietnamese or Salvadoran; as of yet, it is not possible for the Haitian, or Vietnamese or Salvadoran to be one of "us". In Ontario, similar boundary issues prevail (with the previously mentioned crucial difference that Québécois francophones have control of the state and Franco-Ontarians do not). Nonetheless, there have been tensions both within education and without regarding the relationship between francophones of different origins to each other within a collective enterprise of mobilization.

Initially, newly arrived francophones who chose to affiliate with Franco-Ontarian institutions did so within existing forms. In some areas, however, tensions developed, as some groups felt that their voice was being silenced. This was the case in the French-language advisory committee struggles to which I referred at the beginning of this chapter. It also happened within the *Association canadienne-française de l'Ontario*: in 1987, a group of Toronto-based francophones established the *Association multiculturelle franco-ontarienne*, or AMFO, a clear message that the umbrella lobbying group, ACFO, could no longer claim to represent all francophones in Ontario, and specifically, that it could no longer claim to represent francophones of non-Canadian origin. The AMFO has been received as a legitimate voice; it was, for example, invited when Franco-Ontarian organizations were asked by the government to consult on specific issues or documents. On the other hand, not all francophones of non-Canadian origin have forsaken the ACFO for it, and some are members of both organizations.[37]

Within Franco-Ontarian education, there is an increasing concern to provide what is labelled primarily as "multicultural" education, and to understand what forms such social differences take in Franco-Ontarian schools.[38] The Ministry of Education has made multicultural education one of its priorities for French-language schools, and urban school boards frequently cite multiculturalism as an area of concern for pre-service and in-service teacher training.

However, at the same time as there is a concern for including multicultural education in the curriculum, in teaching materials and in ways of teaching students of a wide variety of ethnocultural backgrounds, there remains a search for a distinctively Franco-Ontarian curriculum which also includes the general forms of knowledge with which all Ontario students are expected to become familiar. Franco-Ontarian education faces, in this respect, the same dilemma as that of their colleagues in Quebec. (This is reflected in the Ontario Ministry of

Education's concern to actively develop policies and programmes to promote French language and culture in Franco-Ontarian schools.) On the one hand, the mobilization of francophones and their access to resources depends on their ability to construct a common identity, and they have always tried to do this on the basis of some notion of shared culture. On the other hand, for moral, legal and practical reasons, they cannot exclude francophones whose origins are more varied and who share neither French-Canadian history nor culture.

As we shall see in more detail in the following chapter, francophones in Ontario react in different ways to this dilemma. For some it is a sign of the strength of the group, that others can be so attracted to it. For others, it is a source of concern for the maintenance of what they have come to think of as their particular cultural heritage. For still others, the situation is less a dilemma than it is an opportunity: it represents the possibility of constructing a new identity and way of life which does in fact resolve some basic problems of inequality and identity. If Franco-Ontarians can find a way to construct equal relations among members of diverse origins within the boundaries of their own group, they will have responded creatively to the problems of inequality against which they have been struggling for so many years. By the same token, in so doing, they will create a new cultural form which will still distinguish them from other groups, both from the dominant anglophone society and from francophones elsewhere.

The issue of the *non parlants* and the issue of *multiculturalisme* bring out different sides of what is essentially one dilemma: how to acquire and yet also share power. In order to do so, it is necessary to preserve a boundary which distinguishes francophones from other groups in Canadian society, on the basis of the construction of common cultural forms. At the same time, it is essential to do so in a way which avoids the reproduction of the very relations of inequality against which francophones have, relatively successfully, mobilized. If this is so hard to address in the Franco-Ontarian context, it is at least in part due to the fact that Franco-Ontarians approach the issues of *les non parlants* and *le multiculturalisme* from positions both of power and of subordination. In particular, they are constrained by a state apparatus which they do not entirely control, and by economic and political processes which originate elsewhere but which land up on their doorstep just the same.

The issues of *les non parlants* and *le multiculturalisme* have been useful to the examination of Franco-Ontarian education precisely because they point out so clearly how Franco-Ontarians are caught up in national and international processes, and where they are located in hierarchies of power. These issues, and others like them, will test the limits of the new élite's current strategy of governance within the state system, as well as the limits of mobilization strategies which gloss over major forms of social difference and social inequality within the boundaries of the group.

4.3. Power and subordination: The limits of current strategies

The limits of the possibilities afforded by mobilization within a state system will not, however, depend on local or regional processes alone. Because Quebec is such a powerful force behind the legitimacy of the francophone cause, much will depend on the path that province takes. As I write, debates still rage inside and outside Quebec over whether or not Quebec should be separate from the rest of Canada, and if so, how soon and to what extent. Francophones outside Quebec are thinking hard about what this might mean for them.

In the meantime, francophones continue to mobilize (or, in some cases, to remain mobilized). Their relative success has, however, revealed various forms of social difference within the community, of which *les non parlants* and *le multiculturalisme* are only the most frequently publicly debated. Regional differences have, in fact, always been recognized; everyone knows that living in a rural community where the economy is resource-based and increasingly marginal is radically different from living in an urban community where the major forms of Canadian wealth are generated. Everyone knows that francophones living in communities where they form a majority and where they have access to the resources of Quebec, experience life quite differently from francophones who live in isolated areas where they form small minorities.

But other differences have tended to be minimized, as Franco-Ontarians developed their own sense of identity in opposition to the Québécois, on the one hand, and to English-speakers, on the other. This tendency has been intensified by the increasing interest in French on the part of English-speakers and their increasing presence in Franco-Ontarian schools. It has been also been intensified by the anti-French backlash of English Ontario. For some, the concomitant reappearance of the spectre of Quebec's separation has also occasioned a closing of ranks, in resistance to the notion that such a secession would leave francophones outside Quebec with no options but to assimilate or move to Quebec.

The development of multiculturalism has exploded that myth of commonality. The Franco-Ontarian community has already embarked upon a voyage of discovery of how it may be possible to retain that sense of identity while recognizing not only profound differences but differences bound up in internal relations of inequality (Cardinal – Lapointe 1989). Many such areas require greater exploration, however: notable among them are gender relations and class relations.

Franco-Ontarian feminists have begun to examine how gender relations operate within the Franco-Ontarian community, pointing out that Franco-Ontarian women are doubly a minority, and are affected in particular ways by their class and region of residence (ACFO 1985; Coulombe 1985; Cardinal et al. in press). Some effort has been made to examine the position of female students, who, even more than their male classmates, may encounter insurmountable obstacles to access to social mobility, for example, to careers in science and technology. Little attention has been paid, however, to the role of and consequences for women in processes of mobilization which focus first on commonalities (commonalities which may be defined by others, and not by francophone women themselves).

Class differences have received less attention. Indeed, the first version of the position paper on the development of Franco-Ontarian education prepared in 1989 by the *Conseil de l'éducation franco-ontarienne* took great care to elaborate the concept of the respect of social differences within the Franco-Ontarian community without mentioning class differences at all; they were added further to comments from the academic community. To the extent that they have been taken up, they have been addressed with respect to specific issues. Notable among these have been the consequences for the francophone working class of the increasing marginalization of the resource-based industries of the north, and the high rate of illiteracy among francophone working class adults (Coulombe 1985; Welch 1988). However, while class certainly is involved in processes of selection within Franco-Ontarian education, those processes have never been examined in that light; in general, the relationship of class to the use of language, identity and other cultural forms in processes of social mobility has only begun to be explored.

As these areas are explored, they will certainly have an impact in turn on the forms that Franco-Ontarian mobilization takes and on the relationship between Franco-Ontarians and dominant social groups in Ontario society. It is equally important, however, to delve deeper into the ways in which the ideology of language and mobilization is constructed locally, to examine the ways in which schools, parents and students experience the relations between francophones and dominant society and the relations among francophones of diverse origins and experiences.

The following chapter is devoted, then, to a further exploration of the issues introduced here, that is, how school processes are involved in the regulation of access to the valued resources which the school distributes, including, most especially, the French language itself. Using Toronto's French-language schools as an example (albeit an extreme one), I will examine how social and economic processes brought together, in the course of the 1980s, students from a wide variety of backgrounds, with parents who did not all share the same goals and interests with regard to French-language education.

I will first examine the ideology of language prevalent in the schools in which I worked, and the ways in which the schools articulated to students and parents what its normative expectations were as concerns language choice and language use. I will then examine the ways in which parents articulated their own interests in interviews, and explain them as a function of their experience of French and English. Finally, I will examine how students draw on their varying linguistic resources in order to attempt to gain access to the resources that are most important to them in school: classroom-based knowledge, gained mainly through interaction with the teacher, or at any rate in interactions whose conventions are set by the teacher as representative of the school's normative order, and knowledge of the outside world, mediated through peer relations.

These sets of data show how individual parents and students resolve, in their own practices, some of the contradictions they live every day, and make it possible for institutions such as Franco-Ontarian schools to persist as the participants continue to work on the rules of the game. They also underscore how important the central value of bilingualism is to all concerned; the only question they are working out is the one of regulating access to it.

Chapter 5
Brokers and boundaries: French-language minority schools in Toronto

5.0. The Franco-Ontarian population and the French-language schools of Toronto

The population of francophones in Ontario may be dropping, but the number of francophones in the metropolitan Toronto area is rising. In 1941, there were 7,189 people who claimed French as their mother tongue in Toronto, representing 0.8 percent of the population.[39] In 1986, there were 43,845, and in 1991 49,800 (for both years, about 1.3 percent of the population). In addition, between 1981 and 1986 the number of people claiming both English and French as mother tongues went from 10,130 to 16,600, although this dropped to 12,760 in 1991. With the 5790 who reported French and some other language, or French, English and some other language, as mother tongues, the French mother tongue population of Toronto in 1986 was 66,235 or almost 2 percent of a total population of 3,427,170. In 1991, 6,200 people reported French and a non-official language, or French, English and a non-official language as mother tongues, bringing the French mother tongue population to 68,760, or about 1.8 percent of the total population of 3,893,046.

Drawn to Toronto largely for economic reasons, the francophone population is also becoming more and more diversified, both in terms of regional or national origin and in terms of occupation. Francophones come from all over Canada, with relatively large numbers drawn especially from Quebec. In addition, recent waves of immigration have brought Haitians and francophone Europeans, as well as people from areas where French is an important lingua franca or language of education; for example, there are significant numbers of Egyptians, Lebanese, Somalis and Iranians.

In many ways, this simply represents a continuation of the trend which Maxwell (1977) had already noted in the mid 1960s: francophones move to Toronto because of their jobs, choose to live in certain areas for reasons that have much more to do with their class interests than their ethnic affiliation, and only then make decisions about their participation in ethnic institutions. Of course, in the last twenty-five years another form of immigration has also developed: francophones move to Toronto to provide the services which the government and its agencies are increasingly committing themselves to providing, or to participate in French-language institutions which serve the providers of services and their families.

Not all the new arrivals participate in French-language institutions or activities. A few years ago, a television programme on this topic brought together a number of recent arrivals in Toronto. One single mother, originally from Quebec, pointed out that for her, and others like her, the question was really one of survival. For the first few years, she had to settle into her apartment and her job, arrange education and daycare for her children, find out how to buy food and clothes and other necessities, and learn how to get around the city. Her first priority was to learn English so that she could accomplish her tasks. Only once she was settled in could she begin to think about what it meant to be French in Toronto, and to begin to make decisions about how to spend her free time. Indeed, for most new arrivals, the existence of francophone institutions is often far from apparent; unless one's occupation brings one into contact with other francophones, it is relatively easy to spend several years in Toronto without being aware of the networks that do exist.

Nonetheless, others do seek out these possibilities, at least to the extent of sending their children to French-language schools. For many, especially those arriving in the middle of the year with school-age children, this represents one way of accomplishing the transition with the least amount of trauma possible. The schools thus benefit from a constant influx of francophone students, many of them from outside Ontario.

However, it is not only francophones who participate in francophone institutions and activities. On any given evening at the one French-language theatre many of the patrons will be chatting to each other in English. Many social clubs and professional associations attract people whose first language is other than French. Bilingual businesspeople and local politicians attend monthly luncheons to hear speakers address in French matters of concern to the national business community, and to cement informal ties. While some of them have children in immersion programs, others have enrolled their children in French-language schools.

Indeed, both the number of schools and the number of other types of French-language institutions have increased rapidly over the course of the last twenty years or so. Before 1965, there were activities organized through the parish of Sacré-Coeur, and a benevolent society, the Club Richelieu, which attracted mainly francophone businessmen (founded in 1956).

In the early 1960s, the francophone community began to be more diversified. There were increasing numbers of middle-class francophones in the city, as well as an increasing interest in French-English bilingualism on the part of middle-class anglophones. Between 1966 and 1970 a number of new francophone or bilingual groups and institutions were established, including notably a second parish, a theatre, the bilingual Glendon College, a local chapter of the *Association canadienne-française de Toronto*, and, in 1969, the first high school. In addition, francophones began to develop French-language media. In a recent article, *L'Express de Toronto*, a local French-language newspaper, noted that French radio and television in Toronto date from the early 1970s (*L'Express de Toronto* 6 to 12 March 1990). *L'Express* itself was founded in 1976, although other newspapers had preceded it.

The increasing numbers and diversity of the francophone community began to manifest themselves in the 1970s through the establishment of social clubs and associations, the first of which were formed around 1975. Some of these were formed on the basis of regional or national origin (there are associations, for example, for Haitians, Egyptians, French and Acadians) and some for the pursuit of specific activities (such as community aid, golden age clubs, daycare centres, chorales, leisure activities or the pursuit of religious and political interests). Other associations are primarily of interest to members of certain occupational groups, such as educators, businesspeople or lawyers.

In 1977, an umbrella organization, the *Conseil des organismes francophones de Toronto métropolitain*, or COFTM, was founded to act as an institutional means to provide aid to new arrivals, to provide a meeting ground for francophones who were otherwise isolated, and to allow the burgeoning numbers of francophone groups to formulate common goals and plans for the development of the Toronto francophone community.

Recently, Toronto francophones have been active in establishing province-wide associations of francophones who do not feel well-represented by the ACFO. The *Association multiculturelle franco-ontarienne* and the *Association interculturelle franco-ontarienne* were both founded in Toronto and are most active in that city (see also Chapter 4).

Finally, in December 1989, Toronto became the site of one of the two newly-created school boards in Ontario (see also Chapter 2). The *Conseil des écoles françaises de la communauté urbaine de Toronto* brings together the public French-language elementary and secondary schools which were formerly part of English public boards. Since its inception, it has opened two new elementary schools and incorporated a third which had formerly been private.[40]

With the exception of the schools and a few school- or parish-related extra-curricular activities (such as French-language units of the scouting movement, the *Louveteaux* for boys and the *Jeanettes* for girls), most activities and institutions involve only adults. Evening dinners and dances, noonday luncheon meetings, theatre, dance and musical events, all are primarily aimed at people over the age of 20. Adults thus now have increasing numbers of options in terms of activities which involve the use of the French language, even if they have to make a certain effort first to discover them and then to include them in their daily lives. For most children, French is encountered at school, and possibly at home: their classmates live in other neighbourhoods, and their community- or neighbourhood-based recreational activities are almost always conducted in English.

The francophone community of Toronto is thus not really a community. French-language institutions, even those which explicitly identify themselves as ethnic institutions, serve many people who do not affiliate themselves with the group. Individual participants are involved in many networks and institutions, many of which have nothing to do with francophones or with the French language. There are no francophone neighbourhoods. Among those individuals who count themselves as French, there are few commonalities; indeed, about the only thing in common is precisely that self-identification, although even there, there is no consensus regarding what it means to be French, and many would rather think of themselves as bilingual. Finally, the population is constantly shifting: while there are new arrivals every year, not all stay more than a year or two. In addition, the nature of the immigration may have shifted over the years.

I first became aware of the complex nature of the Toronto francophone population when I began spending significant amounts of time in schools. In each school I visited there were students representing a wide variety of backgrounds. In order to grasp the nature of the school population, and as a way of discovering what social, political and economic processes might be informing what was going on in the schools, I conducted a questionnaire survey of parents whose children were enrolled in Toronto's French-language schools. Since the survey was conducted in 1984, it is undoubtedly somewhat dated.[41] Nonetheless, the results point to some basic sources of heterogeneity in the school population, and help explain both the divergent attitudes of parents towards French-language education and the various ways in which students make sense of some of the contradictions in their experience of French and English.

With the support of the three school boards then responsible for French-language schools in Toronto, 1430 questionnaires were sent out to parents with children in four Catholic elementary schools, two public elementary schools, one public high school and one public French-language instructional unit housed in an English-language school. 485 questionnaires were returned (for a rate of return of 34 percent). To this data I was able to add the results of 123 questionnaires which had been completed in 1983 by parents in a fifth Catholic elementary school where I was conducting fieldwork at the time (a rate of return of almost 50 percent for the population of that school). Finally, I added information from 59 interviews conducted in 1985. The total sample, then, consisted of 667 families (with a total of 2482 individual members), or almost 40 percent of a total population of about 1680 families.

Several things about the demographic profile of Toronto's French-language schools are striking (see Heller 1987a for detailed statistics). First, very few of the families have been in Toronto for more than one generation. Indeed, only 8 percent of the parents were born in Toronto, although over half the children were; a large proportion of families, then, consist of parents who came to Toronto as children, or, more frequently, young adults, while another large group consists of families who arrived together, often with children who have already attended school in their province or country of origin. The majority of immigrants come from Quebec, other regions of Ontario and non-French-speaking areas of Europe.

Second, most of those who immigrated to Toronto arrived after 1964. During the 1960s, most immigrants came from New Brunswick, France and Quebec. Since then, more and more have arrived from Quebec (with a particularly large number in 1983-1984) and from regions outside Canada and Europe, and fewer and fewer from elsewhere. In addition, more of these recent immigrants include families with children. Indeed from 1983 on, in every school I visited, in almost every classroom and at any time of the year, there would be one student who had just arrived, usually from Quebec, and frequently speaking next to no English.

However, only about 30 percent of the families were francophone, that is, consisted of members all of whom, parents and children, claimed French as their mother tongue. About 28 percent of the families included one francophone parent; typically, the children of those marriages claimed English or both French and English as mother tongues. About 20 percent of the families were completely English-speaking, although 31 percent of parents and 42 percent of children claimed English as their mother tongue. 18 percent of parents (but only 8 percent of children) claimed a language other than French or English as mother tongue; in total, about 50 other languages were cited.[42] Again, many children of parents whose first language was other than French or English claimed English or French and English as their own first language or languages.

Generally speaking, French, English or a combination of both languages are used at home. It is probably most striking that fewer than 30 percent of families use only French at home, although it is probably not surprising, given what we know about the dominance of English in Toronto, that almost half the families use some combination of French and English (as well as perhaps a third language) at home. Moreover, almost 20 percent use only English. In addition, it is important to bear in mind that the degree of use of French may have been over-reported: the use of French at home is an important basis for any claim to legitimate access to French-language schools.

5.0 The Franco-Ontarian population

The questionnaire was also used to gather information about the occupations and levels of education of the parents. In general, the francophones are disadvantaged relative to the other groups along both those dimensions. Francophones are over-represented among those with a level of education equivalent to high school or lower, and under-represented among those with any level of university training. Further, francophones are over-represented in occupational categories in the service and skilled labour sectors, and under-represented among managers and professionals. Proportionately fewer francophone than other women are active participants in the labour market.

The questionnaire results reveal some basic dimensions of difference within the school population. First, a significant proportion of parents and children have a first language other than French; indeed, many of the parents do not speak French at all and the children use French and English outside school in widely varying proportions. Second, parents and children have different types and degrees of experience of ethnolinguistic contact, in particular of contact between francophones and non-francophones; some have known only communities where francophones form a dominant majority, others have known communities where francophones form a minority; some have lived through episodes of francophone mobilization while others have not; and so on. Third, there are differences between francophones and non-francophones in terms of occupation and level of education, with francophones tending to be over-represented among those with lower levels of education and less well-remunerated positions.

This wide variety of ethnolinguistic backgrounds, histories of immigration and social positions informs the values, attitudes and expectations of parents and children towards education in general and towards French-language education in particular. The rest of this chapter examines the relationship between the interests and ideologies of the various groups of students and parents present in francophone educational institutions in Toronto as they relate to those articulated through the institutions themselves. As we shall see, the heterogeneity of the client population, and contradictions experienced by many of them in the course of their daily lives, underlie many of the conflicts and tensions experienced by educators, parents and students involved in Toronto's French-language schools.

In order to explore these relationships, I will first examine the ideology of French-language education as expressed by practicing educators in those schools, as well as in positions taken by others within the system as a whole (notably the Ministry of Education). I will then move on to look at the ways parents and students articulate and express their own interests in the context of schooling.

5.1. The schools: Ideology and practice of French-language education

For two years, I would drive up to my daughter's daycare centre just as the first school bus was pulling up. The daycare centre was housed in one of Toronto's French-language schools; as in most such schools, students are drawn from a large catchment area, and free transportation is provided in order to permit them to attend the school. The students who spilled out of the bus, then as today, are clearly from a variety of backgrounds and origins. Some chat, joke or argue in French as they make their way into the school, but most speak to each other in English or in a combination of both languages. When a teacher arrives to supervise the playground before school starts the students crowd around, telling stories, asking for favours; with her, they only speak French.

The entrance to the school is normally decorated with a variety of posters, flags, signs, tapestries and statues. Most prominently displayed are a rotating exhibit of student art (generally on seasonal themes: autumn, Hallowe'en, Christmas, winter, Valentine's Day, and so on), the Canadian flag and religious portraits, statues and sayings. In addition, in the fall of 1989 there appeared a large smiling spider, called *Franco-pattes*. In one corner of the front entrance, there was a drawing of *Franco-pattes*; underneath it was written: "*Hé les amis! N'oubliez pas que je vous surveille*" ["Hey pals! Don't forget that I'm watching you"].[43]

A little further on, a larger paper cut-out *Franco-pattes* perched on top of some lockers. Displayed below was a list of sentences written in shiny script on a black background: *Je joue en français, Je parle français, Je vis en français, J'écris en français, J'apprends le français, J'aime le français, Je rêve en français, Je chante en français* [I play in French, I speak French, I live in French, I write in French, I learn French, I love French, I dream in French, I sing in French]. Posted underneath there was a list of the rules of *Le club de Franco-pattes*: to be members of the club, students had to always speak French. Every day they had to evaluate their own degree of usage. If they heard a classmate speak English, they were enjoined to whisper "*bébitte* 'insect'" in their ear: "*Ça lui mettra la puce à l'oreille de parler français*" ["That will put a flea in his/her ear to speak French"]. Every day and at the end of the week there were special drawings of names out of a hat. If the teacher agreed that the student whose name had been drawn had indeed spoken French, then s/he gained the privilege of belonging to *Franco-pattes'* club: among other things, this included being the caretaker of *Franco-pattes* itself.

For most of the time that my daughter attended that daycare centre, the school displayed brightly-coloured posters all along the walls of the main floor and

5.1 Ideology and practice of French-language education

second floor corridors. These posters, which changed every few weeks, were part of a campaign the school was running to improve the quality of the students' French. Written out at the top of each poster was a sentence representing what one should not say, and which was crossed out. Underneath was the same sentence, re-written in proper French. Many of the posters took up ways of saying things that are more or less influenced by English. At the time of the World Series, most of the posters dealt with the vocabulary of baseball: one shouldn't say "*Le* short-stop *a attrapé la balle avec son* mitt", one should say "*L'arrêt-court a attrapé la balle dans son gant*" [The short-stop caught the ball with his mitt]. One poster had the sentence "*Je voudrais un* soft drink" replaced with "*Je voudrais une liqueur douce*" [I would like a soft drink]; however, the next morning, *liqueur douce*, a common Canadian term, was itself replaced with the European term *boisson gazeuse*.

Other posters dealt with current borrowings or calques: one shouldn't say "*As-tu vu le programme sur la télévision?*", one should say "*As-tu vu l'émission à la télévision?*" [Have you seen the show on television?]. Some deal with common gender errors: one poster had the sentence "*Mon mère le sait*" [My (masc.) mother knows it] with the *Mon* crossed out and *ma* written three times around it, each *ma* with an arrow pointing to the erroneous *mon* in the middle. But others dealt with forms that most linguists would argue properly belong to vernacular Canadian French; many of these forms can also still be found in regional varieties of European French. A frequent such item has been the question particle *-tu*: one should not say "*Ma mère veut-tu y aller?*", one should say "*Ma mère veut-elle y aller?*" [Does my mother want to go?].

This campaign reflects the extent to which the school sees its role, in part, as one of defining and defending specific linguistic norms. These norms define what counts as *le bon français* [good French], and refer principally to two different dimensions of what is usually called *la qualité de la langue* [the quality of the language]. The first has to do with preserving the distinctiveness of French as opposed to English, that is, with defining as "good French" forms which are held to be uninfluenced by the majority language. The second has to do with competing varieties of French; here, European or standard Canadian forms are clearly preferred to Canadian vernacular forms. Interestingly, the influence of English and the presence of features of vernacular or regional varieties of French, as well as developmental or contact phenomena such as simplification, tend all to be treated as equally important, as well as in many respects as equivalent phenomena ("bad French").

The issues of the presence and influence of English, as well as of the value of standard French, emerged over and over again in all the schools in which I was able to spend time, and in conversations with teachers. First, the school should be a place where French is used exclusively, not only in the classroom, but in the corridors, playgrounds and lunchrooms. For many of the teachers (most of whom did not grow up in a minority setting; see below), it is a pleasure and a relief to be able to function completely in French on school grounds, and they hope that the school will represent such an oasis for the students also. Others are sharply aware of the limited opportunities for the use of French outside school, and consider that if the school is going to fulfill its mission of producing French-speakers, it must preserve the French aspect of its own character. This is central to the *mission linguistique et culturelle* of the schools: in a city where English is everywhere, it is crucial to fight to establish domains where French reigns if it is not to disappear entirely. If the schools cannot establish themselves as French-speaking milieux, they will not be able to establish themselves as distinct cultural milieux either, and a critical institutional base of the community will be lost.

Indeed, the current curriculum guidelines for the teaching of French as a first language clearly set forth the importance of the schools' mission under present conditions of change (Ontario Ministry of Education 1987). The guidelines recognize the developing cultural and linguistic heterogeneity of the student body, but argue that this simply reinforces the need for schools to play a central role in the development of the Franco-Ontarian community:

> ...*certaines données traditionnelles se trouvent profondément modifiées: l'homogénéité s'estompe devant le pluralisme et l'assimilation atteint des proportions inquiétantes. Par la force des choses, l'école constitue encore aujourd'hui, souvent plus que le foyer et la place publique, le lieu privilégié de la vie française en Ontario. C'est là, en grande partie, que la collectivité franco-ontarienne s'approprie son passé, vit son présent et construit son avenir.*
> [...some traditional characteristics have profoundly changed: homogeneity is giving way to pluralism and assimilation is attaining disturbing proportions. Of necessity, the school constitutes even today the privileged site of French life in Ontario, often more so than the home or the public arena. It is [at school], in great measure, that the Franco-Ontarian community appropriates its past, lives its present and constructs its future.] (p.16).

The student body may be heterogeneous, and the conditions of life may have changed such that it is harder and harder to use French outside school; all the more reason, the guidelines argue, to pay careful attention to teaching French and teaching in French: "*l'école doit maintenant devenir l'endroit où l'élève utilise la langue, et non seulement où on la lui enseigne*" [the school must now become the place where the student uses the language, and not just where one teaches it to him or her] (p.17). However, it is argued, it is necessary to do so while respecting individual differences and through selecting and integrating the "*éléments culturels qui caractérisent les francophones d'ici et d'ailleurs*" [cultural

5.1 Ideology and practice of French-language education

elements which characterize francophones from here and from elsewhere] (p.17).

However, such a position is difficult to realize, especially as concerns the selection of linguistic elements which are considered valid; it is not clear how one develops a general norm which simultaneously incorporates differences. Indeed, as we have seen, the schools feel they must uphold a single linguistic norm, and that it is by this norm that the community should identify itself. There is no explicit enunciation of what this norm is; nonetheless, in schools such as the one inhabited by *Franco-pattes* there is generally a consensus as to what constitutes *le bon français*. Little attention is paid to pronunciation; indeed, a wide variety of accents can be heard not only among the students but among the teachers themselves. Instead, as reflected on the hall posters described earlier, most attention focusses on vocabulary and syntax. The lexical and structural features that are preferred are the ones that one might characterize as "standard French", the kind that shows up in textbooks and is associated with writing. Only occasionally does this consensus unravel, as when one teacher's Canadian *liqueur douce* was replaced by another's *boisson gazeuse*; indeed, vocabulary is probably the area where the consensus is loosest. Certainly, the curriculum guidelines offer no discussion of the value of different forms nor of the source of that value; it is thus difficult to reconcile a desire to respect individual and cultural differences with a strong sense of hierarchically organized forms.

Teachers and administrators act on their goals in a number of ways. On a daily basis, many regularly insist that students speak French at all times, as do they themselves. For some, this means a continuous refrain of *"Parlez français!"* [Speak French!]; others, coming upon a group of students speaking English in the hallway will, somewhat ironically, ask them what language it might be that they are speaking, or remind them that they are still at school. If a student ever actually addresses a teacher in English, the teacher will usually simply refuse to respond until the student switches to French, or will indicate with a *"Pardon?"* or other utterance that she or he expects to be addressed in French (see also section 5.3. below).

Occasionally, especially when they feel their efforts are not achieving the desired effect, teachers will engage students in an explicit discussion of conventions of language choice at school. One Grade 8 teacher took pains to lay out in unambiguous terms the reasons why he felt it was important for the students to speak French at school and why he therefore made such a big effort to encourage French and discourage English: most importantly, the students were attending this particular school in order to preserve French and to develop their identity as Franco-Ontarians; since school was one of the very few places where the students had the privilege of speaking French, they should take advantage of it.

Some teachers, however, feel that it is not appropriate for them to fight that battle on a daily basis. Most of these are teachers who say they used to try, but rapidly came to realize that their efforts were in vain. They felt that they were wasting energy, energy which could be better spent teaching, and showing students in other, less direct, ways the value that they themselves placed on French. They became less and less convinced that the school was the most important place where the value of French was constituted; instead, they began to argue, they must work with the reality in which the students live. Some will go so far as to argue that English should have its place in the school; to banish it is to alienate students for whom English, as well as French, is central to their activities and their goals.

While teachers are obviously committed to encouraging the use of French, they are equally committed to the encouragement of certain forms of French, whether in spoken or written language. As with the posters, corrections are offered for any form which is different from the variety the teachers wish to uphold, whatever the source of that difference is. In one Grade 9 class, for example, a student was told that her essay about her weekend activities should not include the word *vue*, a vernacular term for movies (instead, presumably, she should have used *film*). Students themselves tend to agree with the notion that their French needs improving; another Grade 9 student, recently arrived from Quebec, told me that she felt that most Canadians *"parlent mal"* [speak poorly]; her model of good French included a classmate from France.

The value of different forms, or, more broadly, of ways of using language, was clearest to me during a period when I was fortunate enough to be able to work with Albert, a French teacher (that is, a teacher of the subject matter *Français*) in a Toronto high school.[44] Ontario high schools are structured according to academic streams: enriched (*enrichi*), advanced (*avancé*), general (*général*) and basic (*fondamental*) (although there is a current trend towards gradual de-streaming). The top two streams are considered preparatory to university. The general level might lead to community college or some other form of skilled vocational training; otherwise, the bottom streams are considered as preparatory to the labour market. Very few high schools contain all streams; the school in which Albert worked focussed on advanced and general level courses, offering modified programmes to the few students who would elsewhere enroll in enriched or basic level courses. Albert himself usually taught only advanced-level classes, but in the year I was with him, he also taught general level classes.

For Albert, teaching general level classes was a challenge, but also a source of frustration. The advanced level classes he taught focussed on the development of literacy and critical thinking skills through reading, discussing and then writing about literary works. Some of these works were European, although a concerted effort was made to include Canadian novels, plays and poems. Students were expected to learn how to talk about and produce texts about texts, with an emphasis on decontextualized forms of language. Their language was expected to be what might be called "standard" French: forms which could be universally intelligible and which respected the highly codified rules of the written language. Interestingly, most of the students in the advanced classes were from Europe or Quebec; in addition, there were a significant number of students for whom French was in many ways a second language. Most came from families in which the parents' level of education was fairly high, and in which the parents held reasonably well-paying white collar or professional jobs (the class included, for example, the children of a judge, a university professor and a high-ranking provincial civil servant).

The general level classes followed the same format. However, the students, many of whom were Franco-Ontarians, Acadians or Québécois from less comfortable backgrounds, had significantly less facility with literary language and with the manipulation of literary texts. As a result, Albert found himself devoting much more time to the correction of small points of grammar and spelling than he had intended or wanted. Using the same approach as with the advanced level classes seemed to lead to the strengthening of the boundary between the two. On the other hand, Albert was extremely reluctant to develop a different content for the general level classes, since that, too, would simply contribute to the development of impenetrable boundaries.

Albert was not sure what the best way out of this dilemma might be. Clearly, the value placed on specific forms of language and specific ways of using language was somehow involved in the persistence of the distinction between the advanced and the general level groups. However, it became clear that, while it might be possible to consider different ways of teaching and arriving at those forms (and the new curriculum guidelines certainly represent such a shift), it is not possible to consider different ways of placing value on forms of language, nor is it easy to broaden or change the forms of language which are considered valuable in the school context.

It is difficult to generalize too far on the basis of my experiences with Albert. However, it does seem possible that the forms of language Franco-Ontarian schools value (just like others in the Ontario school system), have the effect of making it easier for some children than for others to succeed. Certainly, children who already have some notion of what these ways of using language are (whatever language they may have encountered them in outside school), and for whom they represent real avenues for achieving social goals (such as going to university) find themselves in the advanced level classes. Ironically, it can sometimes be easier for a middle-class child who speaks little French outside school to do well than for a monolingual working-class speaker of vernacular Franco-Ontarian, Acadian or Quebec French.

My months with Albert and other teachers also revealed another source of frustration for teachers teaching French and teaching in French in a place like Toronto: the lack of French outside school. Most of the teachers were themselves from other areas: many, like Albert, had come as adults from Quebec or the Maritimes, some were from Europe or French-speaking areas of North Africa or the Caribbean, and others were from parts of Ontario where francophones represented a considerably larger proportion of the population than they do in Toronto (the two French-language teacher-training institutions in Ontario are in Ottawa and Sudbury, and they tend to recruit students from eastern and northern Ontario). They grew up and for the most part were trained in areas where there were French-language resources in the community to draw from. The curriculum and materials to which they have access are also often inspired by (if they do not come directly from) those in use in Quebec, and, to a lesser extent, Europe. The Ontario Ministry of Education, cognizant of this problem, has established programs to encourage the development of materials more appropriate to the Ontario context, but often these materials are developed by national or international publishing houses centred outside the province. Most teaching tends to depend in some way or another on access to resources in and knowledge about the world outside school. Most teachers have techniques and materials which assume that that knowledge is available in French. However, in a place like Toronto (as in other parts of the province), those resources are either non-existent, or they are extremely difficult to obtain.

Finally, most teachers are trained to teach as though their students will have more or less the same degree of mastery of their mother tongue. Further, since most of them, were trained in francophone areas, they expect their students to be, if not monolingual francophones, certainly uniformly highly proficient in the language. It is assumed that the French-language schools which their training prepares them for will be more or less the same no matter what part of the province they are in. Nothing prepares them for the classroom reality they encounter.

Franco-Ontarian schools, then, work hard to create and maintain a specific image of themselves. As guardians of the French language, they must strive to establish a monolingual norm within the school milieu. It is vitally important that only French be recognized as the legitimate vehicle of communication. Further, French is imbued symbolically with specific values: it is the major source of identity and the means through which affiliation to the French ethnic group is

5.1 Ideology and practice of French-language education

accomplished. Learning French and learning in French is not simply acquiring a skill or going about acquiring knowledge: it is the enactment of ethnic affiliation and the construction of ethnic identity.

At the same time, the use of French to teach and to learn in school betrays the value placed on specific forms of French and on specific ways of using French. The role of the school is to transmit and promote *le bon français*: internationally intelligible and based on the written (indeed sometimes literary) code. However, in attempting to accomplish this goal, teachers regularly encounter certain obstacles. First, they depend heavily on students' familiarity with ways of using French typically encountered outside school (by reading books or newspapers at home, say, or by hearing or reading various forms of public discourse). This includes students' ability to extend knowledge acquired in school, by using reference works, or using public institutions like libraries and museums. However, in a place like Toronto, and in other Ontario communities, few of those resources are in fact available in French (only recently has provincial legislation guaranteed services in French in places like museums, but that legislation is far from having been fully implemented).

Second, teaching strategies and materials assume a fairly uniform and high degree of proficiency in French among the students. However, as we have seen, the student body is in fact very mixed. In addition to the fact that students within one classroom can represent a full range of degrees of proficiency in French, the French with which they are familiar covers a broad range of regional and class-based varieties.

Third, the development of curriculum guidelines and materials is constrained by the fact that the schools are part of a province-wide system under the aegis of the Ministry of Education. Franco-Ontarian educators must therefore work within the limits of what is considered universally valid; there are educational goals which are held to be equally applicable to all Ontario schools. At the same time, francophone educators are expected to address the specific needs of Franco-Ontarian schools, including the variation in those needs from region to region.

Finally, as we shall see, not all parents and students share the same set of interests, with the school or with each other. Instead, the schools are themselves the site of struggle among different groups of parents with varied interests in French-language education, while for students they represent only one part of a complex bilingual reality. The schools are therefore scarcely reflections of consensus at any level, but rather must find their way through complex and often conflicting processes and goals.

5.2. The parents: Competing interests in the struggle for bilingualism

Previous chapters and sections have indicated just how heterogeneous the population of Toronto's French-language schools have become, and some of the reasons for that heterogeneity. Certainly, system constraints, notably the need to have a certain number of students in order to open a school or merit certain kinds of services, have encouraged schools to be flexible in their definition and interpretation of admissions criteria. At the same time, different groups of parents are in fact interested in enrolling their children in those schools; in addition to parents of Canadian background (say, whose families have been in Canada for over 100 years), whose first language is French and who speak French at home, one finds mixed marriages, families who use varying degrees of French at home, families of non-French background, and increasing numbers of francophone immigrants.

Clearly, there is something about French-language minority schools that they find interesting. All of these parents have the possibility of sending their children to English-language schools (indeed, often, at some point, they do just that) or to French immersion programmes. In almost all cases, to do that would be to follow the path of least resistance; chances are that the neighbourhood school is English, or possibly French immersion, and most of the neighbours' children probably attend that school. Instead, these parents choose to send their children to a French-language school, even though this means that their children must spend between one and three hours a day on a school bus (of course, most commuters in Toronto devote about that amount of time to travel between home and work, but it is not generally expected of schoolchildren).

Between 1983 and 1986 I attempted to discover what it was about French-language schools that attracted these different groups of parents. In particular, I was concerned to discover the nature of the value parents placed on the French linguistic and cultural resources (capital, in Bourdieu's terms) which it is (uniquely) the school's role to distribute. In 1983, I conducted 20 interviews with parents whose children were enrolled in the French-language Catholic elementary school where I was conducting fieldwork at the time. In 1984–1985, my colleagues and I conducted 44 interviews with parents whose children were enrolled in a public elementary school and/or public secondary module, as part of the study of the two schools which had been requested by their board. In 1985–1986, my research assistants conducted similar interviews with 78 parents whose children were enrolled in one of the other French-language schools in the metropolitan Toronto area (at the time, this included one other public elementary school, one other public high school, and four other Catholic elementary schools).

5.2 The parents

The 1983 sample consisted of ten families chosen at random, and ten chosen to represent the sociolinguistic profile of the school which had emerged from analysis of the questionnaires which about half the families in the school had completed. The two other samples were similarly constructed, although the representative sample was based on a lower rate of return of questionnaires (about 34 percent). The rationale for the split sample was simply to ensure that the representative sample was indeed representative, and to maximize the possibilities for interpretation of those data (since for that half of the sample, at least, we had questionnaire data as well as interview data).

In most cases we interviewed the mother alone, whether at home, at work or in our offices. In a minority of cases we were able to interview both parents, and in two cases the father alone. The choice of participants and locales was left up to the parents; we felt (rightly or wrongly) that it was important that the parents construct the situation in a way that was most comfortable for them.

It is not completely clear why the pattern described above fell out the way it did. Certainly, in cases of mixed marriages, it was almost always the francophone parent who participated in the interview, and, as we know from the demographic profile, in almost all such cases it is the mother who is francophone. In addition, there are more women at home than men, and it is likely that they felt that it was easier for them to find the time to participate in such an interview during the day when the husband was at work and the children at school. Finally, it is possible that in many families the education of the children is seen as the mother's responsibility, although we have no data which directly supports such an assertion.

Most respondents readily accepted participation in the interview, and in a few cases parents sought us out as a way to voice concerns which they felt unable to voice otherwise (or which they felt had been inadequately attended to by the school board). The interviews were mainly conducted in French, although about 25 percent were conducted in English, mainly with parents whose children were enrolled in the two schools which had, for historical reasons, a relatively high percentage of anglophone children. The language of the interview (as well, of course, as what emerged in the interviews) was undoubtedly influenced not only by the language preferences of the parent(s), but also by the fact that two of three interviewers were clearly native speakers of French and our affiliation was with an explicitly Franco-Ontarian organization. If anything, then, the interviews are slanted towards a Franco-Ontarian point of view. The interviews lasted on average about one and one-half hours, and were tape-recorded and transcribed by the interviewer (with the exception of the 1983 interviews and twelve others which we were not able to record).[45]

Two major themes emerged as indices of the nature of the linguistic and cultural resources parents sought for their children through the schools, and of the value placed on those resources: the question of the linguistic, cultural and educational objectives of the schools and the question of rights of access to French-language minority schools. The way in which people define the schools' objectives reveals the nature of the resources which they expect to be distributed there. While they do not necessarily feel that it is uniquely the schools' role to distribute those resources, generally speaking, they agree that the school is a crucial domain in that regard.

The question of rights of access (which are sometimes discussed explicitly in terms of admissions criteria) reveals not only how people define what kind of capital should be distributed in the schools but also who should have privileged access to it. The two are closely linked: people recognize that the resources children bring to the school affects how the school can distribute resources in its own right. For example, the way the school teaches French depends in large measure on the nature of the knowledge of French students bring with them to school. At the same time, the relative ease of students' access to the resources distributed in school is affected by the resources they bring (this is a central insight of Bourdieu's): if the school teaches French in a way which depends on prior knowledge of the language, students who have no such prior knowledge will be at a relative disadvantage. If the school teaches French in a way which does not depend on prior knowledge, students who do have that knowledge will not necessarily be able to use it.

The extent to which the school adapts to the students or to which the students adapt to the school is determined by relations of power among groups with different interests (as reflected in the different resources they already possess). As we have seen, in most Franco-Ontarian schools there are a variety of groups of students who do not share the same point of departure; the question then is, in part, whose interests will determine the schools' goals, programmes and pedagogy? Which group will find its resources to be the most valued in the school context? As a result, who can participate legitimately in the school milieu, that is, what kinds of resources do you have to have in order to be seen as a legitimate participant? What kinds of interests do you have to support (or at least accept as dominant whether or not you actually share them)?

The most striking aspect of the interviews which we conducted was the total consensus among all respondents regarding their major reason for enrolling their children in a French-language school: bilingualism. Certainly, many other educational goals were cited (acquiring basic literacy and numeracy skills, learning to be a good human being, and so on), but these tended to be general, and applied to any form of education. However, respondents of all backgrounds specifically chose a French-language school as a way to help their children become (or remain) proficient in both French and English. Nonetheless, important differ-

5.2 The parents

ences did emerge regarding the nature of the high value accorded to bilingualism and regarding respondents' definitions of rights of access to the school as a privileged path to bilingualism.

These differences fall out along (and sometimes cross-cut) what I will call class and status lines. I am using the notions in the sense defined by Collins (1989: 28):

> La classe constitue la dimension verticale. Dans sa forme générique, elle se fonde non pas simplement sur la propriété des moyens de production, ou sur la position sur le marché, mais plutôt sur la position de pouvoir au sein de l'organisation (dirigeants par opposition à subordonnés, y inclus les positions intermédiaires). Il s'agit cependant d'une distinction qui correspond surtout aux évidences empiriques de variations dans les comportements et les croyances. Le statut est la mesure de l'appartenance à des communautés qui sont conscients d'avoir un style de vie distinctif, il stratifie le long du clivage entre membres et non membres. Ces communautés disposent pour ainsi dire d'un pôle d'attraction, la plus grande proximité avec le centre augmente le statut social tandis que l'éloignement le réduit. En somme, la dimension verticale de "classe" ...provient de processus conflictuels ...Quant au statut, il est le produit des rites d'interaction et des symboles qui y sont associés.
>
> [Class constitutes the vertical dimension. In its generic form, it is based not simply on ownership of the means of production, or on position in the marketplace, but rather on the position of power within the organization (order-givers in opposition to subordinates, including intermediary positions). Nevertheless, it is a distinction which corresponds mainly to empirical evidence for variations in behaviour and beliefs. Status is the measure of membership in communities which are conscious of having a distinctive way of living, it stratifies along the boundary between members and non-members. These communities have, so to speak, a pole of attraction, social status rises the closer one is to the centre, and falls the farther away one is from it. In sum, the vertical dimension of "class" ... emerges from processes of conflict ... As for status, it is the product of interaction rituals and the symbols which are associated with them.]

In order to use this distinction, it has been necessary to make some inferences. The labels "middle class" and "working class" correspond to inferences about the degree of power exercised by the respondent based on their own, and, in some cases, their spouse's, occupation. I have also used level of education as an indication of an orientation to class, especially since in some cases (as, for example, for many immigrants) the actual position occupied does not correspond to the individual's training. At the same time, as Collins indicates, it is necessary to infer class on the basis of different orientations, different ways of behaving and beliefs, and to recognize the conflictual processes that produce it. Differences among language groups, which cross-cut class interests, correspond to differences among status groups. What is interesting is how class and status interests are played off against or used to mutually support each other, creating the basis for shifting alliances and conflicts among parents whose children are enrolled in French-language schools.

In terms of class and status, the population in question here can be characterized along three overlapping dimensions, which all inform the interests of parents and their positions with respect to the role of French-language education in the distribution of the valued resource which bilingualism has become. First, there are parents who consider themselves francophones, those who consider themselves anglophones and those who are native speakers of other languages. However, the population, as indicated earlier, includes large numbers of linguistically-mixed marriages; the position of a francophone father, say, may differ depending on whether his spouse is francophone as well or not. This is important because when one parent does not speak French, the francophone parent tends to rely all the more strongly on the school to support his or her attempts to transmit French to the children. Second, there is class position: in this case, the vast majority of members of what might be called the working class (in Collins' terms, those who take direction) also happen to be francophone; the non-francophone population is made up almost exclusively of people who have power in their working lives, who give direction. Finally, there is the question of the extent to which parents have experienced life in minority settings, that is, have experienced for themselves or are at least familiar with the experience of life as a member of a linguistic minority.

All these dimensions influence the access parents (and their children) have now and have had in the past to the two forms of linguistic capital at issue here, knowledge of French and knowledge of English, as well as the extent to which that capital is valuable to them. Clearly, this capital is of little interest to non-francophone members of the working class; they are not only absent here, but they are also relatively under-represented in French immersion programmes (the other major avenue of access to bilingualism). Since non-francophones in Toronto have very limited access to French, those who want access to it are forced to look to schools to provide it. To the extent that they have never had any knowledge of what it might be like to live as a francophone in a minority setting like Toronto, they tend not to see their desire for access to those schools as in any way problematic.

The perspective of francophones is also influenced by the extent to which they have or have had access to English; this access is especially problematic for recent immigrants from francophone majority areas (indeed, anywhere that English is not readily available). In addition, for those who are working class, English is all the more important as a means of social mobility; most members of the middle class either already have access to English through their jobs, through education or in the community, or (less frequently) do not require it because of the nature of their occupations.

As a result, there are a number of different positions which parents (and their children) have with respect to French-language education. This is reflected not only in the reasons they give for wanting to send their children to those schools, but also in their perspectives on who should be allowed in and on what forms of linguistic capital should be distributed there.

For almost everybody, bilingualism is important because of the opportunities it opens up for their children. This was mentioned most frequently by non-francophones, and, among francophones, those with lower levels of education and lower ranking jobs. In most cases, these opportunities were conceived of as primarily economic, but they included both better access to higher education and access to more interesting and better-paying jobs:

> ... *quand tu vas travailler si tu as deux ou trois langues tu as beaucoup plus de chances à te placer que tu en as juste une*... [when you're going to be working if you have two or three languages you have many more chances of finding a job than if you have just one]
> ... I think the more languages you speak, the better it is ... and I think it really helps later on for more jobs, for anything ...
> ... *les avoir bilingues ça va leur donner une meilleure chance à faire compétition avec les autres*... [having them bilingual that'll give them a better chance of being competitive with the others]
> ... as they grow up with two languages there are just that many more doors open to them, it's a very competitive world.... French is one of the advantages ...

Members of what I might qualify as the middle class (that is, people with relatively high levels of education and holding well-paying jobs in positions of power) also appealed to general principles. Both francophones and non-francophones mentioned national unity:

> ... I think they should be brought up bilingual all of Canada ... since we are a bilingual country...
> ... *on veut vraiment être Canadiens unis bien il faut y travailler au bilinguisme*... [if we really want to be united Canadians well you have to work at bilingualism]

For some francophones in this group, however, this unity depends on francophones being able to preserve their language, and in order to do so, they must have exclusive access to their schools. Although they sometimes phrased it in politicized and mobilized terms, they did have in common with other francophone parents a concern for the maintenance of language and culture:

> *Les parents francophones, nous, on veut une école française parce que nos critères sont que le français soit la langue première, que le milieu soit ... on compte sur l'école en somme pour renforcer la culture qu'on transmet à la maison*

[We francophone parents, we want a French school because our criteria are that French should be the first language, that the milieu should be ... that is, we count on the school to reinforce the culture that we transmit at home]

...*c'est un bel héritage*... [it's a beautiful heritage]

...*nos sources, nos racines, nos traditions, notre culture, ce que ça entraîne avec ça, c'est quand-même plus que la langue parlée*... [our sources, our roots, our traditions, our culture, all that goes along with that, it's more than just the spoken language all the same]

...*je ne voulais pas que les enfants soient coupés à un moment donné de la famille*... [I didn't want the children to be cut off at some point from the family]

However, in addition to the economic and national unity advantages of bilingualism, non-francophones mainly spoke about the cultural and cognitive advantages of bilingualism:

... I feel that when you go to a school of a different language than your mother tongue, that it is conceptually enriching, that I think it adds to one's intelligence base ...

Indeed, for many non-francophones the fact that the school functioned in French, rather than any other language, was almost immaterial.

I don't see the language, I see education in general and I believe that the languages in themselves are education because children who can explain in different languages ... can see life from different angles ...

Some said that, quite frankly, the language of instruction could have been Russian or Italian or anything else, and it would have been almost the same from a cultural and cognitive point of view, although from a practical perspective such parents did prefer that their children learn another world language.

The value of bilingualism is thus simultaneously expressed in terms of simple economic value and in terms of ideological symbols. Different groups of parents place different weight on the strictly economic, as opposed to symbolic, resources at stake: on the whole francophones tend to stress symbolic issues more than non-francophones. There are also differences in the nature of the symbolic resources stressed by different groups of parents, and in the ideological positions they adopt in order to legitimate their presence in the schools. Non-francophone parents tend to focus on universalistic principles, whether political, cognitive or cultural, and thus take the discussion out of the realm of ethnic interests. Francophone middle-class parents tend to stress issues concerning the advancement of francophone minority rights; they argue that the very existence of the schools must be based on the need to address the distinctive position, needs and interests of francophones. This position helps advance the interests of this group, especially insofar as they are in competition with non-francophones.

Many francophone middle-class parents do indeed see themselves as in competition with non-francophones, most particularly with anglophones:

5.2 The parents

> ...*ce qui est très très intéressant, c'est que je vois que l'école francophone, cette école ici, c'est une école qui est bien pour les francophones, mais c'est une école qui est bien plus avantageuse pour les anglophones, ma chère, ce sont les anglophones qui bénéficient probablement plus...* [what's really really interesting is that I see that the francophone school, this school here, is a school which is fine for the francophones, but it's a school which is much more advantageous for the anglophones, my dear, it's the anglophones who probably benefit more]
>
> *[cette école] ne doit pas servir d'école d'immersion de luxe pour les élites anglophones...* [[this school] should not serve as a deluxe immersion school for the anglophone élite]

These parents argue in particular that the presence in the school of non-francophone children affects the quality of teaching and the possibility of creating a French-language milieu in the school:

> ...*[les enfants francophones] sont pénalisés ... parce que le rythme de l'enseignement est ralenti...* [[francophone children] are penalized ... because the rhythm of teaching is slowed]
>
> ...*quand c'est devenu la mode pour les anglophones d'avoir une éducation en français, ils les envoyaient à nos écoles au lieu de les envoyer dans les écoles d'immersion et ça baissait la qualité de la classe...* [when it became fashionable for anglophones to be educated in French, they sent them to our schools instead of sending them to immersion schools and it lowered the quality of the classes]
>
> *il y a eu aussi un choc psychologique par rapport à [mon fils], dès qu'il est entré dans l'école il ne pouvait plus fonctionner en français, il fonctionnait en anglais parce que chaque fois qu'il parlait français les petits anglophones se moquaient de lui...* [there was also a psychological shock with respect to [my son], as soon as he entered the school he could no longer function in French, he functioned in English because each time he spoke French the little anglophones made fun of him]
>
> ...*[ma fille] est arrivée en première année et je pense qu'ils étaient quatre dans sa classe qui étaient vraiment des francophones. Ça fait que là, elle est arrivée en pleurant, elle m'a dit, "Maman, je ne comprends pas mes amis, qu'est-ce qui se passe? Tu m'avais dit que c'était une école de langue française"...* [[my daughter] arrived in the first grade and I think there were four in her class who were really francophones. So she came in tears, she said to me, "Mummy, I don't understand my friends, what's going on? You told me it was a French-language school"]

This competition is based on different positions which anglophone and francophone members of the middle class have with respect to access to French and English. Francophones maintain that in order to be bilingual they have to work at preserving French, not learning English:

> ...*pour moi il est évident comme Franco-Ontarienne que si on étudie pas notre langue, on la perd...* [for me, as a Franco-Ontarian, it is obvious that if we do not study our language, we lose it]
>
> ...*parce que automatiquement on savait bien qu'ils apprendraient l'anglais à cause du milieu, donc l'important c'était de conserver l'autre, de ne pas perdre

une pour avoir une autre, mais d'en acquérir une et de conserver l'autre... [because automatically we knew well that they'd learn English because of the milieu, so the important thing was to keep the other, to not lose one in order to have another, but to acquire one and to keep the other]

...ben moi je dis que c'est important d'avoir les deux langues et puis s'il n'y a pas d'école de langue française les enfants l'auront pas... [well, *I* say that it's important to have the two languages and if there's no French-language school the children won't have it]

However, as one Franco-Ontarian parent pointed out, francophones who are newly arrived in Ontario, who speak little or no English and who have always lived in an area where French is the dominant or only language, often have a different point of view. Frequently, when such families arrive in Toronto, they enroll their children in English-language schools. This is seen to be the case, typically, of Québécois, who are used to living in a French monolingual community and who are often in Toronto for a limited period before returning to Quebec, as opposed to Franco-Ontarians, whose entire lives are informed by the experience of being a minority:

...il faut faire la distinction, les Québécois font ça, les Franco-Ontariens font pas ça. Les gens qui arrivent du Québec insistent pour apprendre l'anglais, puis moi d'expérience, je savais pertinemment bien que t'as pas besoin d'aller à l'école anglaise pour apprendre l'anglais. L'anglais, ça s'attrape en Ontario... [you have to make the distinction, Quebecers do that [i.e. enroll their children in English-language schools], Franco-Ontarians don't. People who arrive from Quebec insist on learning English, but from experience *I* knew particularly well that you don't need to go to an English school in order to learn English. English, you *catch* it in Ontario]

Indeed, some parents we interviewed who had arrived in Ontario as monolingual francophones had in fact initially sent their children to English-language schools. However, after a certain amount of time, they realized that while their children had acquired fluent English, they were in the process of losing their French, and so they switched them to a French-language school.

Other such parents opt initially for a French-language school, often feeling that this will ease the transition for their children. However, unlike other francophone parents who have grown up in or lived for a certain amount of time in an English-speaking milieu, these francophone parents voice a great deal of concern for the opportunities their children will have, through the school, to learn English:

je crois que c'est pas beaucoup, étant dans un milieu anglais ... ils parleront l'anglais, c'est pas du côté parlé, mais j'ai peur du côté écrit... [I think it's not much [the amount of time devoted to teaching English in school] being in an English milieu ... they'll speak English, it's not with respect to speaking, but I'm afraid about the writing]

5.2 The parents

Working class francophones, even those from minority areas, often share this concern that their children master both French and English through school:

> *il faut absolument qu'ils parlent l'anglais et qu'ils puissent l'écrire, il n'y a pas seulement le français, on vit dans un endroit anglais (...) et je ne veux pas être bornée...* [they absolutely must speak and write English, there isn't only French, we live in an English place ... and I don't want to be narrow]

Non-francophones, of course, rely on the school for their access to French. Those who have little experience of what it is like to be a linguistic minority tend to believe that if children learn a language early, they will learn it well, and will be therefore able to participate in the school in exactly the same way as francophone children. Thus for them the first language of a student is immaterial in terms of the effect it might have on the way language is used within the school; no matter what the first language, the language of communication at school will be French. As a result, it makes little sense to them to worry about whose interests the school is most likely to be serving; as long as everyone speaks French equally well and equally often, no one group will be favoured:

> ... so many children whose families come from Europe and all over, the parents don't speak and the small children do speak the language very fast...
>
> ...*ils apprennent tellement vite, ils se mettent dedans je pense comme une semaine et puis ça donne une chance*... [they learn so fast, they put themselves in there I think like one week and it gives [them] a chance...]
>
> ... even if they don't speak French, it's up to the teacher, let's say from kindergarten and on, I am sure they will learn it, I think if they go to higher grades, they should have a test in my opinion, otherwise they can't follow...

The presence of non-francophone children is also often justified through appealing to democratic principles (all schools should be open to all residents) or to the practical problem of numbers (having enough students to maintain a school with a range of services and programmes is a higher priority than being highly selective in terms of the nature of the admissible student body). Indeed, while many non-francophones will appeal to these arguments, many francophones are also prepared to make compromises along these lines:

> ...*pour avoir la qualité il faut avoir la quantité, il faut une masse critique*... [to have quality you need to have quantity, you need a critical mass]

Francophones from majority settings also interpret the situation from the perspective of French as a pole of attraction, as a source of value which can compete with English. They do not see French as threatened and in need of protection, as francophones from minority settings do:

> ...*on voit même des Anglais lesquels envoient leurs enfants dans des écoles françaises. Alors cela explique beaucoup de choses, qu'ils veulent quand même leur inculquer la langue française. Ça fait plaisir par exemple... il faudrait*

encourager cela parce que si on se limite par exemple, à mettre des lois, ou bien des restrictions, à mon point de vue, on ne donne pas libre cours au français de s'élargir comme on le veut... [one even sees English people who send their children to French schools. So that explains a lot of things, that just the same they want to teach them French. It's a good thing, though ... we should encourage it because if we limit ourselves, for example, making laws, or restrictions, from my point of view, we won't be giving French the freedom to expand the way we want to]

Non-francophones who have some experience of French communities in minority settings frequently come to have sympathy for the concerns minority francophones have for the survival of their language. As a result, they have to resolve what they acknowledge to be a conflict of interest between francophones and non-francophones:

> ... I can understand the reservations that parents of French kids can have: they feel that the French standard is lowered and watered down. Well, it is obvious, and I would feel the same way if I was them, but I think it is a question of the numbers; if you have enough francophone kids to make a viable class, and all I know is that in [this school] there was not the number there ...

Of course, this position itself encounters the defence of anglophones who fail to understand the source of francophones' disquiet:

> I have two kids who are fluently bilingual in a bilingual country and not only have I no guilt I sort of felt proud of it ... we made a commitment to that for their good, not for anyone else's good, but in a way it is a commitment to the fact that there are two languages and two cultures. That's why I feel so strong about anyone questioning whether it's the right or wrong thing; it's perfectly right, it's perfectly moral

French-language schools thus seem to have become at least a potential battleground, an arena where parents of different backgrounds, and hence different interests, fight for their rights of access to this privileged path to bilingualism, and for their right to have the school facilitate this access in a way which best corresponds to the linguistic resources which they and their children bring to school. The potential for conflict emerges from the specific nature of the heterogeneity of the school population, which is in turn produced by a combination of large-scale social, economic and political processes and local bureaucratic and legal constraints within which schools must operate. The success of francophone mobilization has enhanced the value of the economic and symbolic resources to which one can gain access by participating in those schools, not only for francophones, but for non-francophones as well. Criteria of admissions and requirements for enrollment levels make it possible for non-francophones to be there. Often this combination of factors has been the basis of alliances, as when the two groups joined forces to lobby for the establishment of one of Toronto's French-language elementary schools. Subsequently, however, as we have seen, that alliance also laid the groundwork for the emergence of conflict.

Everyone agrees that the schools should function in French and should provide a French-speaking milieu. However, different groups of parents have different reasons for wanting this, depending on the value of bilingualism to them for the advancement of class interests, on the ways status can be used as a means for advancing class interest, and on the linguistic resources they bring to their participation in French-language education (that is, the capital they have to invest and hence the nature of the return they expect to gain from their investment). In addition, experience of life in French-language minority and majority milieux affects the perceptions different groups of parents have of the possibilities for becoming bilingual through schooling, and the strategies they are prepared to adopt in order to achieve their goals.

Differences arise concerning what it is that will ensure that school remains (or becomes) monolingual and concerning the kinds of compromises that it may be worth making in order for the institution to function. Parents who have no access to French outside school are more likely to argue that the language background of the children is not an important factor in ensuring that the school remains a French milieu: after all, languages can be learned. Parents who have access to French outside school tend to disagree; they see the power that English has outside school, and feel that that power has an effect on the willingness of non-francophone children to use French (whatever motivations their parents may have). They do not see their own (francophone) children as operating from a position of strength inside the school, and seek to protect them from yet another source of English domination. Even so, both francophone and non-francophone parents, while recognizing that the presence of non-francophone children in the school may increase the power of English within the school, may be prepared to accept that presence. This acceptance springs largely from a recognition of the problem of enrollment, that is, the need to have certain numbers of students in order to have a school at all.

In addition, francophone members of the working class tend to have a position which overlaps with both those of francophone members of the middle class and of non-francophones: they are not in direct competition with non-francophone members of the middle class, and have perhaps the most to gain from an alliance with them. While valuing their own language and culture, they place more emphasis than do other francophones on the importance of the school in distributing knowledge of English as well as French, since school-based knowledge of both languages is crucial to their economic success and they are more dependent on the school than are others for access to such competence in English.

Finally, parents who have lived most or all of their lives as a member of a majority (whether anglophone, francophone or otherwise) and have had little or no contact with members of minority groups, tend not to see the same issues as parents who must or are at least able to adopt a minority perspective. For them, English and French operate on a basis of equality. As a result, not only is any discussion of who has a right to be at the school completely moot, but the school also is seen as having an obligation to provide access to both French and English.

These are questions of status because they revolve around the setting of symbolic conventions of membership. The disputes are, however, intimately tied to class interests, both symbolic and material (and, of course, the two are closely linked). Bilingualism is an essential component of the advancement of middle class interests for both francophones and anglophones; a form of symbolic power, it is used to create and wield political and economic power. The question is who may have privileged access to that bilingualism, and by what means. Francophone and anglophone middle class parents are involved in a dispute over whether French-language schools should serve the interests of both.

This analysis places the school at the centre of cross-cutting symbolic interests, some of which overlap and some of which conflict. While these interests found some form of expression in the interviews, they are also expressed in other ways. They are given voice when parents run for election as school trustees, and they are expressed in meetings of parent-teacher associations. They have even been institutionalized through the founding of rival parent associations; in one school, francophone middle-class parents who felt that anglophones had too much power in the school founded a parent association which they felt would better represent their interests than the APE. Such mobilized parents have also gone to the press, and their mobilization has touched off broader disputes about language rights such as those in Thunder Bay and Sault Ste. Marie. In other areas, in earlier times, disputes among francophones along class lines have affected the establishment of bilingual or homogeneous French-language schools (as in Sturgeon Falls or in Welland in the 1970s; cf. Chapters 2 and 4).

The question remains as to what actually happens in these hotly disputed institutions. Parents have their own interests, shaped by their own experiences, and these may or may not be shared by their children. In the next section, I will examine the way students in French-language schools in Toronto use French and English to construct their own social world. In particular, I will look at the ways in which their use of French and English at school reveals the value those languages have for them, particularly in terms of the ways in which using French or English allows students of different backgrounds to gain access to situations which are important in their own lives.

5.3. The students: Language choice and social boundaries

In the winter of 1983, I began spending time in French-language schools in Toronto. The period of most intense fieldwork covered the two years of 1983 and 1984, but since then I have spent at least some time in schools, and continue to do so (see Chapter 6 for a description of our classroom-based action-research in the period 1986–1989). The fieldwork began in a Catholic elementary school, which I have elsewhere called St-Michel (Heller 1984, 1987a,b). From January to June 1983 I spent three days a week there, sitting in classrooms, hanging out in the teachers' lounge, standing in the playground at recess, sitting in on after-school arts and crafts programmes, helping with rehearsals of school plays, attending science fairs and cultural events in the school as well as the year-end graduation, and accompanying teachers, parents and students on outings to fairgrounds and nuclear power plants. About the only thing I did not do was to take the school bus, although a Grade 6 student named Christiane and I often travelled part-way home together on city bus and subway.

In 1984, I began spending time in a school which I will call here Samuel de Champlain. It was then the only "homogeneous" high school, that is, the only French-language high school which was an administrative entity on its own, not attached in any way to any English-language school (although, of course, at the time, it was in a school board that was almost exclusively English). For a little over a year, I went to classes once or twice a week. Most of these were advanced-level French classes (*Français*), but I also attended general-level *Français* classes, advanced-level English classes (in which, given the high level of English-language proficiency of the students, the programme was the same as that offered in English-language high schools), *Anglais (langue seconde)* classes for the minority of students who spoke little or no English on their arrival at school, and classes in History and Biology. Since the school was considerably larger than St-Michel (about 600 as opposed to about 300 students, and about 30 full-time and part-time teachers and specialists as opposed to 12) and students rotated from class to class, rather than having almost all their subjects taught in the same classroom by the same teacher, it was considerably more difficult to participate in the life of the school than it had been at St-Michel. Nonetheless, it was possible to get to know some groups of students, and to spend considerable time with teachers in their offices and in the teachers' lounge.

In 1984, together with a team of colleagues, I also began work on a project requested by another school board. This project concerned the school board's two French-language "instructional units", Jeanne-Sauvé, an elementary school and a secondary-level module housed in an English-language high school. As indicated earlier, the project was in some respects a response to the complaints of some francophone parents that anglophones had too much power in the school and that the school was principally serving their interests and not those of francophone parents. However, it was officially phrased as a descriptive statement of the situation of the schools on the occasion of the tenth anniversary of the elementary school. As part of this project, I was able to spend several weeks in both schools, again, principally sitting in on classes (in Grades 1 and 8 in the elementary school and Grades 9 and 13 in the secondary school), but also hanging around the elementary school playground and the secondary school lunch room.

In 1986, again with a team of colleagues, I began the collaborative project focussed on the development of an innovative pedagogical approach which is the subject of Chapter 6. Through this work, my colleagues and I spent several months working with Grade 7 and 8 teachers and students at Samuel de Champlain; this involved participation in the classroom as well as meetings with the teachers (for a variety of administrative and pedagogical reasons, the seventh and eighth grades of the board's French-language elementary school had by then been moved to Samuel de Champlain). This was followed by three-week long field trials of the material we had developed in a Grade 6 class at Jeanne-Sauvé (a public elementary school) and Grade 2/3 and 5/6 classes at Ste-Anne (a Catholic elementary school). In 1989, we undertook the filming of a teacher-training tape which involved several weeks' work in the Grade 2 and 3 classes of another public elementary school. This work principally allowed me to keep verifying the hypotheses which I had initially developed at St-Michel, elaborated at Samuel de Champlain and verified at Jeanne-Sauvé and the secondary-level module.[46]

In all these cases, data on students' language use was collected through two means. Most of the time, it was collected through observation and field notes. On some occasions, however, I was also able to tape-record students. At St-Michel, four Grade 7 and four Grade 8 students (two boys and two girls from each grade) wore mini-cassette recorders for two school days each, from the time they entered the classroom in the morning to the time the last bell rang in the afternoon. The students were selected on the basis of their observed patterns of language use, and included students who used mainly French, students who used mainly English, and students who regularly used both. The same was true three years later of four Grade 3 and four Grade 6 students at Ste-Anne, where we were simultaneously conducting a field trial of our materials. In addition, during the materials development phase at Samuel de Champlain, and during field trials at Jeanne-Sauvé and Ste-Anne, we recorded small-group interaction as the students participated in the activities which we had designed.

5.3 The students

At St-Michel, I began by identifying patterns of language choice, both in terms of the situations where language use might vary, and in terms of the variation among students within or across those situations. The patterns I identified there were subsequently borne out in other schools, and the following examples are taken from most of the schools in which I did fieldwork. In the broadest terms, situations could be divided between those focussed on peer-group activities, and those controlled by school or school-related authorities.

The English-language milieu of wider society provides most of the elements of popular culture which are used in the construction of peer-group relations: games and toys, television and movies. The popular culture of these schools differs little from that found anywhere else in English-speaking (indeed French-speaking) North America, whether it revolves around Go-Bots (those model cars and trucks which can be transformed into robots, ca. 1985) or Teenage Mutant Ninja Turtles and Garfields (ca. 1990). Tokens of, and knowledge about, these forms are traded on the social stock exchange of the playground and school bus. At the same time, of course, the distinction between French and English can be used to reinforce the distinction between the world of school, controlled by adults, and the world of play, where children set the rules.

On the other hand, academic success (or at least the avoidance of outright failure) depends on the ability to use French in situations, defined and controlled by the school, where performances are evaluated in academic terms. In addition, in these schools, the legitimacy of any student's presence is dependent on his or her ability to use French, not just in strictly academic terms, but in other situations calling for the display of competences which are symbolic of the school and of school life, such as informal interaction with teachers, school outings or participation in regional contests such as science fairs or debating tournaments.

This distinction is based primarily on the empirical evidence of shifts in language use, that is, English is used among students in situations which they primarily control, while French is used with adults in situations which the adults control. At one level, the use of English is connected to experiences outside school which most students share, to a solidarity based on life in the world of baseball and Barbie dolls. The use of French is based on the experience of life in situations controlled by adults. The separation is therefore not neutral, but intimately bound up with the relations of power between the world controlled by peers and that controlled by adults, between the meaning and value of popular culture and the value of institutionalized official culture.

My claim for the existence of this relationship is reinforced by some explicit evidence, of two kinds. The first emerged during the taping of one of the Grade 3 students at Ste-Anne. One of the girls, Sophie, went out into the playground at recess, wearing her tape-recorder. One of her classmates told her (in French) that she couldn't play with the others, because she was wearing a recorder and the game was going to be in English. The tape-recorder, which two adult researchers had asked Sophie to wear, with the obvious support of the school, was, in the mind of this child, only allowed to capture French; the world of adults and the world of children could not be allowed to meet.

In large part, of course, this is because of the children's recognition that English is illegitimate in French schools; this equally revealed by the second form of evidence, the students' indication of the illegitimate nature of the use of English. They whisper, they hide, or, in moments of daring, use English explicitly to resist school authority. In many schools, the use of English is almost covert; at the sight of an approaching adult, students will warn each other to speak French.

One afternoon, I was walking down the stairs of an elementary school behind two girls who were chatting with each other. Turning the corner, one caught a glimpse of me over her shoulder; she began insistently tapping her friend's arm until her friend caught on and switched to French. At St-Michel, one morning, the Grade 8 teacher told one of the students in the classroom to speak French; the student replied (in English) that it wasn't nine o'clock yet, that is, the school frame had not yet been officially called into play by the bell marking the ritual beginning of the school day. In a Grade 9 class in another school, the teacher asked a student to read out the day's announcements, which the student began to do in French. The teacher was called away; as she went out of earshot, the student switched to English. All the students recognized this switch as illicit; whispering and giggling, they kept an eye out for the teacher's return, as the announcement reader tried to gauge the point up to which she could retain deniability as the teacher re-entered the room.

In the Grade 8 class at St-Michel, during class time, I observed this exchange between a teacher and a student:

Teacher: *parlez français! vous êtes à quelle page?* [speak French! what page are you on?]
André: page forty-three
Teacher: *André!*
André: *page quarante-trois* [page forty-three]

At the same time, other forms of behaviour indicate the students' acceptance of the legitimacy of school-sanctioned behaviour: they do, after all, speak French most of the time, when they are supposed to. Still, it is not always easy or possible to keep each frame strictly separate, and much of what students do reveals the work they undertake to manage the constant passage from one to the other.

5.3 The students

This "work" consists principally of two forms of language use: bilingual puns and code-switching, that is, the use of both French and English within short stretches of discourse or even within single utterances. What both forms of language use do, of course, is to neutralize the opposition between languages and the frames they index. Bilingual puns are funny because they juxtapose forms which are generally held to be mutually exclusive; the humour is also a release. Code-switching provides the same kind of juxtaposition, but through the creation of ambiguity. By speaking both languages at once, it is possible to operate in both frames simultaneously. In addition, there were occasions when students drew on various frames to create forms of artistic expression, the force of which derived precisely from their ability to move across different linguistic and cultural frames.

I heard bilingual puns from students of all ages, from kindergarten to Grade 13. By way of illustration, I will provide the puns that I consider the funniest, generally because they are the most complex (however, even simpler ones relying only on straight word-for-word translation were still considered hysterically funny by their originators and audiences). The first was reported to me by the kindergarten teacher at St-Michel. A little boy had asked her what the expression *je m'en fiche* meant (it means, more or less, "I don't care"). She suggested that he ask one of his classmates. A short while later, the boy returned, and reported that he knew, now, what it meant. "*Quoi alors?*" [what, then?], the teacher asked. "*Je m'en poissonne!*", he replied. The teacher, expecting a straight answer, couldn't understand what he meant; to help her, the boy explained: "*Je m'en fiche, je m'en fish, je m'en poissonne!*" The second is from a Grade 8 class, during a *dictée*. Anyone who has been schooled in French will associate that word with a certain atmosphere: dead silence, and the slow, rhythmic utterance of each word of a text chosen to exercise students' written language skills. In the middle of the *dictée*, into the silence, the teacher provides the next word: *tantôt* 'by and by'. One beat later, from somewhere in the back of the class, comes the theme music from *The Lone Ranger*, evoking that Western hero's trusty Indian sidekick, Tonto.

Code-switching was generally used in situations where, for external reasons, the separate English and French frames were collapsed. A typical situation was the oral report: students had to stand up and give a report in the classroom in front of the teacher and all the other students. The official nature of this performance entailed the use of French, but at the same time, it was a performance in front of peers. By using English for side comments and pauses, hesitations and gap-fillers (umm, let me see, etc.), students could neutralize the tension between the two frames. In this instance, code-switching is one of several role-distancing strategies; part of the balance between the authority of the school and the solidarity of the student involves not performing too officially, not entering too greatly into the school-sanctioned role. By embedding French discourse in English commentary, a student can legitimately turn in a good official performance. This is underscored by the following example: in the middle of a Grade 7/8 class at St-Michel, a Grade 6 boy knocked on the door and entered. Addressing the teacher, he said: "*Je m'excuse de vous déranger, monsieur*, I know I better be, *mais est-ce que je peux avoir le poids rond et le poids à distance?*" [I'm sorry to bother you, sir, I know I better be, but may I borrow the round weight and the distance weight?]. In this case, the English phrase, distancing the student from the obsequiousness of his utterance, was clearly addressed to the other students in the classroom.

In other cases, when the teacher is not present but the students are nonetheless engaged in official school activities, or are supposed to be, code-switching has less of a role-distancing function, but serves nonetheless to manage the contradiction between school work (French) and peer-group interaction (English). Here, the switches tend to be more syntactically integrated into the discourse, and can also operate turn by turn in conversation. A typical case is small-group work (this will be discussed further in Chapter 6). The following example is from a small-group discussion during a twelfth-grade chemistry class in the secondary-level module:

Anne: ... *que l'examen au microscope est inutile* [... that examining through the microscope is useless]
Marie: no
Anne: yeah
Daniel: shoot her
Anne: *c'est vrai* [it's true]
Daniel: *non* [no]
Anne: that's *c'est ce que vous nous avez dit l'alcool est sous forme de liquide?* [that's that's what you told us the alcohol is in liquid form?] I don't understand

In addition to such everyday uses of language, on several occasions students took opportunities presented to them to work out aspects of the relationship between the different frames of their experience, specifically, to create an object of interest by juxtaposing the frames, and thereby contributing to the resolution of tension between them. Two examples will illustrate what I mean.

In the first case, the Grade 8 students at St-Michel were asked to prepare humorous skits to be presented at the year-end graduation ceremonies. In one skit, a student emerges from the wings, and asks the audience: "*Connaissez-vous l'histoire de Pierre et le Loup? Non? Eh bien, regardez!* (Do you know the story of Peter and the Wolf? No? Well, watch!)" The curtain then opens onto a scene of four eighteenth century French soldiers playing cards. A fifth soldier comes running in from stage right, shouting: "*Wolfe est là! Wolfe est arrivé!* (Wolfe [that is, the famous British general who captured Quebec from the French in 1759] is here! Wolfe has arrived!)"[47] The soldiers jump up from the table and grab their weapons. The lookout bursts out laughing: it had all been a joke. The disgruntled soldiers return to their game, and the lookout returns to his post. A few minutes later, he rushes back in, insisting that this time Wolfe really *has* arrived. No one believes him, although, of course, this time it is true; the soldiers are therefore unprepared when the British arrive, and hence are easily defeated. This revisionist history of the British conquest of Canada depends for its effect on the unstated association of *Pierre et le Loup*, presented in the introduction and providing the plot line, with Wolfe (*loup* being the French for wolf). Anyone who cannot do the translation, or recognize that it is in the translation that the key to the skit lies, fails to grasp its originality.

The second example comes from a small-group activity which formed part of the action-research phase of our work. A Grade 7 class at Samuel de Champlain was engaged in the production of an ad; it was up to them to decide the nature of the product, the market, the medium, as well, of course, as the form of the ad itself. Most groups simply developed French-language versions of ads, or types of ads, with which they were familiar from English-language television. One group chose to do an ad for an Oriental sauce, based on an American product of that nature. In developing the ad they found themselves confronted with the problem of reconciling the Oriental nature of the sauce, the American English ad format with which they associated it and the French language which they were constrained to use for their own version. Most other groups confronted similar problems (at least as far as the English and French frames were concerned) but circumvented the issue through direct translation. This group, whose work, significantly, was considered qualitatively much better by the other students than that of any other group, found a more original solution.

In the final version of the ad, three students, two girls and a boy, enter an Oriental restaurant. When the waitress arrives, they order steak (American) and rice (Oriental), as well as the sauce in question. The waitress brings the order, but forgets the sauce. When she finally returns with it, she trips and the sauce flies into the air. The boy produces a baseball mitt, and catches it with a flourish. In unison, the students shout the name of the sauce, slap each other's hands in the American gesture of satisfactory completion, and then, palms together, bow and vocalize ("a:h") in a stereotypically Oriental way. Each aspect of the ad unites elements of Oriental and American culture within the French-language text, permitting a particularly satisfying resolution of the difference between the three frames.

This form of behaviour, the separation of French and English mediated by bilingual puns, code-switching, and other forms of expression and neutralisation of the tension on the boundary, characterizes the use of language by the vast majority of students of all ages in all the schools in which I worked. Essentially, I would argue, it can be explained by the importance of the students' experience of life in English and life in French. It is a reflection of the extent to which they take seriously both the value of English and the value of French, as a source of prestige and of economic status. While in the terms of their immediate experience, the value of the two languages have different sources, they are nonetheless concerned to maintain their participation in both worlds. However, it was also clear that these patterns did not characterize everyone's behaviour. Indeed, there were two groups of students whose behaviour did not fit this model, precisely because their experience of French and English was different. The difficulties they had with the world they encountered, as I have just described it, and the eventual recruitment of most of them into the majority group, serve, however to illustrate further the strength of the conventions developed by the majority.

The two other groups were functionally monolingual. The French-dominant students generally had just arrived in Toronto from a region where French was the majority or only language. The English-dominant students had generally not been in their current school very long either (although there were some exceptions to this); in some cases they had been in immersion programmes, but in general they came from homes where no French was spoken and had little prior experience of French.

It is important that it is not language background, but rather experience of French and English which is at the basis of the distinction among these three groups. The ways in which each group used French and English goes some way toward explaining why this might be so. Most importantly, it became apparent that, while the principal convention of language choice in activities which might be described as official school activities involved the exclusive use of French, peer-group activities centred around the use of English.

French-dominant students, then, arrived in a world where they had no difficulty participating in official school activities, but where their access to peer-group relations became immediately problematic. As students, this placed them in a difficult position; it is never good to be seen to be collaborating too much with the authorities, even if, in the end, you go along with their values and goals. On the other hand, their ability to interact with the teacher was also considered valuable by other students, and could serve as a basis for negotiating status among the peer group. The ability to speak French was the major form of valued capital these students could offer others.

Most of these students experienced their entry into these schools as difficult, even painful at times. They felt isolated and alone, they felt that others were making fun of them. Christiane, the girl who often took the bus home with me from St-Michel, talked about this: she had arrived earlier that year from Quebec and spoke little English. By the winter, she had still not made any friends, and felt lonely and still, in her words, "*dépaysée*" (literally, out of one's territory or country). By spring, she was talking about changing schools, ostensibly because she and her mother and sister would be moving, but clearly she had no reason to feel tied to St-Michel.

However, not all such students were like Christiane. Some were able to use their French to accrue status, some were lucky enough to arrive in classes where the peer-group network was not as closed as it happened to be among the Grade 6 girls of Christiane's class, and others had more gregarious personalities. Marc, a Québécois monolingual boy, arrived in Christiane's class at about the same time as she did. He quickly made up his mind to break into the boys' circle, and possibly the nature of the boys' activities and of their relationships made it easier for him to do so. During recess, he would hang around the edge of ball games, learn the rules of the game, and begin to play, occasionally interjecting the kinds of verbal routines which marked the games' episodes. By spring, he was fairly adept at using routines such as "Shut up!" and "Leave me alone!" in appropriate and functional ways, although his phonological and paralinguistic treatment of these phrases as single, unanalyzed wholes betrayed his lack of understanding of the meaning and composition of these routines.[48]

Marc's younger brother, Eric, entered Grade 3. His approach to his situation was similar to Marc's. In addition, Eric, who, if anything, was more gregarious than Marc, indeed, assertive and at times almost aggressive, carved out an important role for himself among the boys: he became their spokesperson, their broker in a way, with respect to the teacher. He argued the boys' various causes (permission to bring various forms of contraband, such as balls, into the classroom, say) and in a variety of non-academic ways acted as their representative. (Other similar students in other schools adopted similar roles, and in addition frequently acted as brokers in academic matters as well.) In return, other boys acted as his broker with respect to English-dominant students. Eric got into a fight one day with another boy, Alex, over who had the right to hang his coat on a particular coat hook. The argument, such as it was, mainly in French on Eric's side and in English on the part of Alex, was going nowhere until a third boy, Robert, intervened. Robert collected the evidence, interrogating Alex in English and Eric in French. He finally rendered his judgement in Eric's favour, saying to Alex, in English: "Does it [the coat hook] have your name on it?"

Marc and Eric had an older sister, Josiane, who was in Grade 7. Somewhat less gregarious than Marc and Eric, she was nonetheless able to make friends with Sylvie, a bilingual girl from northern Ontario, who had arrived at St-Michel at the same time as Josiane. For all practical purposes, Sylvie became Josiane's language broker, explaining to her what was going on around them in English, and doing for her whatever English-language interaction needed to be done. The other students in the class thought of Josiane as francophone; one girl explained to me that she only spoke French with francophones, like Josiane, although in practice what this meant was that very few students interacted with Josiane at all unless they absolutely had to, in which case they either spoke French to her or operated through Sylvie. In turn, Josiane and Sylvie categorized the other students as English. For example, Josiane and Sylvie sat talking together on a bus during a school outing; Josiane said it would be nice if everybody sang songs together. Yes, Sylvie, said, "*mais eux-autres ils connaissent juste des chansons anglaises* [but they only know English songs]".

At St-Michel, there were not many such French-dominant students, and only in the case of Marc and Christiane were there ever more than one per class. In the larger high schools, however, there were more, and in both there developed small parallel peer networks composed only of French-dominant students. However, unlike the main peer networks which tended to be divided by age group and, at least to some extent, by gender, the French-dominant networks cut across several grade levels.

Thus some French-dominant students, like Marc (and indeed, eventually Josiane, although in her case the process took much longer), became bilingual and members of the main peer-group networks, while others remained isolated, literally alone or with a small group of friends. The variety of outcomes can be seen as a product of the kinds of strategies individual students were prepared to adopt (linked at least in part to the social and communicative resources they felt they could draw on and their degree of confidence in doing so) in interaction with the concrete possibilities presented to them.

Just as every year, in most classes, one or two French-dominant students would arrive, so there were a few English-dominant students in each school. These were generally students who, while of French origin, had attended English-language or immersion programmes, although occasionally, especially in the earliest grades, their non-francophone parents had simply made a decision to enroll their children in a French-language school. English-dominant students, of course, faced the opposite set of problems from those faced by French-dominant students. While they had no difficulties making friends, their interaction in situations where the use of French was expected could be compromised by their relative lack of proficiency in French.

At St-Michel, this happened to a Grade 6 student named Patrick, who had recently arrived in the school, having attended an immersion programme for several years previously. One day, the teacher decided to do some role-playing as an exercise in the development of language skills. Each student had to stand in front of the class and act out a situation which the teacher proposed. Patrick was given the situation of a little boy who comes home later than he was meant to, and has to explain to his angry and distraught mother what he was doing and why he was late. For several minutes, Patrick hesitated, then finally said "*Je jouais au parc* [I was playing in the park]". The teacher pushed for more, but the more the teacher insisted, the less was forthcoming: "*je jouais au parc*" became "*je jouais*", then "*jouais*", and, finally, nothing at all.

These kinds of situations, where students were asked to perform without preparation in front of the class in direct interaction with the teacher, were, however, relatively rare. Usually, English-dominant students could fairly successfully avoid direct interaction with the teacher. Often, like the French-dominant students, they relied on bilingual brokers. At Jeanne-Sauvé, one English-dominant Grade 1 student, Nancy, became friends with Catherine, a fluently bilingual student originally from France. One day, they were standing near me in the playground. Nancy said to me: "What are you eating?" I replied, "*Je ne mange rien, qu'est-ce que tu manges, toi?* [I'm not eating anything, what are *you* eating?]" Nancy seemed confused, and repeated her question, in English, several times. Finally, she turned to Catherine and said: " Ask her what she's eating!" Catherine then turned to me and said: "*Elle veut savoir ce que tu manges* [She wants to know what you're eating]". In similar ways, students like Catherine acted as brokers within the classroom, clarifying for students like Nancy what was going on (for example, what exercises they were supposed to do, what the homework assignment was, and so on) and hence facilitating their access to the academic processes of the school. While some English-dominant students could function in this way for some time, for most this kind of support acted to help them stay in the game long enough to learn at least enough French to function in school, that is, to use it well enough so that they no longer would feel the stress that students like Patrick felt under pressure to perform.

If the French-dominant and English-dominant students have difficulties, it is because they do not possess the linguistic resources (and in some cases the cultural knowledge) necessary to make the bridge between the two major frames of school experience, the world of peers and the official world of the school. The fact that most students eventually start acting like those whom I have called here the bilinguals, is an indication both of the stability and of the importance of the boundary. If the students did not value, at some level, both worlds, they would refuse to participate in one or the other. Certainly some do; they remain isolated from their peers, or, alternatively, choose to leave the French-language school. But most do not; while they express certain forms of resistance to school authority (so satisfyingly easy to do simply by speaking English), this resistance is no different from that of most other school children in the Western world. Indeed, for the most part, just as teachers' distancing themselves from their role legitimates their dominance (Bourdieu and Passeron 1977), so the students' resistance legitimates their acceptance of that dominance (Willis 1977).

Students do not talk very much about why they so assiduously pursue participation in both worlds, at least not until they near the end of high school and begin thinking about their future. This is not for lack of opportunities: teachers, and often, by their own account, parents, bring the subject up frequently. Teachers often ask "*Pourquoi est-ce que je veux que vous parliez français?* [Why do I want you to speak French?]" Students learn to respond in unison: "*Parce que c'est une école française!* [Because it's a French school!]" Occasionally, the discussion goes a little deeper, exploring the question of identity and the ideology of bilingualism (cf. section 5.1.).

For some students it clearly is, at some level, a question of francophone identity as well as a strategy they adopt in order to gain access to the resources of bilingualism. They speak French at home, they participate in French-language activities, and eventually many of them become active in francophone student or community organizations and choose to attend French-language universities in Quebec or bilingual ones in Ontario. For others, the interest is mainly instrumental; for example, some students in the public secondary-level module were outraged to discover that the school board and the province considered them francophones on the basis of the fact that they were in a French-language instructional unit. Most of the students have accepted the notion, shared by their parents, that it is important to be bilingual, and that being in a French school while also living in an English-speaking community is one way to achieve that goal, perhaps the best, or maybe the only, path open to them. Indeed, the experiences that they have in managing the boundary between French and English at school can provide valuable training for similar brokerage roles in the future.

Whatever their interests and points of departure, almost all the students in Toronto's French-language schools showed, through their use of French and English, their interest in maintaining a foot in both worlds and their ability to act as brokers across the language boundary. Their language practices, then, raise some interesting questions about the role their schools actually play in the formation of the boundary between French and English. While educators, and many parents, see the school as having to be situated squarely on the French side of the boundary, students' linguistic practices betray another reality. It is to this issue that I turn in the following section.

5.4. Brokers and boundaries

Toronto's French-language schools are arenas for the construction of the ethnolinguistic boundary between French and English. This boundary emerges in a discourse of struggle: the school and some parents attempting to create an exclusively francophone milieu, while non-francophone parents try to gain access to bilingualism through participation in Franco-Ontarian institutions, and students live in both French- and English-speaking worlds (as well as, often, in communities of other origins).

The school, as a minority institution, and those parents who have experienced what it is like to be part of the francophone minority, perceive that the persistence of French depends on the existence of milieux where French is the most valued form of linguistic capital. Perhaps more importantly, they have invested in the persistence of French as a way of gaining access to or maintaining those domains where knowledge of French is essential; in order for institutions like schools to serve those interests they have to be controlled not just by French-speakers but by people who see their broader interests as collectively expressed and served through the medium of French. Not that they deny the importance of English, but simply that for them it is clear that they do not need English-language education in order to learn English.

However, the very mobilization of francophones around those collective interests allows them to be seen by others as being in a position of power, not a position of powerlessness. While many francophones (and the schools) engage in a discourse of defence, others seek access to the resources those francophones are trying to protect, because they, too, have learned to treat them as valuable. Their bewilderment at the often hostile reaction of many francophones has many sources. One is the simple inability of those who have power to see inequalities in the distribution of power. If Canada is bilingual, then necessarily French and English are on an equal footing; if francophones can go to English schools then anglophones can go to French ones. For many immigrants, of course, it certainly appears at first blush that French and English *are* equal, or at least both more privileged and more valuable in the Canadian context than their own languages.

Another source has to do with the ways in which Canada's ideology of bilingualism hides a struggle between francophones and anglophones for political and economic power and for social prestige. The notion that individual bilingualism is valuable, that it will lead to good jobs and to social prestige, entails that some people will be bilingual and others will not, since, of course, if everyone in the country were fluently bilingual, in the absence of any functional distribution of languages, there would scarcely be any reason to remain bilingual. If bilingualism is to be a relatively rare, or at least restricted, commodity, the issue arises of who will have privileged access to it.[49] When bilingualism was a mark of domination, of course, francophones were the almost exclusive proprietors of this form of linguistic capital. The challenge that they face is the retention of this privileged access now that bilingualism has become central to access to power or prestige. On the other hand, for the experience of French-language education to be truly valuable to anglophones it should be as close to "authentic" as possible, that is, it should be a legitimate participation in an institution that is seen to be of the Franco-Ontarian community. The question there is the extent to which anglophones can use that institution to pursue their interests without damaging that authenticity.

For some, the authenticity must come from inside, that is, it is institutions such as schools which must be truly francophone (in whatever sense they may give that concept). For others, the authenticity is external. Many participants in French-language schools, whether their first language is French, English or both, think of themselves and of the schools as bilingual. The core areas which provide the significance and value of the two languages are elsewhere (presumably in Quebec for French and in the rest of Canada for English); they themselves are on the boundary, and feel their public as well as their private lives should reflect that.

Thus the struggle over who should have privileged access to bilingualism is a question of which group's interests should prevail in more than one sense. For some, it is a question over who should have access to the exclusively francophone institution of the school, and a question of the extent to which the school can adapt its curriculum and pedagogy to varied interests and still retain its francophone identity. For others, the struggle is over the nature of the identity of the school itself, as a francophone or, in contrast, a bilingual institution.

These struggles emerge out of the differences in the social position of different participants and hence in the linguistic and cultural capital which they bring to this arena. The differences underlie the definition of their interests and their needs. For middle-class francophones, the acquisition and maintenance of class position derives from their investment in French, or, more precisely, from their control of francophone institutions and of the resources which underlie the value of the French language. Others see their role as lying principally in the form of brokerage; the value of bilingualism derives from the ability it gives them to move back and forth between two worlds.

For everybody, school is essential to providing access to the forms of linguistic capital they need in order to achieve their goals. The problem is that not everybody arrives at school with the same forms of capital, and not everyone agrees about what forms of capital should be distributed at school. As a result, those who control the school, parents and administrators, find strategic means of defining whose interests are primarily to be served by the school. These means include decisions about the language of instruction, the language of communication with parents, the pedagogy of teaching French and in French, criteria of admission and streaming. They do this through the institutional structures of the school, the parent-teacher associations and the elected school board.

In the meantime, the students have found their own solution to the tensions over the definition of the boundary which so engage their parents and their teachers. Unlike the majority of the adults, most of the children have, or quickly acquire, an intense experience of what it is like to grow up in a world dominated by English, but where the value of French can be brought to the foreground under certain circumstances. Few of them have experienced the stigmatization of French which many of the adults knew as children (although most of the students who are native speakers of regional varieties of Canadian French still feel that the quality of their language is inferior to that of the Europeans). For them, the boundary is clear, and their job is to straddle it.

At the moment, then, the schools are producing two things. At the level of the students, they are producing a generation of language brokers, who are adept at moving back and forth between languages and between domains controlled by different groups of people. Further, these brokers, at some point in their school careers, encounter the kinds of decision-making which are crucial to the development of boundaries, that is, they are made to become aware of their own position with respect to the boundary and of the strategies that are available to them in the use of language to pursue economic, political and social interests. At the level of the broader society, they are raising fundamental questions about the nature of bilingualism. Through the expression of educational ideology, clear class and ethnic interests are being pursued; the schools provide an important arena for the formulation of those interests and for the playing out of the contradictions and conflicts among them.

For the researcher, this analysis poses an interesting dilemma. It is possible, of course, to present the analysis, and let it take its course. But it must also be seen as a form of discourse in itself, as a contribution to the debate, as an avenue for the privileging of certain interests over others. Certainly, parents and teachers with whom we spoke were very open about this; for them, participation in the research was only meaningful to the extent that it might enable them to pursue their own interests. For us, it was very clear that the maintenance of a fiction of objective and neutral research was not only groundless but also dangerous, in the sense that research presented in that light can then be taken up by others and exploited for their own purposes. Preferable by far to us was the open acknowledgement of the role of research in the social and political debate over the value of bilingualism and the role of French-language schools in defining the value of linguistic resources as well as in distributing them. This stance has allowed us to declare our interests; in essence, it is a means for us to accumulate evidence which convinces us of the legitimacy of certain goals and of the strategies one can use to attain them.

The following chapter is an account of that end of the research process: the formulation of our own interests and the grounds which that gave us for developing ways to further those interests. Having arrived at an analysis which we found plausible, even persuasive, we had to ask ourselves: now what? What do we do about that? What do we give back to the schools, the parents, the administrators, the students? The answers we found to those questions are, of course, partial, but the experience then raises new questions and feeds into a cycle of research which is, at the same time, an act of commitment to Franco-Ontarian education.

5.4 Brokers and boundaries 179

Photograph 1. Students at l'École du Sacré-Coeur, the first French-language school in Toronto, in 1907

Photograph 2. L'École du Sacré-Coeur, 1943

180   5   French-language minority schools in Toronto

Photograph 3. L'Église Sacré-Coeur, the first French-language church in Toronto, ca. 1955

Photograph 4. The Sacré-Coeur parish-based Lamarche hockey team, named for the *curé*, 1956

5.4 Brokers and boundaries   181

Photograph 5. Le Centre francophone, the first secular francophone community centre in Toronto, ca. 1977

Chapter 6
Projet "Coopération et découverte"

6.0. From ethnography to action-research

The relationship between a researcher and the people she or he works with is always complex. Certainly, explicitly or implicitly, there is always, somewhere, a notion of exchange or reciprocity. The researcher gets something out of this activity, and it is only right that the other participants do too. One can argue that we all benefit from deeper knowledge and understanding, but those are rather long-term rewards. Clearly, there is no one way in which to address this question; we each must decide for ourselves what seems right. For me, a path developed slowly, out of the relationships I established and the experience I was able to acquire.

Toronto schools tend to get studied backwards and forwards and upside down. The few French-language schools in the system experience this scrutiny in an intensified manner; there are only a few tokens of this type, and so participation in studies cannot be rotated among schools. In addition, there are, on a regular basis, province-wide studies of Franco-Ontarian education, and all French-language schools are called upon to participate one way or another. However, the results are often not immediately available or useful; the schools sometimes get the feeling that they are giving considerably more than they are getting back. Their willingness to let me work with them was therefore clearly contingent on my delivering something that might be useful to them; I imagine that I am scarcely alone in having had this experience.

At any rate, it seemed reasonable to me. At first, of course, there were real limits to what I could give. So I gave my time, a willingness to talk, a helping hand, whenever possible. What seemed to matter most was the time I spent in the schools; I went from being a researcher to being a person, and the purpose of my work, I think, became clearer, at least to the teachers I spent time with. Initial results, especially the demographic profiles of the student population, were well-received; certainly the demographic information could be used immediately in thinking about a variety of policies, from admissions to curriculum planning (whether it was or not is less clear to me).

By 1985, the data was starting to get saturated. The hypotheses I had initially generated were borne out in each of the kinds of French-language schools found in the Toronto region, elementary and secondary, public and separate. Among other things, what emerged was a picture of schools in which strategies for carrying out the mission of preserving French language and culture were predicated on assumptions which no longer held. In a number of ways, school personnel acted as though they were operating in a milieu in which all students mastered the same variety of French and to the same degree; there was also an implicit assumption that students did, or at least should, have access to French outside school. The forms of language and culture that were valued corresponded to standard, if not élite, forms. The shadow community invoked by school attitudes was a homogeneous, relatively stable and locally concentrated population with deep roots in Canada.

The reality of the classroom was, however, very different. For one thing, despite the fact that over time shared experiences of life in Toronto gave many of them something in common, the students scarcely formed a homogeneous group. There were students from francophone and anglophone families, from families of other language backgrounds, as well as from mixed families. The francophones came not only from a wide variety of Canadian regions (rural and urban, majority and minority) but also from around the world. Many, but not all, students from non-French backgrounds came from parts of the world where French was a language of instruction or otherwise served as an important second or third language. Only about half the students had been born in Toronto, and every year each school admitted newcomers, sometimes part-way through the year. The students thus mastered a wide range of regional and class-based varieties of French, and to varying degrees of proficiency. They themselves identified to a greater or lesser extent with some notion of francophone identity. And they had a wide range of degrees and types of experience of life in francophone majority or minority contexts.

Second, the student population, even the francophone population, was far from being geographically concentrated. There is no French neighbourhood in Toronto; at best, there are a few areas where the francophone population is large enough to support parish activities or meetings of social clubs and youth groups more or less from the neighbourhood. Generally speaking, however, participation in French-language activities outside school required effort on the part of both students and parents, and, with the exception of some homes, students' exposure to and use of French outside school could range from minimal to nonexistent, especially as they grew older and less involved in their nuclear families.

This mismatch explained a lot to me about the frustrations teachers were experiencing, and about the difficulties the schools seemed to be having in achieving their linguistic and cultural goals. Some elements of the situation were already matters of public debate: the presence of English-dominant students, the increasingly multicultural nature of the student body. However, the solutions that were being sought were primarily structural and political. I do not wish to argue that such solutions are inappropriate; I did however feel at the time that they were partial, in the sense that certain elements of the situation were unlikely to change radically, and further, in the sense that none of them addressed the set of characteristics I have just described or the school milieu in which they become salient as a systematic whole. Notably, very few addressed the kinds of strategies teachers could adopt in the classroom to respond to the reality they were experiencing.

It seemed to me that it should be possible to begin giving something back to the schools precisely in this area; a contribution which grew directly out of the ethnographic work I had been doing. The rest of this chapter is devoted to a description of this stage of work, and to a discussion of the extent to which it might or might not make a difference, given the goals we set ourselves.

6.1. The development of a teaching approach

At about the time I began thinking that it should be possible to develop a teaching approach more appropriate to the classrooms I knew, two things happened. First, I used Shirley Brice Heath's *Ways With Words* (1983) in a graduate course I was teaching on language, culture and education. The content of the book, and, perhaps more importantly for me, the use my students made of it, convinced me of the feasibility of using ethnography not only as a research tool, but also as a teaching strategy. What captured my attention was the possibility of turning students into ethnographers in order to have them discover the various ways in which they themselves used language, the ways others around them used language, and then to understand and exploit that diversity in terms of people's social experience and social goals.

This struck me as critical in the context in which I was working. Neither students nor teachers really grasped the extent to which there was diversity along these dimensions among students, even in a single classroom, nor what the characteristics of that diversity might be. Students and teachers tended to dismiss their knowledge of anything other than standard French as illegitimate in the school context, if not illegitimate in any context. Students' knowledge of English was valuable to them, but they knew it had no place in official school settings outside English class. Canadian students felt that they spoke French badly compared to the Europeans. Teachers and students could not build on the knowledge that they did possess in order to widen its range, because that knowledge was literally invisible. In addition, while the schools insisted on the importance of the identity and cultural dimensions of their goals, they in fact favoured only one version of French language and culture to the detriment of others. As a result, they were rendering illegitimate forms of French identity which, under other circumstances, might be considered perfectly legitimate.

It occurred to me that using ethnography might be one way to destigmatize entire sections of students' verbal repertoires, indeed to introduce the notion of repertoire as one way to help students and teachers redefine their pedagogical goals in the light of their lived experience. Further, it struck me as a way to deal flexibly with the fact that each student's point of departure was likely to be different from that of his or her classmates; the whole-class pedagogy that most teachers favoured normally made this next to impossible.

In the fall of 1985, I tried out some of these ideas with the collaboration of Albert, the high-school teacher mentioned in Chapter 5 and responsible that fall for a Grade 9 advanced-level *Français* class. The students kept some field notes about the language they were exposed to outside school; this had the effect of making them notice some uses of language they were otherwise quite unaware of. They tape-recorded an interview and transcribed it, in order to become aware of some of the features of ordinary spoken language. Finally, they looked at the language of advertising, in order to connect both verbal communication to visual images and form to communicative purpose.

It was an interesting semester, but unsatisfying in some ways. First, neither Albert nor I were able to quite figure out how to deal with the masses of data the students generated in each exercise, most importantly, how to help them make generalizations on the basis of it. In part, we thought, this may have been because our approach had been too "top-down": we had presented the general principles, then had students do some fieldwork, and expected them to link the two, instead of allowing a grasp of general principles to grow out of an apprehension of the regularities of their own experience and a comparison of the realities of the students in the class. Second, we were unable to find really satisfactory ways to evaluate this activity, since it differed radically from what Albert (or any other teacher) was used to doing. As a result, the students had the impression that Albert accorded this activity less importance than others, since it had less weight in the calculation of their grades.

While I was struggling with these problems, I began talking to one of my colleagues, Graham Barker. Graham had been working with one of the other faculty members in our centre, Michael Canale, on the development of problem-solving strategies. Working from a basis in cognitive learning theory, they were trying to find ways to help students learn to use language to learn, specifically, to solve problems. They had become interested in cooperative learning strategies as a means to structure these activities, to achieve their goal of helping students take more responsibility for their own learning, and to integrate cognitive, linguistic, metalinguistic and affective dimensions of the learning experience. However, just as I was coming up against the limitations of an anthropologically oriented approach to teaching strategies, Graham was beginning to feel the limits of one structured primarily in terms of cognitive frameworks. He couldn't attach the materials they were developing to the lived reality of the classroom, nor build in the interactional dimensions of the students' work, because he lacked an understanding of who the students were and of the social dimensions of their interaction. Our problems seemed complementary, and so we thought maybe our approaches might be too.

What developed out of our talks was a teaching approach which combined elements from the ethnography of communication with cooperative learning techniques in order to achieve a number of goals (cf. Heller – Barker 1988; Heller et al. 1990). Our primary goal was to help students expand their verbal repertoires in French. For us, this had to be a crucial component of teaching French and in French in a minority context. Given the limited range of activities in which it is possible to use French in Ontario, we argued that schools needed to take on the responsibility for expanding students' repertoires in that language. What this meant from the point of view of the schools was admitting as legitimate a wider range of varieties and uses of French than had hitherto been the case.

We felt that this combination of techniques would allow us to achieve this goal (as well as some others which flow out of it) in a number of ways. First, it would allow us to maximize the potential and minimize the obstacles presented by the two fundamental characteristics of the classrooms: the heterogeneity of the student body and the lack of access to francophone life outside school. Students would be able to share the resources they collectively possessed and discover others outside the walls of their classroom, indeed, outside the walls of the school. They would be able to participate in common tasks while each focussing on their own specific needs. As a result, we hoped, they would be increasingly able to take responsibility for their own learning, ties between school and community (so important in a minority context) would be strengthened, and the diversity of the student body would become a source of learning and a basis for the development of common goals rather than a source of strife and fragmentation. I will readily admit that we have been idealistic, but we have consciously chosen that path.

In 1986, together with several colleagues (Laurette Lévy, Françoise Pelletier and François St-Pierre) we put together an outline of what such a teaching approach might look like. With Albert, I had put the language-related goals well into the foreground of our activities, but I hadn't been entirely satisfied with the results. We decided instead to embed those goals into the structure of the projects, and to organize them around thematic content related to our overall goals. The projects, as might be expected, have gone through one or two incarnations over the years; the three that have crystallized are as follows:

Projet Reportage. The major goal of this project is a mini-ethnography of a situation outside the classroom (elsewhere in the school or outside the school) where French is used as a medium of communication. The idea is mainly to discover different ways in which French is used in settings outside the students' immediate experience (or to bring students to some degree of awareness of resources which may have escaped attention), and to help the students forge stronger links with the francophone world around them. Students communicate the findings in a number of ways, both oral and written, linguistic and visual (notes, transcripts, skits, drawings, oral or written narrative reports, etc.). Students can choose different formats and different combinations of modes of communication.

Projet Publicité. In this project, students look at the language of advertising, and create their own ads. The goal here (as it was in the embryonic version Albert and I had experimented with) is to examine the relationship between situations and modes of communication, as well as between communicative forms and functions.

Projet Histoire. The goal here is to examine the history of the local francophone community, or perhaps, one elsewhere. As in *Projet Reportage* there is a strong emphasis on strengthening links between school and community, and on bringing to light resources that are otherwise invisible, but with a diachronic rather than a synchronic focus. Students present the results of their research in ways similar to those of the first project.

All the projects share a structure which is based on the cooperative learning technique known as the jigsaw (Sharan – Sharan 1976; Aronson 1978; Kagan 1985).[50] The basic idea is that the class is divided into small groups, each of which has a specific goal related to the overall theme of the project. For example, in *Projet Reportage*, each group will focus on a different setting. If the students are staying within the school, they may choose such settings as the playground, the principal's office, the caretakers' room or the daycare centre (many French-language schools, in Toronto at least, provide space for a non-profit daycare centre). If they can work outside school, they may choose a church, a radio station, a youth club, or any other community setting, institutionalized or otherwise.

Within each group, each student has a specific role to play, that is, becomes an "expert" in a specific area crucial to the realization of the project. This way, the group cannot function without the participation of each student, and it is possible to avoid the classic problem of group work, namely, that one or two students do all the work while the others do nothing. The domains of expertise are the same in each group. It is here that we have focussed most explicitly on the language- or communication-related goals of our projects. In *Projet Reportage*, the experts are: the observer (who goes to the setting chosen and takes field notes), the interviewer (who interviews key participants in the setting), the artist (who develops visual representations of the activities observed) and the scriptwriter (who uses the basic ethnographic information as a basis for the development of a dramatic rendering). *Projet Publicité* shares the scriptwriter and the artist; in addition, there are a language expert (reponsible for the verbal form of the ad produced) and a marketing expert (responsible for collecting information about the audience aimed for on which decisions about the communicative form of the ad can be based). In *Projet Histoire* there is an interviewer and an observer, as well as experts responsible for extracting information from visual and written documents. What all these domains of expertise have in common is a focus on using language or non-verbal communication to acquire information and then to transmit it.

The projects follow the same basic five-step structure:[51]

Step 1: Whole class
Presentation of the project: the concept of cooperation, the structure and functioning of the project
Explanation of the Jigsaw method
Creation of base groups
Warm-up Jigsaw activity

Step 2: Base groups
Examination of evaluation methods and criteria
Preparation of group task: choice of final product and distribution of domains of expertise among group members

Step 3: Expert groups
Creation of expert groups and examination of work methods for each domain of expertise
Preparation of a report to be presented to other base group members

Step 4: Base groups
Presentation by each expert concerning the techniques learned in the expert group phase
Evaluation of each report

6.1 The development of a teaching approach

Reflection concerning cumulatively collected information
Organization and undertaking of group work

Step 5: Whole class
Presentation and evaluation of each group's final product
Comments, reflection and discussion on the learning
processes involved; general discussion concerning the project

In both the content and the structure we have built in opportunities to use language in a variety of ways. Students must use both spoken and written language over the course of the activities, must listen as well as speak, and read as well as write. They do so in a variety of communicative situations: with people they know as well as people they don't, with peers as well as adults or even sometimes younger children, on a one-to-one basis, in small groups or with the whole class.

What I have just presented is the final form the projects took. Initially, we sketched out both the form and the content of the projects, and took them to teachers we knew in one of Toronto's French-language schools. Working with several teachers and their Grade 7 and 8 classes, we fleshed out and modified them based on what happened in the classroom. We set up a lesson plan with each teacher, observed their classes while they taught, then drew up the plans and the materials for the next stage based on what had happened.[52]

The initial development resulted in the specific format described above. Once the activities had been developed and the resource materials written up, we tried them out again in other classrooms, modifying the language, and, in a few cases, some aspects of the format, until teachers and students felt comfortable with them. Following this phase, we decided to examine the extent to which the approach might be usable for students both younger and older than the twelve- and thirteen-year olds who had originally been involved.

We were interested in exploring the extent to which the *Projet Reportage* could be used by older students to examine situations outside the school milieu. We were able to work once again with Albert and his Grade 10 class, setting up groups which looked at a church, a theatre, a television station, an elementary school and a daycare centre. We were also interested in how the approach might be used by students too young to work directly with the written student materials we had developed for the older children. Here, we were able to work with a teacher of a combined Grade 2 and 3 class, and, later, with two teachers in another school, one responsible for a Grade 2 class and the other for Grade 3.

Finally, during the presentations we had begun to give in a variety of teachers' professional development contexts, we began to receive expressions of interest from French immersion teachers, that is, teachers responsible for using French as a language of instruction with students whose first language was other than French. Since two members of our team (Laurette Lévy and Françoise Pelletier) had had prior experience conducting research in an immersion context, we undertook to work with a small group of teachers and consultants to adapt the materials to this specific second-language environment.

In the end, the basic format we adopted as a result of our initial collaboration held, and we found ways of modifying the materials so that they could be used at a variety of grade levels and in both French-as-a-first-language and French-as-a-second-language contexts. In order to help students unfamiliar with group work become accustomed to it, we developed a kit of short preparatory activities to be used as a warm-up before beginning the projects; most of these activities were adapted from materials being circulated in networks of educators interested in cooperative learning.

We also developed the evaluation component of the activities. Since our focus was on helping students discover strategies for expanding their verbal repertoires, we necessarily had to argue both for a greater emphasis on learning process (as opposed to outcome) than most teachers and students were used to, and also for a shift of some responsibility for learning from the teacher to the students: we worked within a model in which the teacher did not act as the privileged source of information, but rather as a resource for student-driven activity. The consequences for evaluation are obvious: evaluation could no longer be based solely on student products (summative evaluation), nor could it continue to rest solely in the hands of the teacher. Instead, it was necessary to build in evaluation components focussing on the process of learning (formative evaluation) and to entrust aspects of evaluation to the students themselves. If there were problems with the implementation of the approach, it was here, and the resistance came not from the teachers but from the students. They had difficulty accepting the notion that they could be responsible for their own evaluation, and difficulty accepting that the learning process can be as important as the product.

I mentioned earlier that once the initial trials had been completed, we began to present our work to other educators, people who had not been directly involved with the development phase. In the context in which we work, as is common elsewhere, research and development of this kind is normally presented to practitioners in a variety of settings. The standard format is the workshop, which normally lasts one to three hours (exceptionally, full-day workshops can be scheduled). Material is presented, ideally with a hands-on component at some point during the presentation, and educators are then left to experiment with what they have learned on their own in their classrooms, with little or no possibility for further discussion with others who may have been present or with the presenters themselves.

6.1 The development of a teaching approach

In our case, on the one hand, we conducted workshops with Franco-Ontarian teachers, sometimes on the level of one school, more frequently at a regional level in the context of a professional development day, or at a provincial level in the context of educational conferences. With very few exceptions, cooperative learning was a relatively new concept for most of the educators we encountered. On the other hand, we also conducted workshops within the network of educators interested in cooperative learning, at a local or regional level. Here it was striking that we seemed to be the only team working in a francophone context, and it was here that we encountered the few Franco-Ontarian, immersion and occasionally Québécois educators who had begun to explore these concepts.

We were highly motivated to undertake this dissemination phase of our work, not only because we were convinced of its usefulness in terms of the specific goals we had set (in the next section I will take up some of the evidence for this claim), but also because some of the teachers with whom we had worked had gone on to use the approach to teach other subjects in ways which, they felt, allowed them to achieve multiple objectives which were difficult to achieve using more traditional teacher-centred whole-class methods. We thus felt that the approach could be readily adapted to respond to a fairly wide range of needs and to focus on a wide range of pedagogical objectives.

For example, Pascal, a Grade 8 teacher, used the structure of the projects to teach components of both the geography and the mathematics programme. In geography, he had the base groups take on as a task the description of the ecology of a specific region, each group focussing on a different zone. Experts learned about specific aspects of any regional ecology, knowledge which they could then apply to researching their aspect of the ecology of their region. The results of each expert's research were then combined to present a comprehensive report on the group's region. In geometry, each group had to build a scale model of its own design. Experts were responsible for specific operations necessary to the design and construction of the model (artistic design and calculations of angles and areas). This teacher felt strongly that it was possible for the students to master the content more efficiently (that is, in a shorter period of time) and more effectively in this way; in addition, he felt it developed students' independence and both social interactive and leadership skills. Finally, it expanded their language skills by engaging them actively in the exploration of domains for which they generally lacked knowledge of appropriate ways of talking and writing.

Armed with this knowledge, and with the results of our own experiences, we developed workshops which simultaneously gave us some time to simply present the approach, and also included one of the warm-up activities as a hands-on way to show the educators more or less what we meant. I won't say we fell flat on our collective face, but we did encounter problems for which we were not prepared. Teachers had a hard time grasping dimensions of the structure of the activities, let alone what motivated the particular structure we proposed. They were concerned that they would not be able to monitor what the students were doing, and, in particular, that the students would use this opportunity to speak in English. Our counter-arguments (principally that it is not necessary to constantly monitor students in order to find out how they are doing, and that the structure of the projects forces students to exploit any linguistic resources they have in order to expand their proficiency in French) remained unconvincing to them.

Finally, in one workshop, a teacher expressed her wish to actually see how this worked out in the classroom. As a result of this comment, we began to realize that a major source of our difficulties resulted from the institutionalized structure of the professional development workshop, which effectively cut off the real hands-on experience of using these materials from the situation in which they were presented. If we had been successful in the past, we began to feel, it was probably because we had lived through the implementation process in the classroom with the teachers, and had had the time (however brief and snatched at lunch-time or on the way out to the school buses) to go over what had happened that day and how it might be modified the next. If Pascal was able to adapt the approach to radically different content, it was because he had used the materials once through from beginning to end and had seen what resulted from that experience.

The professional development process, however, made it unlikely that these experiences could be repeated, never mind the fact that our team was too small, and engaged in too many other activities, to possibly continue to play a coaching role in our own region, let alone across the province or elsewhere. We remained (and remain) frustrated with the institutionalized structure, but in the meantime began to use the insights we gained from this frustration to work on some ways around it (see Fullan – Connelly 1987 for a discussion of the structural limitations of in-service training in Ontario).

The first was to work on the literal content of that teacher's comment, namely, that she wanted to see how this approach actually worked. We spent a year producing a half-hour video which not only provided animated graphics as a way of visualizing the structure of the activities, but more importantly showed how two different projects were used in three classrooms (Grade 2 and Grade 3 classrooms in a Franco-Ontarian school and a Grade 7 classroom in a French immersion school). This video has proven invaluable in allowing educators the vicarious experience of living the activities; they may not be able to visit someone's classroom themselves, but they can eavesdrop on one, as it were. It has also, unexpectedly, proven useful in presenting our work outside Canada, with the added dividend of acquainting others with some of the realities of francophone minorities and of second language learners in this context.

The second strategy we adopted was to attempt to develop a network of resource persons around the province, to whom we could present the material and who could then act as contact persons in their own region. With the support of the *Association des enseignantes et des enseignants franco-ontariens*, the Franco-Ontarian teachers' association, we spent a year conducting workshops around the province. In the end, I suspect that our hope of creating a network of resource persons was probably not realized. In large measure, we were unable to overcome the limitations of the institutionalized structure in this way; to set up the kind of network we had envisaged we would have had to have had the time to conduct much more in-depth work than the workshop structure allowed us, and there should have been a follow-up and an infrastructure for cross-regional communication which simply does not exist. Nonetheless, we were able to reach a geographically dispersed audience and to examine the ways in which the approach might be adapted to the different social realities of each region.

The third approach is one we are currently exploring, although doing so has taken us away from the content areas which spurred this reflection in the first place. Instead, we are focussing on a school-team model for action-research and reflexive practice, in which small groups of teachers work together with school board and consultants and members of our team to identify issues of concern, develop strategies to address them, reflect on and subsequently modify those strategies, and then work with other teachers in the school and across the board to further develop their ideas.

The development of the approach thus took us from contemplating what interventions might be appropriate to address issues revealed by basic ethnographic research, to collaborative development of a specific teaching approach and teaching materials in conjunction with teachers and students, and finally to a consideration of the professional development and dissemination dimensions of developing a new approach to teaching and learning practice. Many questions remain, especially those regarding the consequences of our activities for the students and for the teachers, in the short- and long-term, and within the bounds of the institutional structures within which we work. These questions certainly include ones which touch on the impact of such teaching and learning strategies on the ability of students of different backgrounds to learn about each other, understand each other and share resources among themselves; on their ability to use a wider variety of forms of French to good effect in and out of school; and to come to a greater awareness of the relationship between language use, ethnicity and social mobility (to mention some of the issues raised in previous chapters).

In the next section, I will take up the question of the short-term local consequences of our activities, that is, an exploration of what actually happened in the classroom. I will look specifically at the ways in which students drew upon their linguistic and cultural resources to accomplish the tasks. This will be used as a basis for arguing that the projects did achieve what we wanted them to, at least in terms of opening up opportunities for new ways of using French, as well as in terms of facilitating interaction among students of different backgrounds and acquainting them with dimensions of the world around them about which they otherwise knew little. Finally, I will argue that beyond these goals, the projects provided contexts for creative solutions to problems of competing linguistic and cultural frames, which perhaps might lay the groundwork for going beyond the major obstacle to Franco-Ontarian education, namely the unequal relations of power which obtain not only between the anglophone majority and the francophone minority but also within the francophone community itself.

In the final section, I will place these considerations within the context of the institutional structures which both constrain and make possible our work. The question here is primarily one of the extent to which purely pedagogical interventions of the kind I have described here can make a difference within the confines of an unchanged institutional structure.

6.2. *Projet Coopération et découverte* in the classroom[53]

In order to get a sense of the extent to which (and in what ways) our projects might be achieving our goals, we took care in the implementation and trial phases to create appropriate conditions and to closely examine the workings of the projects. In addition, we had access both to student and to teacher formative and summative evaluations as sources of information regarding the sense the participants made of the activities and the extent to which they felt their own goals were met.

The conditions we were concerned with had mainly to do with the composition of the groups: we wanted to make sure that the groups contained students who normally interacted little and in addition possessed different degrees and types of proficiency in French and English (in practice, as we knew, the latter characteristic almost always entailed the former). This meant that in most cases the groups were assigned by the teacher, and consisted of both boys and girls, students relatively proficient in and relatively weak in French or English, and students of a variety of ethnocultural backgrounds. Most frequently, the number of boys and girls was equal, but the number of Toronto-born or -raised bilingual children was generally greater than the number of recent immigrants (generally French-dominant) in any single group.

In order to examine closely how the projects worked in practice, we observed and tape-recorded in each of the twelve classrooms in which we conducted this work. We generally observed every session in which the project was conducted, from beginning to end; in a few classes, the teacher decided to devote extra time to the project or to assign components of it as homework, and we did not have access to those episodes. During the group work segments, we generally chose to follow one or two groups through their activities (Steps 2 and 4 for the base groups, Step 3 for the expert groups). However, since there were usually two of us in the classroom at any one time, we could not follow all the experts from one group into their respective expert groups. In addition, especially in the initial development phase of the work, we were frequently called upon by both students and teachers to provide clarification or additional information, or to participate in resolving some new problem which had arisen. In the classes engaged in *Projet Reportage* it was frequently difficult (and, in the case of the Grade 10 class doing fieldwork outside the school, impossible) to follow groups into their target settings. As a result, we only have complete data sets for a few groups (in the sense of continuous records for one group from the beginning to the end of a project). Nonetheless, we have approximately twenty audio recordings of entire episodes or even steps of groupwork, as well as videotapes of all phases of the project in three classrooms, along with field notes for all observation sessions in all classes (notes and recordings generally covered full class periods, which ranged in length from forty to ninety minutes).

We concentrated principally on interaction among students during the group-work phase in order to discover how they would draw on their linguistic and cultural resources to accomplish their task, given the changed communicative structure of the situation in which they found themselves. Specifically, while for the most part they were used to speaking French to the teacher in the classroom and English to peers outside it, they now found themselves in a classroom situation but with peers as interlocutors, faced with a task in which the resource material and final product were necessarily in French.

What we found was that the French-dominant students often acted as key structuring agents in the activity. Engaging the others, or being engaged by them, they offered opportunities for their less-proficient peers to discover ways to contribute substantively to the linguistic expression of the activity. In exchange, they had a certain measure of control over the situation, but, perhaps more importantly from their point of view, they were able to engage in French in sustained interaction with the peers from whom they were often isolated.

Second, group work often became an occasion for metalinguistic discussion; in order to conduct and produce their work, the students had to arrive at some consensus regarding form, and to integrate forms of language with which they were relatively unfamiliar. This caused them to confront diverse linguistic expressions explicitly, and to debate the acceptability or appropriateness of these forms in the context and for the purpose of the activity in which they were engaged.

Third, the activities provided occasions for symbolically confronting the contradictions which characterize the experience of these students, precisely because the activities collapse frames of reference which are normally kept separate. Individual students confronted this situation in ways commensurate with their social position; that is, French-dominant, bilingual and English-dominant students, starting from different viewpoints, responded differently to the same conditions. At the same time, in some groups, collective responses emerged which drew on the experiences and knowledge the students had in common.

In what follows, I will illustrate each of these dimensions of group work with examples taken from recordings and observations in a variety of the classrooms in which we worked.

It is possible to see what happens to French-dominant students most clearly in the interactions of two groups. As was typical of most classes, in these groups there is one French-dominant student together with three or four bilingual, or even English-dominant students. Group 1 consisted of five girls in a Grade 6 class (one of the few where students were allowed to self-select group composition and so where most of the groups consisted of only girls or only boys). (Grade 6 students are normally about 11 years old.) Selina had arrived from Quebec a few weeks prior to the recording analyzed here. She was of mixed French/Danish origin, and spoke English and sometimes French at home. She had been enrolled first in English, then in French schools in Quebec. She considered English to be her mother tongue, but she had a much broader experience of life in French than any of the other four girls, all of whom had been born and brought up in minority settings.

Laura was of mixed French/English origin. Although French was sometimes spoken at home, Laura considered English to be her mother tongue. She was born in a small city in western Ontario, and had been in Toronto, and in this school, for about four years. Terri, Rachel and Alicia were all from Toronto, and had all been in the same school together since Grade 1. Terri was of mixed anglophone/Hungarian origin; both Rachel and Alicia were of anglophone background. All three spoke little or no French at home and considered English to be their mother tongue.

6.2 In the classroom

Group 2 consisted of two boys and two girls in a Grade 5 class in a different school. Ricky's case was mentioned in Chapter 4: he was from an anglophone Ontario background (although one of his grandparents was francophone). The family had been recruited to a suburban French-language school by a principal who was trying to boost enrollment, and who made sure that the children stayed in French-language schools when they moved into the city. Ricky spoke little, if any, French outside school. Pierre had arrived from Quebec about five months before the episode to be discussed here was recorded; he spoke little or no English when he arrived. The family came for one year in order for Pierre's father to obtain medical treatment unavailable in Quebec. Pierre was somewhat older than the others, having been kept back a grade (Ontario and Quebec have different educational systems). Julie had a francophone mother, although she lived alone with her anglophone father, her mother having recently returned to her native Quebec. In addition to regular visits to Quebec, the family had also lived for several years in a francophone region of New Brunswick. Julie had always been educated in French. Finally, Nora was of mixed anglophone/German origin. At home, English, German and French were spoken (in that order of frequency). Nora was born in Toronto, and had always been in the same school.

Group 1 was engaged in *Projet Reportage*. The situation they had chosen was the school office; at the time of the recording they were in Step 4 of the project, producing the drawings, notes, transcripts and script for the final product. Two of the students had finished their work; Alicia was helping Terri complete the drawings and Selina was working on the script. The basic plot of the script had to do with an imagined scene in which a mother accuses the principal and vice-principal of negligence because her son had apparently been beaten up in the schoolyard.[54] Throughout the episode, Selina engages the other students in this activity, mainly through the use of questions, but also through other, explicit framing devices:

l'élève, comment voulez-vous qu'il s'appelle? [the student, what do you want him to be called?]
has anybody haven't talked yet?
on commence la saynète [we're starting the skit]
okay guys I'll read it
écoute [listen]
okay guys listen listen

It is significant that Selina uses French and English, frequently even French and English semantic equivalents, here. By doing so, she taps into her classmates' linguistic resources and conventions of peer-group interaction, which are dominated by English, and is thereby able to engage them in her work. At the same time as she meets them on the common ground of English, she continues to assert the French convention of the script-writing task, and to turn her classmates' contributions towards the accomplishment of the production of a text in French. She thus uses her own linguistic resources in a way which then draws the resources of the others into action within a framework in which French is conventional. Her codeswitching bridges the gap between French and English, between the four other girls and herself, and between the informal social relations of the group and the official nature of the classroom task.

In the following example, we can see how Selina's engagement of the others provides an opportunity, in this case in particular for Rachel, to have input into the script development, and to learn how to lexicalize her ideas in French.

Example 1.
Rachel: *je suis l'élève*
Laura: Rachel is *l'élève*
Terri: Rachel's *l'élève*
?: I'm {xx} I'm
?: Selina
Laura: is there a mother in that Selina?
Selina: Rachel
Rachel: *je suis* wounded *mhm j'ai fait mal je suis mal et je viens*
(…)
Selina: *"eh bien eh bien c'est que mon enfant est terriblement blessé" dit la mère "alors" dit Madame "alors alors"* {laughter} *dit Madame Langley "qu'est-ce qui se passe?" "eh bien c'est que j'étais dehors et je jouais tranquillement avec mes amis et soudain un grand garçon m'a poussé parterre*
Rachel: *hm hm elle marche non l'élève fait comme ça* {Rachel imitates someone limping}
Selina (to Terri): yeah yeah this you you have a lot to say here see wait (to all) *non non l'élève fait*
Terri: what about Valiquette let Valiquette come in
Selina: *dit l'élève en marchant tout croche dit l'élève en*
Terri: let Valiquette come in now

Rachel: I'm the student
Laura: Rachel is the student
Terri: Rachel's the student
?: I'm {xx} I'm
?: Selina
Laura: is there a mother in that Selina?
Selina: Rachel

Rachel: I'm wounded mhm I did badly I am badly and I come
(...)
Selina: "well well it's that my child is badly hurt" says the mother "so" says Madame Langley "so so" {laughter} says Madame Langley "what's going on?" "well it's that I was outside and I was playing quietly with my friends and suddenly a big boy hit me and pushed me to the ground"
Rachel: hm hm she walks like no the student goes like this {Rachel imitates someone limping}
Selina (to Terri): yeah yeah this you you have a lot to say here see wait (to all) no no the student goes
Terri: what about Valiquette let Valiquette come in
Selina: says the student walking all crooked says the student while
Terri: let Valiquette come in now

Selina thus draws on her own linguistic resources to tap into those of the others, and in so doing makes it possible for them all to realize a collective task in French. Her knowledge becomes valuable to the peer group in ways she had not yet experienced, and she is able to make ties that had been difficult to construct up until then. She can also draw on the others' ideas to develop a script which is richer and more compelling than what she may have been able to produce on her own. The others gain access to a linguistic domain and means of expression which provides them with an opportunity to expand their linguistic resources.

In Group 2, it is Julie, aided by Nora, who is responsible for script development, not Pierre, the one French-dominant student in the group. This group also had chosen to do a *reportage* on the school office, but with a focus on the secretary. The plot revolves around a love triangle: the secretary and the principal are caught *in flagrante delicto* by the secretary's husband, who happens to be the mailman, and his dog.[55]

Pierre is at a triple disadvantage; not only is he marginal to the group (as a newly-arrived francophone monolingual), but he is structurally marginal to the script-writing activity, which is in Julie's hands. Further, he is obliged to leave the activity for a considerable period of time: the school nurse has arrived to give shots to a few students who had not yet received them. Nonetheless, during the time he is present, he is called upon, principally by Nora, to contribute. As in Selina's case, he has knowledge which the others need, and he is motivated to provide it, since he gets something in return as well.

Example 2.

(On a day that Julie is absent, Nora is working through different aspects of the development of dialogue for the script as set out in worksheets provided to each group).

Nora: *le verbal*
Pierre: *le verbal c'est quand tu parles*
Nora: *okay la voix uh*
Pierre: *la voix c'est ça*
Nora: *la volume*
Pierre: *le volume wa:h*
Nora: *l'articulation*
Pierre: *si tu parles comme il faut*

Nora: the verbal
Pierre: the verbal it's when you talk
Nora: okay the voice uh
Pierre: the voice is this
Nora: the volume (fem.)
Pierre: the volume (masc.) wa:h
Nora: articulation
Pierre: if you talk properly

Example 3.

Julie (to Pierre): *elle est ton* boyfriend *elle est ton boyfriend*
Ricky: *oui*
Nora: *elle est ta ta uh blonde* I don't know
Julie: *ils se bataillent?* how do you say that? *et tu* {xx}
Pierre: *je sais*
(…)
Pierre: *woé wô wô j'comprends pus là j'suis la secrétaire pis c'est ma uh ma* girlfriend *c'est ça? j'suis en amour avec une fille*
Nora: *t'es um t'es une fille*

Julie (to Pierre): she's your boyfriend she's your boyfriend
Ricky: yes
Nora: she's your your uh girlfriend how do you say that? and you {xx}
Pierre: I know
(…)
Pierre: whoa whoa whoa I don't understand anymore I'm the secretary and that's my uh my girlfriend is that it? I'm in love with a girl
Nora: you're um you're a girl

At the same time, Pierre sets up an alternative conversation to the one dominated by Julie and Nora and the script development. The fourth member of the group, Ricky, is working on writing up his interview with the secretary while all the script development work is going on; although he participates actively, he too is somewhat marginal to this process. As a boy, he is probably also a natural ally for Pierre, or at least easier to approach. At times when Julie and Nora are absorbed in their task, Pierre engages Ricky in other conversations and verbal activities, including a discussion of the visit to the school nurse and the horror of shots, and a musical riff which plays on the form of people's names. The particular conditions of this episode allow Pierre and Ricky to form a tie, one which is carried out in French. This is of particular benefit to Ricky, who learns how to talk about things like braces and shots; later, Pierre's help is more concrete, as he makes a specific effort to help Ricky learn and produce his lines during the rehearsal of the script:

Example 4.

Ricky: *laisse-moi voir tes dents fais comme ça t' as besoin de* braces
Pierre: *des quoi?*
Ricky: *des choses comme Michel d' accroches*
Pierre: *des broches non*
Ricky: *oui oui*

Ricky: let me see your teeth do like this you need braces
Pierre: what?
Ricky: things like Michel "accroches"
Pierre: braces no
Ricky: yes yes

Example 5.

Pierre: *tu es aussi belle qu' une rose*
Ricky: *tu étais tout belle comme une rose toujours*
Nora: what? what? what?
Pierre: *tu es toujours aussi belle qu' une rose*
Julie (to Nora): and then you come in

Pierre: you are as beautiful as a rose
Ricky: you were all beautiful like a rose still
Nora: what? what? what?
Pierre: you are still as beautiful as a rose
Julie (to Nora): and then you come in

There is also benefit to Pierre. Not only is his contribution valued, but, like Selina, he gains access to peer relations without having to do so through English. His knowledge of French no longer confines him to the role of broker between students and the teacher (although he does eventually play that role as well, acting as spokesperson for his group when the teacher calls on them to summarize what they have done so far); such a role is one students often feel ambivalent about, because its value derives too much from the authority of the teacher, and not enough from the peer network. Instead he can begin to operate in his own right within the peer group, and our recordings of his activities in the playground show that even there students like Nora continue to draw him into their activities by approaching him in French.

Of course, Pierre also takes this as an opportunity to begin to learn English, precisely the kind of development so many parents and educators fear. My response to this is that in a minority context the best way to preserve the minority language may not be to isolate it from the language of the majority, but rather to ensure the continued value of the language of the minority. In that sense, what has happened in the micropolitics of Pierre's class is not that French has been protected from English, but rather that it has acquired a value among the students which it had not previously enjoyed.

Not all groups had students who were as clearly French-dominant as Selina and Pierre. In the classrooms in which we worked, however, among themselves the students were able to pool linguistic resources to achieve their communicative ends, and, where necessary, sought them outside the group in the human and documentary resources to which they had access in the context of the project. Clearly, the structure of the project necessitated, for most students, reaching beyond their individual resources; they found what they needed most frequently close at hand, but if not, were able to find it elsewhere.

The second dimension of interest in these activities concerns the development of metalinguistic awareness, particularly as concerns how one uses specific forms of French in the specific communicative context at hand. In some cases, this took the form of simple debates regarding the appropriateness of individual lexical items. One pair of Grade 6 boys engaged in a lengthy debate over the relative merits of two competing variants of the French term for peanut butter: the Canadian standard (*beurre d'arachides*), or the Canadian vernacular (*beurre de pinottes*). In others, discussion centred more on the ways in which people talk in specific situations. In Group 1, for example, in developing the dialogue for their skit, the students had a discussion about the way in which a principal might talk to a vice-principal:

Example 6.

Alicia: then Madame Langley she said *"oh je m'excuse monsieur c'est {xx}"*
Laura: I said like a ba ba bla {xx}
Terri: looks like a clown Rachel
Rachel: look she shouldn't say *"oh je m'excuse"*
Laura: oh yeah oh yeah okay

Selina: no they're both *patrons*
Rachel: stupid she's his *patron*

Alicia: then Madame Langley she said "oh I'm sorry sir it's {xx}"
Laura: I said like a ba ba bla {xx}
Terri: looks like a clown Rachel
Rachel: look she shouldn't say "oh I'm sorry"
Laura: oh yeah oh yeah okay
Selina: no they're both bosses
Rachel: stupid she's his boss

This kind of awareness can be seen as the first step to understanding both the concepts of linguistic variability and the concepts of linguistic repertoire. It is a base upon which students can build a familiarity with the ways in which people of different backgrounds use language, as well as an appreciation for the ways in which they themselves can draw on linguistic resources to accomplish specific communicative purposes in specific communicative contexts.

The third area of interest here has to do with the ways in which students drew on their linguistic and cultural knowledge to address the social and communicative problems posed by the collapsing of frames in these activities. As indicated earlier, in many cases students reacted as one might expect given their social position. Thus bilingual children frequently produced precisely the kinds of puns and wordplay I had discovered elsewhere when frames were collapsed for other reasons (see Chapter 5). In Group 1, Alicia and Laura in particular initiated such games:

Example 7.

Selina: then the mother listen then the mother should say *"je demande que vous me donniez dix dollars pour ce qui s'est passé"*
Alicia: *dix dollars? cent dollars* I can sue you
Rachel: *mille dollars* yeah *mille dollars*
Laura: *je vais te souer* (laughs)
Alicia: (laughs) *je vais te souer*

Selina: then the mother listen then the mother should say "I demand that you give me ten dollars for what happened"
Alicia: ten dollars? a hundred dollars I can sue you
Rachel: a thousand dollars yeah a thousand dollars
Laura: I'm going to "souer" you (laughs)
Alicia: (laughs) I'm going to "souer" you

Example 8.

Selina: you guys you know what we should do we should start sticking the sentences and finish it in a different way
Rachel: like okay *on va faire* Mickey Mouse built a house
?: okay that's for fun
Terri: no no don't stop it just keep going Mickey M
(laughter)
Alicia: Mickey Mouse built a house
Laura: these two aren't going to win the prize
?: no Rachel stop pressing the pause
Laura: *mais non* you pause the record
?: ah
Rachel: it doesn't record
Terri: *d'accord qu'est-ce qu'on va faire* Mickey Mouse built a house
Alicia: (laughs) *non non non on ne va pas builder un house on va faire un Mickey Mouse*
Rachel: *Alicia ne fais pas la la folie*
Laura: *la folerie*
Rachel: *la folie pas folerie*
?: why not?
?: *je suis d'accord*
Terri: *est-ce que vous buildez un house comme Mickey Mouse?*
Rachel: *vous faites des stupidités*

Selina: you guys you know what we should do we should start sticking the sentences and finish it in a different way like you know like you go
Rachel: like okay we'll do Mickey Mouse built a house
?: okay that's for fun
Terri: no no don't stop it just keep on going Mickey M
(laughter)
Alicia: Mickey Mouse built a house
Laura: these two aren't going to win the prize
?: Rachel stop pressing the pause
Laura: but no you pause the record
Rachel: it doesn't record
Terri: okay what are we going to do Mickey Mouse built a house
Alicia: (laughs) no no no we aren't going to build a house we're going to do a Mickey Mouse
Rachel: Alicia don't do craziness (from *faire la folle* = act the fool)
Laura: "la folerie"

Rachel: "folie" not "folerie"
?: why not?
?: I agree
Terri: are you building a house like Mickey Mouse?
Rachel: you are doing stupid things

Similarly, as might be expected, the French-dominant students did not engage in these sequences. Interestingly, however, in Group 1, although Rachel understands perfectly what is going, she takes a disapproving stance. At the same time, of the four bilingual girls in the group, she is the one who is making the most effort in (and deriving the greatest benefit out of) interacting with Selina to produce the officially sanctioned product. The French-dominant students instead reacted, as we have seen, by drawing on their linguistic resources to engage others in talk. How this occurred was a product of the local configuration of roles and responsibilities in each group combined with the linguistic resources the students had to draw on: in Selina's case, she had control of the script-writing activity and enough English to make a bridge to the others; in Pierre's, he was marginal to the activity, and had little or no English to draw on.

In some groups, the actual content of scripts revealed ways in which the students tried to make sense of the activity. One Grade 10 group consisted of four students of Canadian francophone background. They chose in their skit to recount their experience of fieldwork: their group had focussed on an elementary Catholic school in a western suburb of Toronto, and had done a group interview with a Grade 8 class. Michelle had been the interviewer; she began the skit, in formal French, somewhat nervous and a little stilted. Paul played the roles of the different students, providing equally formal and stilted, frequently monosyllabic, answers to Michelle's questions. Then Chantal and Marc came in, Chantal standing behind Michelle and Marc behind Paul. They each began to provide, in vernacular Canadian French, the inner comments of Michelle and Paul as they spoke: "What a stupid question I just asked!"; "I'm really making a fool of myself!"; "What does she want anyway?". The students were able to play off the conventional distinction between standard French (formal, institutional, public) and vernacular French (informal, private) to signal the difference between Michelle's and Paul's public performances and their inner thoughts. That contrast then allowed them to make a point about constraints on the kind of data you get depending on how you set up data collection activities, activities which are socially meaningful. The Grade 7 skit of a television ad for selling an Oriental sauce provides another example (see Chapter 5).

The skits presented by both these groups were extremely well-received by their audiences. They are clearly satisfying in an important way: they speak to the problems of resolution of tension across linguistic and cultural boundaries which the students experience in their everyday lives, and which the structure of these activities forces them to confront.

In this respect, the activities were successful. We wanted them to force students out of their routine, to use the linguistic and cultural knowledge they had to go beyond them, both in terms of expanding their skills in and knowledge of language, and in terms of understanding how language is connected to a culturally- and socially-constrained experience of the world. In having to interact with other students with whom their interaction was otherwise limited, and in having to examine and participate in activities which were either unfamiliar or completely taken for granted, students did encounter such opportunities, and strove to make sense of them in a number of ways.

The content of their skits, their patterns of use of French and English, their bilingual word-play, their heated discussions regarding the shape of dialogues, all reveal a heightened awareness of the ways in which English, standard French and Canadian vernacular French play a role not only in their own lives but in those of the people around them. They also reveal the students' ability to expand their own repertoires to confront the communicative exigencies of new situations and new social relationships.

In the short-term, then, there are many signs of the kinds of opportunities activities like these can open up in the kind of pedagogical situation we were addressing. We cannot evaluate what the long-term consequences may have been, largely because we have not been able to systematically follow up the ways in which these students developed. However, there are other reasons why it has been difficult to get any more than a glimpse of what it might mean to reorganize a classroom in this way, reasons which more than anything else are linked to the institutional structure of the school system in which these classrooms were located and its relationship to university-based researchers like us. I will close this chapter with a consideration of the limitations of such pedagogical interventions from this perspective.

6.3. The limits of pedagogical interventions

An undertaking such as the one I have described here clearly depends not only on a reasonable relationship between university-based researchers and schools, but also on a certain degree of flexibility within the organization and functioning of classrooms. The extent to which it can make a difference in broader terms depends on the nature of the relationship between students' experiences inside schools and those which they have outside the school setting, a relationship which is constrained by the nature of the school as a social institution in any specific community. In this section, I would like to briefly reflect on what participation in *Projet "Coopération et découverte"* has taught us about each of these things.

When I began the cycle of research which eventually led to the project described in this chapter, I was often at a loss to know how to respond to educators' requests to know how my research might benefit them, in particular, how it might be useful to the proverbial teacher trying to figure out what to do on Monday morning. My answer had to be fairly abstract, in the sense that I knew what issues I wanted to face and why they were relevant to the Franco-Ontarian school system, but it was impossible to be more precise without having done the basic research first. The result has been that in many ways that research has remained private, or at least pushed into the background in my developing relationships with educators. The eventual product, however, the materials and workshops, have been extremely public.

Of course, within the Franco-Ontarian school system alone, the nature of the classroom varies radically from one area to another. The kind of research involved here demands intensive involvement over fairly long periods of time, and it simply isn't possible for a small research team to have that kind of involvement all over the province, let alone the city of Toronto. In order for the results and outcomes of our research to have any kind of pertinence outside a small area, it has to be possible to make the links without repeating the fieldwork.

From our point of view, one way in which to do this is to render explicit the ties between the (generally hidden) basic ethnographic work and the actions that might be taken on the basis of that work. The second step is to give up ownership of the approach, and to train educators to undertake similar cycles of research and curriculum innovation themselves. This is, of course, what many researchers in the field of education have been talking about, whether under the rubric of "teachers as researchers" (a now institutionalized feature of an annual conference on ethnography and education sponsored by the University of Pennsylvania's Graduate School of Education, for example), or "reflexive practice" (cf. Fullan – Connelly 1987), or anything else. The growing sense that the gulf between educational practice and educational research must be bridged finds its echo here, based in an appreciation of the ways in which the processes at issue are socially and historically contingent. Any model, such as that offered in our materials, can only be a model, since the specific ways in which relevant factors come together for any group of students and their teachers has to be a local manifestation of variable processes.

However, the currently institutionalized forms of educator-researcher relations, at least in Ontario, do not always facilitate such processes. In-service training is conducted through workshops; educators and researchers are taken out of their workplaces to discuss innovations, and rarely meet again. Further, educational research (like any other kind of social science research) tends to get funding on a short-, or at best medium-, term basis. Once the project is over, researchers have no time to go back. Finally, the institutionalized patterns of the lives of both educators and researchers make it next to impossible to achieve long-term implication even on a local level. We are all participants in systems which make us accountable over the short-run for verifiable, and usually quantifiable, results.

As a result, it was difficult for us, in the first instance, to ask for anything more than for teachers to somehow fit this project into a relatively short period of time in a way that could be shown to link explicitly with programme objectives as set down by government and school board authorities. The top-down processes of change which characterize the school system make it difficult for classroom teachers to act on any issues they may be able to identify nor experiment too wildly with programmes and teaching techniques; instead they are accountable for implementing changes and achieving objectives which are largely determined for them. For teachers to devote more than, say, an hour a day for three weeks, would seriously jeopardize their ability to remain accountable for other programme and institutional goals.

Similarly, the workshop model of in-service training has made it difficult for us to have any sense of how teachers make use of what we have presented to them, nor of the kind of support they may need in order to do so. Yet even where, more recently, we have been able to experiment with other models of in-service training which, theoretically at least, give us (teachers and researchers together) all the time we need to experiment with and reflect on innovations, institutional constraints make it difficult to maintain any kind of critical distance on our work. Not only do teachers have to be very present in the classroom in a way which makes critical distance difficult, but they have to produce results which fit specific objectives (for example, which can feed into the preparation of report cards, or directly implement a programme objective).

Third, of course, there is the issue of trust. To undertake a programme of critique means to let go of current structures and to be open to the frightening limbo of the unknown. While colleagues of various kinds can provide support in this process under the best of circumstances, they are also representative of the worst that can happen: losing one's sense of competence not only alone, but also in public.

Finally, there is the question of what difference such an innovation might make to Franco-Ontarians even if its implementation in the classroom were not fraught with the difficulties I have just discussed. What if it were possible to make more than isolated, punctual use of such a way of organizing classroom activities? Would it make a difference to students' awareness, use and mastery of different varieties of French, to their relationships with each other and with members of other groups, to their sense of what it means to be Franco-Ontarian?

Clearly, this depends entirely on the kinds of social goals schools set for themselves and hence the kinds of relationships they maintain with other institutions and with the networks which link them to a variety of other social situations and social relationships. Explicit in our materials is a vision of the school as engaged not only in the unexamined preparation of an élite for higher education and of everyone else for vocational training, but more importantly as engaged in the development of a community which can critically examine and decide on the kinds of resources it holds valuable, what one needs to be able to do in order to produce and distribute those resources, and who is responsible for developing and distributing the symbolic resources which are so intimately tied to the production and distribution of material ones.

To the extent that activities such as the ones we have described here are embedded in such processes, and feed into other activities where the resources people consider valuable are produced and distributed, they can contribute to the ability of the school to play such a role. Currently, the Franco-Ontarian population faces a number of interrrelated issues which are forcing it to re-define itself, and hence to re-define what it expects from its schools: the changing nature of relations between Quebec and the rest of Canada, the increasing integration of francophones into the global economy, the increasingly multicultural nature of the Franco-Ontarian student body. The activities I have described here may seem at first blush to be light-years away from such momentous changes, but such changes only happen in local sites, and in interactions in real time and among real people. In the final chapter, I will return to the broader questions which have informed this book, and consider the ways in which the examination of the situated experience of individuals helps us understand what is at stake for Franco-Ontarians as a whole.

Chapter 7
Franco-Ontarian education and the possibilities for pluralism

7.0. Power, boundaries and the distribution of resources

Franco-Ontarians find themselves now in the web of two sets of relations of power. First, they must struggle to find their place in Ontario, as well as in Canadian and international society. They fight to find a way to participate equally, to equally enjoy the fruits of success in education and in the job market. They have accepted the general rules of the game; unlike some segments of Canada's Native population, they do not strive for a return to past practices. This makes a certain degree of sense: the image of Franco-Ontarians' past is one of domination either by the British conquerors or by the élite of New France. It is not a past that has much allure. At the same time, that past is what Franco-Ontarians have in common, and it represents ties which have provided support and comfort in many ways from one generation to the next. To leave that behind is risky; it is hard to re-invent ties which will at the same time release people into the new global marketplace and also maintain the local support networks which provide a safety net in case life out there gets too rough.

Nor do Franco-Ontarians strive for building an alternative world, one which they might invent for themselves. In part, this is because they do not have the resources which would allow them to do that; there is nothing in the development of Franco-Ontarian society which would provide an alternative resource base. In part, this is due to the relative success Franco-Ontarians have in fact achieved in gaining access to resources previously exclusively controlled by anglophones; the success of that strategy has obviated the need for finding another.

Franco-Ontarians therefore share, on the whole, a vision of participation in the national and international marketplaces which shape their lives. Their struggle is to find a way to do so which does in fact allow them full advantages, and which also protects them while they embark on this risky endeavour. In their struggle they have adopted certain strategies; although many have assimilated, many others have engaged in ethnic mobilization and the pursuit of integration through the establishment of institutions similar but parallel to those of the dominant anglophones.

The consequences of these strategies are several. First, many of those who have assimilated have had to pay a price. Rewards sometimes have to be post-

7.0 Power, boundaries and the distribution of resources 211

poned for generations, and in the meantime people experience the pain of lost connections, the isolation of those cut off from familiar worlds and not yet at ease in new ones. They also must come face-to-face with those who have chosen the alternate path of mobilization, and who often blame them for weakening the francophone cause.

Those who have mobilized also walk a fine line. They often wonder whether the struggle is worth it, or whether it would not simply be easier on them and on their children to speak English. They may be conscious of the risks they are taking, of the possibility that by setting up parallel institutions they may be cutting themselves off from the resources of the dominant group, without having an alternate resource base to fall back on. They must resolve the contradiction between adhering to the past which they all have in common and which holds their mobilization together (but which represents the very realities they have mobilized to escape) and constructing a new way of being francophone in the global village.

In addition, mobilization holds within it the possibility of reproducing relations of inequality within francophone society. Those who have led the process of mobilization have invested their lives in it. The legitimacy of the mobilization is based on a certain sense of what it means to be francophone, or perhaps more accurately, who counts as francophone. This notion of shared francophone identity has been based on a concept of continuity, from France to eastern Canada, and from various parts of eastern Canada to the farthest reaches of Ontario and beyond. The image is of a long uninterrupted process through which francophones first came to North America and then slowly spread out across the continent, especially its northern portion. Initially, such mobilization had to face the fact that being francophone was stigmatized in wider society; the major problem francophones faced (and in some respects still face today) was a problem of inclusion, that is, how to make sure that people who were born francophones continue to affiliate themselves with the francophone group.

However, two developments have recently changed the situation of Ontario's francophones. First, Franco-Ontarian mobilization has been partly successful, and so the group has become attractive to others in a way never previously encountered. English-speakers and immigrants want access to the French language in order to compete in the job market, and in order to gain social status associated with the rising value of bilingualism in Canadian society. In addition, changes in the nature of migration and immigration have provided a potential pool of French-speaking members who previously were not on the scene. French-speakers from Europe, Africa, Asia and the Caribbean are among the new groups arriving in Canada. As others appear who wish to affiliate with the group, the principles of inclusion which allowed mobilization to occur can easily turn into principles of exclusion. These principles of exclusion in turn produce relations of inequality, and yet mobilization protested just such unfair discrimination. The old guard of militant, mobilized Franco-Ontarians has to face the possibility of sharing newly won powers in newly formed institutions.

These then are the contradictions: how to be francophone (and therefore different) and a citizen of the world (and therefore the same) at the same time; how to maintain and legitimize mobilization on the basis that francophones are disadvantaged (which many continue to be) while enjoying the fruits that successful mobilization brings (to some); how to wield power without reproducing relations of inequality. For most Franco-Ontarians these are contradictions experienced in everyday life, and it is in everyday life that Franco-Ontarians look for, and sometimes find, the means, if not to resolve, then at least to temporarily neutralize them.

Sometimes this means becoming invisible, walking the streets in English, singing the songs of the dominant culture. Sometimes this means playing off one language against the other, using French to resist the hegemony of English and English to resist the authority of francophones and francophone institutions. It can also mean moving back and forth between languages in order to participate in more than one world. Finally, it can mean using French and English to build bridges or create walls between Franco-Ontarians and Québécois, between Québécois and Somalis, between Franco-Ontarians and Lebanese, between Iranians and Haitians.

How people use their languages, and which languages they use, is not something that can be determined in any simple or straightforward way. The languages and language varieties in their repertoire are attributed value through the experiences one has of the consequences of using them, and through the possibilities one imagines opening up before one through their use. That value is also a function of the degrees of mastery of them that one has, as opposed to the mastery possessed by others in one's entourage.

Because of Bill 8, major provincial institutions operate at least partly in French, and French is now part of their public image. It is possible to go to the museum and come upon someone who will explain in French to one's children how many different kinds of bats there are, or read in French the text that is part of all exhibits. At the same time, the flow of francophone immigration to Toronto continues, and people are less ashamed of speaking French in the streets. The lady in the store where I buy my socks is from Quebec; the gentleman at the parking lot near the market is also francophone. It seems "normal" to speak French with them.

On the other hand, contradictory messages abound. The provincial government must provide services to the francophone public in French, but the working

7.0 Power, boundaries and the distribution of resources 213

language of government is English. Francophone civil servants therefore find that while they can speak their language with clients, they cannot speak it with colleagues at work. Francophone children growing up in Toronto receive compliments from strangers as well as acquaintances on the fact that they speak French, but they continue to assume that they will learn English and use it with their playmates on the street or with other people in the neighbourhood and around town; it never occurs to them to teach their friends to speak French, and it is a source of surprise to find a shopkeeper who understands what they thought were secret conversations with a parent or sibling. Employment equity programs exclude francophones from the list of target groups on the grounds that such measures are no longer needed, but francophones still have less education than the norm and are underrepresented in white-collar and management positions.

There is also increasing conflict within francophone institutions. Parents argue about criteria of admission to their children's school, some worrying that too many children come speaking French as a second language, others shocked that francophones could consider excluding or providing differential treatment for such students. People from countries outside Canada fight for representation in Franco-Ontarian institutions, and argue that current ideologies systematically exclude them. Others reply that the whole purpose of mobilization was to preserve a language and a culture that already existed and that was threatened from the outside by the dominant anglophone majority, and that they find it hard to give up their notion of what that language and that culture is in order to accommodate the very different cultures and varieties of French they now find in their midst.

These conflicts are both abstract and ideological and very concrete. They include discussions of principle, concerning the nature of what it means to be francophone, and the rights and obligations a francophone should have. Many of these discussions revolve around the label to which francophones wish to attach themselves; a seemingly superficial issue, but one which is in fact rife with significance for those concerned. The most heated and lengthiest such argument I have ever witnessed took place in a workshop sponsored by francophone lobbying organizations. The purpose of the workshop was to formulate goals in the area of race and ethnic relations: most of the time was taken up discussing the term *franco-ontarien* and whether or not it included all those present who wanted to be seen as part of the group, and not as one of the group's interlocutors. Most of the participants who were not born in Canada, and in particular members of visible minorities, argued that the term *franco-ontarien* systematically excluded them; others argued that a term can be made to mean whatever one wants it to mean, and that *franco-ontarien* was a neutral descriptor of people who speak French and live in Ontario. The issue was only resolved by choosing a term and explicitly defining it. Certainly all those concerned spoke of the importance of not reproducing relations of inequality, yet many present continued to feel that such sentiments rarely were transformed into practice.

While such questions of principle are clearly important, they are also accompanied by discussions of practice, of what to do and how to do things in daily life. These include questions of participation in francophone institutions and francophone networks, and the ever-present issue of language choice.

For most francophones in Ontario, the ease of participating in francophone institutions is at least matched by the ease of participating in English ones, if it is not actually harder. This is particularly true of education, but includes other institutions (the media, the church, and so on). For example, does one send one's child to the nearest French-language school, or to the local school around the corner where all the neighbourhood children go? Does one watch the news in French despite the knowledge that all one's co-workers will be discussing tomorrow what they have seen tonight on the English channel? Does one go to the French church despite the fact that one's husband attends an English church and one isn't particularly fond of the *curé*? The issues here also touch on other ethnic institutions, or ones based on race or gender: does one participate in francophone lobbying institutions whose leaders are all white or ones that bring together visible minorities but which function in English? Does one participate in local feminist activities in English, or attempt to form similar activities in francophone institutions dominated by men?

At another level, there are questions about the constitution of one's social network: does one invite both francophone and anglophone friends to one's house together, knowing that that means that all conversation will be in English? Does one hire the first good baby-sitter one finds for one's child, or does one hold out for a francophone? Does one make friends with anglophones at work knowing that one's colleagues are militant francophones? Does one seek out other visible minorities or women despite the fact that they are anglophone?

For those whose lives are directly bound up in Franco-Ontarian institutions, the conflicts concerning questions of practice are often acute. On the one hand, the way in which one does one's work influences what francophones can do collectively with respect to the anglophone majority; through what one does on the job it is possible to advance collective rights. This includes issues of participation in institutions and networks, as well as of language choice, and goes beyond them to touch on the content of one's work, whether that be the drafting of position papers, the formulation of parliamentary bills, lobbying, or anything else. On the other hand, one has to examine ways in which one's practice may reproduce relations of inequality within the francophone community. One has to ask whether what one proposes or does is in the interests of all francophones, or only some. The role of French proficiency evaluators working for the provincial government illustrates this paradox well.

When the provincial government enacted its law on French-language services, it thereby created the need for civil service positions whose incumbents would, in effect, implement the law by providing those services and by supervising their provision. However, the government did not assume that candidates for those positions would all be equally competent speakers of French. As a result, the government would require some way to assess a candidate's proficiency in French (although candidates for other positions are not required to undergo formal assessment of their ability to speak English). It therefore established an agency[56] whose members would evaluate the proficiency of candidates for positions designated under the law as requiring a civil servant able to provide services in French. The evaluators therefore existed, on the one hand, to ensure that the government would be able to implement its own law, and thereby increase the scope of what Ontario francophones can do in French; on the other hand, they were also there to select appropriate candidates from among the pool presenting itself for specific positions.

Criteria of evaluation become crucial here, since different kinds of people have privileged access to those jobs depending on what counts as good French. In addition, that access depends on candidates' abilities to display their proficiency in the specific situations which the evaluation agency chose as occasions for that display. In specific terms, this meant mastering a variety of French which corresponded to what one finds in francophone monolingual areas, and being able to display it in an interview. Franco-Ontarians who are used to using a bilingual codeswitching variety, and who may have little experience of interview situations, are not likely to do well under these circumstances; this is probably also true for any speaker of a non-standard variety. However, well-educated Europeans and Québécois are more likely to do well. While this is a specific and very restricted example of some of the issues, it is nonetheless important, given the role of both the federal and provincial governments in providing employment for bilinguals with at least a high school, and more often a university education.

The same kinds of dilemmas attend the Franco-Ontarian educational system. It is a major source of employment for francophones, and is responsible for producing students who will be able both to participate in anglophone-dominated networks (locally, provincially, nationally and internationally) and take up the francophone cause. It must unite francophones against the influence of dominant society, and tie them to some common notion of what it means to be francophone. At the same time, it must ensure that all its students are treated equally, and have an equal chance of succeeding at school, no matter how different they are one from the other. Franco-Ontarian schools must therefore somehow provide a curriculum which is equivalent to that available in English-language schools and which addresses the specific needs and interests of Franco-Ontarians taken as a collectivity with something in common, as well as addressing the needs and interests of the different groups which include themselves under the Franco-Ontarian umbrella.

Beginning in about 1990, the Ontario Ministry of Education has undertaken to develop a policy regarding Franco-Ontarian education which brings out into the open all these issues. Its initial purpose was to examine ways in which it could ensure a common degree of proficiency in French and a common degree of identification with the Franco-Ontarian community in Franco-Ontarian schools, in order to help francophone students strengthen themselves as a group vis-à-vis the anglophone majority. It has encountered the problem of the complex ways in which external and internal inequalities interact: on the one hand, some educators want to focus on programmes which will help francophone children learn to function effectively as francophone monolinguals (it is assumed that such a tactic will not in fact in any way jeopardize students' access to English; the kind of bilingualism that is envisaged here is the capacity to function as a monolingual would but in two language environments). They assume that the monolingual language norms and cultural practices to be favoured are those with which they are familiar from their own experiences in Canada. They thus construct the problem as one of protecting Franco-Ontarians, seen as a homogeneous group with specific and uniform linguistic and cultural practices, from the assimilating influences of English.

Other educators, while agreeing on the importance of expanding students' abilities to function in French, are less clear as to what kind of French that might actually mean. And while they agree that francophones must have something in common, they are less sure that that should include solely or principally the linguistic and cultural practices of Canadian francophones. They worry that to do so reproduces the relations of inequality that francophones have fought against for so long. These educators maintain that francophones must appreciate that their group occupies a position of weakness (although not inferiority) with respect to the dominant group which necessitates special measures to right; at the same time, however, they must also appreciate the incipient hierarchy of power that exists within Franco-Ontarian communities and which must be transformed into internal egalitarianism.

Just as the provincial government evaluators' dilemma revolves around issues of linguistic varieties and occasions for the display of competence, so does that of Franco-Ontarian education. Success at school necessitates the acquisition of whatever variety of French the school considers valuable and legitimate, and it necessitates the ability to display not only competence in that variety but mastery of it in order to display other forms of knowledge through it, on occasions and in ways determined by the school. The ministry's dilemma is how to define what counts as legitimate forms of French in school, and how to go about evaluating that in a fair and equitable way.

What does one do with students who are culturally legitimate Franco-Ontarians or Québécois or Acadiens, but who speak vernacular varieties of French (whether they call them *bilingue* or *joual* or *chiac*)? What does one do with African or Haitian students who speak French as a second language, but who speak no English, and who may master the written variety better than the oral or vice versa? What does one do with immigrants from outside Canada who, in the terms of a monolingual norm, speak French "better" than Franco-Ontarians, but who have no knowledge of Franco-Ontarian linguistic and cultural practices and ideologies? What does one do when students arrive at school expecting to display their knowledge through written tests and exams, or by reciting texts by heart, and have never had the experience of preparing and presenting the oral narratives or expositions which are so often used as occasions for display of competence in Ontario classrooms?

Franco-Ontarian education is thus, as an institution, facing some of the most difficult questions which emerge from ideologies of democracy and pluralism. It is far from clear how it is possible to be different but equal, either as francophones in a society composed of many different groups, or as one or another of different kinds of francophones among the set of people identifying themselves with and participating in Franco-Ontarian institutions. These are contradictions which have to be lived out on a daily basis, and at least dealt with, if not resolved. But they also have implications for the future of francophone mobilization in Ontario, as well as elsewhere in Canada, and for the possibilities for pluralism which Franco-Ontarians are well-placed to recognize and maybe even to achieve.

7.1. Language practices and the contradictions of Franco-Ontarian education

Through the eyes of individuals it is possible to see, at least in part, how the contradictions of Franco-Ontarian education are lived out in the lives of those who study and work in those schools. I will tell this story from the perspective of Marie-Paule, a Haitian high school student, and through her attempt to show the different ways students and teachers use language to confront the contradictions of daily life at school. Marie-Paule does not exist; she is a composite of many different students, but she represents a set of views and practices that many students in her position share.

Marie-Paule was born and brought up in Haiti. She spoke Creole at home, and learned standard European French at school. She is confident of her French; she knows it is a prestigious language, and her experiences at school in Haiti showed her that she had mastered it well. Her school placed a great deal of emphasis on rote learning. For her, mastering a subject meant learning a lesson and being able to recite it in front of the class by heart. She did well at school, and formed an image of herself as a good student. She lived with her extended family, and stayed behind in Haiti when her parents emigrated to Canada until she could join them several years later. She has fond memories of Haiti, and remains in touch with relatives there. However, in her mind she will never go back there to live, since she sees it also as a place where she would run great risks of encountering violence.

When she arrived in Toronto, her father had already chosen which school she would attend. Although she is Catholic, and could have attended the Catholic high school, her father had already become active in the area of race and ethnic relations, and through that activity with public school boards (which tend to be more racially mixed than Catholic schools). Marie-Paule was thus enrolled at Champlain.

Her first months at school were difficult; she was unprepared for the numbers of students who spoke English to each other, and indeed, her first day at school she wondered if she hadn't entered the wrong building, since Champlain is beside a large anglophone high school. She also found it hard to make friends among her classmates, many of whom had known each other since elementary school. In addition, some of them treated her differently because she was black, or thoughtlessly made racist remarks in her presence; she was thus reluctant to make overtures to many of the white students from Toronto. She eventually found friends among similar recent arrivals in other grades, and also befriended two other girls who later arrived in her class from francophone regions outside Canada, who spoke a variety of French close to Marie-Paule's and who also spoke no English.

Neither was Marie-Paule prepared for the kinds of teaching she encountered at Champlain. No one ever asked her to memorize anything. Instead, she was frequently called upon to write pieces based on her opinion or to make oral presentations concerning her analyses and understandings of course materials. She was expected to make drafts of texts and revise them, and in various other ways to pay attention to her learning process rather than focussing exclusively on its product.

Finally, the variety of French many people, including the teachers, spoke was not one she herself was familiar with, and not one which she had been taught to value. She was not interested in learning this Canadian French, and found it frustrating that it often made understanding teachers and classmates difficult. When other students found it hard to understand her, she reacted by re-affirming the value of her French, and down-grading that of her classmates. She disputed classmates' choice of words, and argued vociferously that her choice was more logical, and in other ways better; she told them that she was used to hearing *le bon français*.

Her two friends eventually left Toronto. Although by this time Marie-Paule had learned quite a bit of English, she remained reluctant to enter the bilingual networks. She tried to befriend some students newly arrived from Somalia, who spoke standard French, having been educated in that language at home. However, the religious and cultural differences were great. The Somalis were refugees from civil war; while Marie-Paule could somewhat share their experience of violence, she did not share the view of the Somalis that exile was temporary.

The Somali students frequently used their own language to talk amongst themselves; just as the bilingual students who dominate the school excluded Marie-Paule through their use of English, so Marie-Paule felt excluded by the use of Somali. The Somali students explained to her that their use of Somali was natural for them, and a way for them to cope collectively not only with their condition of exile but also with the same exclusion through English that Marie-Paule herself had encountered. Unlike Marie-Paule, who had but few francophone monolingual students to choose from, there were many Somalis who arrived more or less at the same time, and thus were able to constitute their own networks. Nonetheless, their use of Somali made it impossible for Marie-Paule to fully participate in those networks. Her attempt broke down one day when she became angry with Zahra, one of the Somali girls, and found herself using English to express her anger. Marie-Paule told Zahra in English that she didn't like the way Zahra had been acting, nice one day, cold the next; speaking simultaneously, Zahra countered that it really didn't matter what Marie-Paule said. (Of course, this strategy allowed Marie-Paule to retain deniability; since Zahra spoke no English she could not get angry with her for what she said, merely for how she said it. At the same time, that language choice underlines the rift between the two.) In an ironic turn, Marie-Paule found herself using the language which had excluded her to confirm a wall which had arisen between her and Zahra.

Marie-Paule puzzled her teachers. In their experience, students who did poorly usually spoke French poorly; they were not used to a student who, they agreed, mastered the language, and yet seemed not to use it in expected ways. They liked the fact that she always spoke French, and enjoyed speaking French; they never had to nag her not to speak English. They liked the fact that she mastered basic elements of French morphology and syntax; they never had to correct her conjugations and she never confused masculine with feminine. She could write well-formed sentences. And yet they consistently found that the way she answered questions seemed not to the point, and her oral presentations did not follow the form they were trying to teach their students to adopt. Marie-Paule, in turn, felt that she was wasting much of her time in her classes, since providing her opinion scarcely qualified as learning something, and it sometimes seemed to her that her teachers did not understand what she was trying to say.

While Marie-Paule retained her pride in her identity as a Haitian, a black and a francophone, she also increasingly, as she grew older, had to confront the realities of life in Toronto. Any sort of odd weekend job, even local babysitting, required English. Entertainment on television or radio, in newspapers and magazines and books, in movie theatres and clubs, was much more readily available in English than in French. Eventually, she learned English, although she rarely used it with the bilingual students at school from whom she already felt alienated, reserving it for her life in the broader community, or for the rare moments such as her fight with Zahra when English and only English directly served her communicative purpose.

For the most part, then, Marie-Paule dealt with her problems of cultural identification through seeking out others as much like her as possible. While the academic side of school remained a puzzlement, she did well enough to pass, and turned increasingly to art and music as a source of satisfaction. She did her best to separate French from English, although her bilingualism became a resource she could use when she needed or wanted it.

Marie-Paule came to Champlain expecting to find a place where others valued standard European French as much as she did, and in the same ways. She was not prepared for the complex relations that existed among English, Canadian French vernaculars, standard Canadian French, standard European French and other mother tongues spoken by members of the student body. She was unprepared for the ways in which other francophones focussed on their struggle as a minority, since for her standard French at least always had represented a language of power. More than anything, she was unprepared for the little value accorded to what she already knew and the forms of language she already mastered.

While ostensibly evaluating her on the basis of merit, the school nonetheless quite clearly had to choose between valuing what Marie-Paule and other students like her had (which would mean, first, being able to discover what that was, and second, modifying the curriculum and teaching practice accordingly) and evaluating their performance against existing expectations. The school, and parents and students along with it, are living through the contradictions of this place and time: the necessity of providing an excellent education to all students while judging some to be better than others; and of molding *la relève*, the new cohort to whom francophone militants will pass the torch, while also molding citizens of the world.

Through their use of language, Marie-Paule and other students, as well as Marie-Paule's teachers, find ways to display their competence and to evaluate each other's performance. They find ways to open doors for each other, or to close them, and they find ways to both build and burn bridges. However, they also find ways to live with the contradictions they experience, specifically the contradiction of the ways in which inequality does exist within an ostensibly egalitarian institution. Marie-Paule keeps her languages separate, and finds zones of activity (art and music) where her performances can be evaluated without recourse to language. Other students and teachers find other solutions: codeswitching, deliberately failing so as to be able to change schools, resisting the authority of French by only speaking English, building exclusively monolingual French-speaking networks, and so on. As long as they can do that, the processes which underlie the existence of those contradictions will remain.

7.2. Conclusion

Walking the streets of Toronto now, ten years after I arrived, I can hear and see the difference. Much of that has to do with knowing where to go; if I go into that church, this school, that theatre, I will find people who not only can speak French, but will actually do so in public. Much has to do with the social networks I have developed both through work and through my children; I know who to call if I need a referral to a doctor, a travel agent, a daycare centre. But much has to do with what has happened to Franco-Ontarian mobilization over these ten years, and the attitudes of individuals towards it.

If I leave my house and walk east, I will pass neighbours who are francophones. Our children play together in the park in the summer, and take skating lessons together in the local arena. We spoke to each other in English first, until we heard each other speaking French to our children. Some of the other children in the neighbourhood go to a local French immersion programme; they like at least to begin conversations with us in French, although usually anything lengthy reverts to English. Most of our neighbours speak to us in English. On the whole, we expect to speak English outside our homes; French is for those who specifically identify themselves, by returning French in conversations, as eligible for inclusion in whatever rudimentary francophone network locally exists. We don't know each other very well; the fact of speaking French is not enough to bind us together in any highly meaningful way. However, we do trade information, and enjoy an amiable chat now and then.

If I turn south from my immediate neighbourhood I come to Bloor Street, the major east-west thoroughfare. The part of Bloor Street near where I live, and continuing towards the centre of the city, is lined with shops and little restaurants. Many people choose to live here when they first arrive in Toronto, and others come in the evening or on weekends. Along with many other languages (especially Hungarian, Polish, Cantonese, Italian, Portuguese and Korean, as well as English) it is increasingly possible to eavesdrop on conversations in French, spoken with both European and Canadian accents. Because of the status French has gained thanks to the mobilization of francophones, people are less reluctant to speak openly with their friends in French on the street; also, many are new arrivals who have never known the pressure of living in a community where French is a subordinate language.

If I continue east along Bloor, close to the university I come across a building maintained by the government of France. It offers many kinds of programmes about France and in French, including French lessons which, of course, focus on the European standard. However, because it really is the only programme of its kind in Toronto, many anglophone adults interested in learning French go there, even if their motivation is primarily linked to communication with Canadian francophones.

A little farther east there are the buildings of the institute where I work and those of the university. I frequently use the university's athletic centre; with increasing frequency I see in the women's locker room young students whom I first met eight or nine years ago when I began doing fieldwork in French-language schools in Toronto. The bilingual or French-dominant or anglo-dominant eighth graders I once knew have turned into young women, studying in an English-speaking post-secondary institution. They sometimes recognize me, and we chat in French; they are pursuing their interests, and for the moment French does not seem to be an important part of their lives.

In my institute one hears French sometimes in the elevator or in the cafeteria, but always from someone one already knows to be francophone. Sometimes francophones who enter the building for the first time drop by our centre, as a way of establishing some ties with other francophones. Most other people speak English when they come through our door, although increasingly they will use a symbolic "*bonjour*" when they arrive and when they leave. Because of Bill 8, more and more signs are in both English and French, including the large one on the street; still, French has to be sought out and specifically asked for if one wants to use it. Also, since we are employees and not clients, as in any government office, we are obliged to use English as the language of work when communicating with others in the institute.

If I leave my institute and continue south, I come to the buildings housing the Ontario government. Because of Bill 8, more and more francophones work here. Bill 8 stands as a symbol of the power of the state in regulating ethnic relations, and of the faith francophones have had in the state as a means of gaining equality. It also thereby stands as a symbol of the kind of mobilization francophones have favoured, one which places them in the heart of the state bureaucracy to seek majority resources but as francophones. They must explain the specific conditions under which Franco-Ontarians live, while sharing a common policy or programme goal with anglophones; they must argue for programmes and policies which at once take difference into account and at the same time provide exactly what anglophones are getting.

At the entrance to one of the buildings, a sign at the information desk proclaims "English/Français". Unfortunately, a request for information in French produces a puzzled stare; I only get my information if I repeat my question in English. A phone call to the number for French-language services in another ministry produces an anglophone who informs me that "the lady who speaks French isn't here right now". The burden of providing those French-language services rests on a small number of people, none of whom can use their language in their place of work.

If I leave my institute and continue east, I come to the major intersection of the city (it's hard to imagine a city of close to 4 million having one major intersection, but Toronto does). South of that intersection lies the heart of francophone Toronto, the old Catholic working-class neighbourhood which still contains a church and a school, as well as a retirement home. North lies the new area of settlement, middle class neighbourhoods attracting the new middle-class francophones. There is another church there, and all but one of the remaining schools. Beyond the city, in the suburbs, more francophones settle, some middle-class, but many factory workers as well, come from other provinces or other parts of Ontario to seek work.

Much farther east lies the heartland of French Canada, and, of course, across the ocean, France itself. Those too are ties that can be strengthened through the global village. But at the intersection there are also some guys with a boom-box playing rap music from the U.S., and a fellow in a kilt playing a bagpipe. The languages one has to know in order to eavesdrop effectively are legion, but only one is necessary if you need to know where something is. Somewhere in this maze of languages, French is trying to find its place.

Notes

1. MacLennan took the title from a poem by Rilke, in which two solitudes were taken as the basis of love. It is revealing that the term has come to stand instead for the distance and lack of mutual understanding which are thought to characterize French-English relations.
2. Population statistics come from the 1991 federal census for Thunder Bay and the 1986 federal census for Sault Ste-Marie, published by Statistics Canada. 1991 figures were not yet available for all census districts at the time of writing. In 1986, Thunder Bay had a population of 113,344, of which 1.3 percent, or 3,520, were francophone.
3. Statistics Canada allows single and multiple answers to census questions regarding language. The figures reported here are based on single answers only since they represent the vast majority of responses.
4. At moments of high tension I frequently get letters and telephone calls from friends and colleagues outside Canada, asking me whether the country is going to break up. From inside Canada, the view is quite different; we seem engaged in a long slow process of decentralization, but one which entails maintaining a balance between federal and provincial governments, between territorial nationalism and pluralism. The moments of tension seem artfully produced, and, given the public's reaction to the 1992 referendum, may be less and less convincing.
5. The native population suffered in particular when, having conquered New France in the last half of the eighteenth century, the British began circumventing the middlemen and dealing directly with the hunters and trappers. As Wolf (1982:194) argues:

    ... as the European traders consolidated their economic and political position, the balanced relation between native trappers and the Europeans gave way to imbalance. The decline of international warfare diminished the politically motivated flow of goods from European authorities to native American allies. The native Americans themselves came to rely increasingly on the trading post not only for the tools of the fur trade but also for the means of their own subsistence ... Abandoning their own subsistence activities, they became specialized labourers in a putting-out system, in which the entrepreneurs advanced both production goods and consumption goods against commodities to be delivered in the future. Such specialization tied the native Americans more firmly into continent-wide and international networks of exchange, as subordinate producers rather than as partners.

6. In exchange, the French received territory in the Caribbean. Voltaire is said to have remarked that the French came out the better in this exchange, the sugar plantations of the Caribbean being clearly more valuable than the "*quelques arpents de neige* [a few acres of snow]" they were giving up to the British.
7. Gagnon (1989), however, points out that within French Canadian society, there were struggles over political control, first between the rural and the urban élites, the *seigneurs* as opposed to the professionals, and then between the élite and the farmers

and petty bourgeoisie. Nonetheless, whatever access to political power and social mobility the French rural population may have had (through election to the legislative assembly or entry into the clergy), this occured within the confines of French-speaking society.
8. In addition to construction, especially, for part of the nineteenth century, in shipbuilding, the lumber industry was an important component of the pulp and paper industry. Construction and pulp and paper are still essential domains for the Canadian economy today.
9. Sources are: Statistics Canada (for census data), Lachapelle and Henripin 1980, Bernard 1988 and Arnopoulos 1982. Note that the Canadian government began keeping census records in 1851, but did not add a question on first languages until 1931. The question on language use at home was added in 1971.
10. However, Lieberson (1970) notes that the gap in rates of bilingualism between males and females is typical only of communities where francophones are a majority, and as long as men are more affected by labour market conditions (I would add, and as long as anglophones control that market).
11. Initially, the Commission endorsed a policy of bilingualism and biculturalism. However, indigenous and immigrant groups felt that such a policy disenfranchised them. The resulting compromise allows francophones to feel they have a special and protected position within Canadian society, without excluding other groups. Nonetheless, the federal policy of multiculturalism still makes francophones uneasy, since they feel it threatens the specific rights of francophones, and opens the door to renewal of anglophone domination of all groups different from their own (Berthelot 1990).
12. Certain aspects of this legislation have, more or less unofficially, been noted to be unenforceable, such as oral communication and communications with foreign companies. In addition, criteria are somewhat different for companies of different sizes.
13. Nonetheless, recent years have seen the development of strong intercultural and antiracist education movements in Quebec. These movements have clearly enunciated their relationship to Quebec nationalism. For example, Québécois deliberately use the term *intercultural* rather than *multicultural* education, in order to distance themselves from the federal policy of multiculturalism which they feel undermines the legitimacy of francophone rights. Berthelot (1990) provides an excellent example of the adaptation of francophone nationalists to the need to integrate immigrants within the education system; in particular, he argues that Québécois cannot become tolerant of others unless they themselves are in a position of strength.
14. All translations are mine.
15. In 1992, however, most francophone lobbying groups outside Quebec officially supported the Charlottetown Accord on the grounds that it, unlike Meech Lake, contained sufficient provisions for the protection of official-language minority rights.
16. The most extreme version of such a position is reflected in the discourse of some Québécois nationalists who have referred to francophones outside Quebec as "*cadavres encore chauds*" [warm corpses] or "dead ducks". Others have proposed a "*loi

de retour" [law of return] which would facilitate migration by francophones outside Quebec to an independent Quebec. The change in the name of the FFHQ was, in fact, a reaction to such moves, an explicit attempt to divorce claims for francophone rights outside Quebec from Quebec nationalism. FFHQ members, recognizing the damage to their cause that Quebec independence would bring, assert thereby their claim to rights in the provinces in which they make their home; they are not "outside" anything, they say, their home is "here".

17. In the winter of 1990 the Alberta courts decided in favour of a group of parents who had sued a school board on the grounds that the board was refusing to provide French-language education to which they were entitled by virtue of Article 23 of the Canadian Charter of Rights and Freedoms (see below for a more detailed discussion of the provisions of Article 23).
18. Bernard (1988) shows a rate of language transfer of 34 percent and a rate of exogamy of almost 40 percent in 1981.
19. In a parallel case, a parent in the Penetanguishene area took the province to court in a battle over the quality of the services offered; this successful challenge, discussed further in Chapter 4, had the effect of rendering void the constraint regarding the number of children necessary to justify the provision of services.
20. I am grateful to Glenn and Suzanne Humphreys for providing much of the local data used in this chapter concerning the debates in Sault Ste. Marie.
21. The text is presented as it was printed.
22. Laurentian University in Sudbury, one of six bilingual campuses in Ontario, has a programme permitting students to study for a semester or a year in Nice, similar to many study-in-Europe programs run by universities all over North America.
23. It is worth noting that the number of anglophone children in immersion programmes in Quebec had been steady at between 17,000 and 19,000 (or about 8 percent or 9 percent of the population of English-language schools) between 1977 and 1989. In 1989–1990 the numbers jumped to over 28,000.
24. The choice of language of instruction is complicated, however, by the confessional basis of organization of the school system. In most provinces in the mid 1960s, French-language schools were to be found only within Catholic boards of education. Non-Catholic anglophones therefore could not gain access to those schools. It would, however, have been possible to lobby for the creation of French-language schools within public or Protestant boards, alone or in conjunction with secularized or non-Catholic francophones (as happened, in fact, in Toronto in the early 1970s). However, while more and more French-language public schools have been created (for a variety of reasons), anglophone attraction to French-language education has not necessarily increased; the immersion option seems to remain the preferred path for those anglophones interested in bilingualism.
25. Most of this research showed that indeed students' English-language skills and academic achievement did not suffer as a result of French immersion (Swain – Lapkin 1981; Lapkin et al. 1983). However, as Olson and Burns (1983) have pointed out, this is scarcely surprising, given that the students not only come from the middle

class but are also members of the dominant ethnolinguistic group in Canada. They thus have ample support and opportunities outside school to learn and use English, as well as to acquire the knowledge and skills base which facilitates school success (Bourdieu – Passeron 1977). Learning French in no way threatens them.

26. Researchers at the Ontario Institute for Studies in Education have, however, attempted to analyze the extent to which the job market offers opportunities for immersion graduates (Lapkin et al. 1988; Hart et al. 1990). On the whole they find that immersion graduates are most likely to be interested in management level jobs, but that the majority of such bilingual positions are to be found in a shrinking public sector which is decreasingly recruiting from outside its own ranks. Other such jobs are in teaching, a domain which is not of particular interest to immersion graduates. The best opportunities may be in entry-level private sector positions in sales or other areas requiring contact with the francophone public, although employees' French-language skills seem to be less and less important as one moves up the hierarchy (and away from direct contact with the public). At the same time, it is not clear that immersion graduates, as opposed to bilingual francophones, are considered qualified candidates for these positions (despite francophones' fears to the contrary). Finally, on the job, while French may be used with clients or customers, it is not always used among employees or between employees and their hierarchical superiors.

27. Although most anglophones interested in bilingualism favour immersion over French-language schools, their presence in French-language schools can be important enough in proportion to francophone students to have a significant impact (Mougeon et al. 1984).

28. A typical career path would involve several years of teaching, followed by promotion to the rank of vice-principal, then principal. At that point, some individuals move higher in the ranks of the school board hierarchy to become superintendants, or even directors of education. At almost any point, however, an educator can move to the ministry; this is considered in many ways to be the most desirable and most prestigious of the available educational occupations. It is certainly important to have spent at least some time working there, for example, through a temporary secondment.

29. Below I refer to this as a tension between universalistic values, that is, values taken to be shared in much of the Western world in mainstream society, and which underlie francophone attempts to participate in national and international networks and activities, and particularistic ones which legitimate francophone mobilization and specific interests.

30. Some of the results of that study are presented in Chapter 5. The situation never did explode, but rather tensions have remained unresolved, and there continue to be periodic crises.

31. However, as noted in Chapter 2, French-language education at the secondary level could be funded through the public system only, and not through Catholic schools.

32. The following account of the Marchand case is drawn from a discussion with Daniel Marchildon, a Penetanguishene journalist, on 23 March 1990, as well as from Marchildon 1990.

33. The board in Ottawa contains a Catholic and a public section; there remain tensions there, due to problems in negotiating distribution of resources (among other things, the public tax base, which includes all corporate and commercial entities, is always larger than that of the separate system). In Toronto, the French-language schools within the Catholic board chose to remain there; as a result, the new board brings together those schools which were formerly divided between two public boards. Technical problems (such as how to assure representation on all board sub-committees) have been discovered as boards try to function according to the new system. In most areas, the definition of rights of access under Article 23 and its application in the voting process have been problematic. For example, the enumeration process in Toronto encountered three snags. First, it was discovered that the wording of the enumeration form discriminated against those wishing to declare themselves francophone electors. Second, some who had were counted as anglophone electors by mistake. Third, no definition of the term "francophone elector" was provided, and many voters were unsure of how to classify themselves. As a result, it is likely that fewer francophone electors were in fact enumerated than should have been; at the same time, some who may not have fit the Article 23 definition may have counted themselves in.
34. As noted in Chapter 2, Canadian citizens whose first language learned and still understood is the minority language of their province of residence, or who themselves were educated in that language in Canada, or any of whose children have been educated in that language in Canada, have the right to enroll their children in minority language schools.
35. This attempt was never realized. In addition, one board's attempt to implement similar criteria was opposed by a group of parents.
36. From a televised debate on education in the series *Le lys et le trillium*, TVOntario, 21 October 1984.
37. In 1990 yet another association was founded, the *Association interculturelle franco-ontarienne*, or AIFO. The AIFO acts as an umbrella organization for francophone multicultural associations, making a distinction between itself and the AMFO, which it sees as being an association of individuals. More importantly, it appears that the AIFO was established in reaction to perceived selective representation within the AMFO.
38. The term "intercultural education" is also often used, especially in Quebec, precisely to avoid the connotations of the term "multicultural" alluded to above, and to emphasize the building of bridges rather than the maintenance of difference. This distinction can also be related to the distinction made in English-language education between "multicultural" and "anti-racist" education, although the terms have different histories and are not referentially equivalent.
39. All statistics in this section come from Statistics Canada and are based on the census for the year indicated.
40. The French-language schools in the separate, Catholic, board, unlike those in Ottawa, elected to remain where they were.

41. Among other things, since the time the data were collected, three public elementary, one Catholic elementary and one Catholic high school have opened within Metropolitan Toronto. In addition, some of the students who would otherwise have attended schools in Toronto now have access to newly-opened schools in communities outside the metropolitan area.
42. Languages other than French and English claimed as first language include (terms used here are my translations of the ones provided by the respondents): Afrikaans, Arabic, Armenian, Batak, Chinese, Creole, Cree, Czech, Dutch, Estonian, Finnish, Gaelic, German, Greek, Gujurati, Hebrew, Hindi, Hungarian, Indonesian, Icelandic, Italian, Japanese, Kabyle, Korean, African languages, Latvian, Lebanese, Lithuanian, Macedonian, Malay, Maltese, Persian, Pilipino, Polish, Portuguese, Romanian, Russian, Sinhala, Spanish, Swedish, Swiss-German, Tagalog, Tamil, Thai, Turkish, Ukrainian, Urdu, Vietnamese, Yiddish and Yugoslav.
43. Examples and quotes in French are in italics, in English in regular typeface. The translation of French examples is also in regular typeface.
44. All names have been changed.
45. All 12 exceptions concerned the same two schools referred to above, those with a high anglophone enrollment. In some cases, because the interviews were conducted at a time when there was overt conflict between some francophone and anglophone parents, parents were uncomfortable with being recorded. In others, the setting of the interview made recording difficult. In all 12 cases, notes were taken and subsequently written up.
46. My current research, underway since 1991-1992, focusses on language, social difference, school success and cultural identity.
47. Wolfe is, of course, a powerful cultural symbol for francophones, since he led the British troops at the Battle of the Plains of Abraham, from which francophones date their subordination to the British conquerors.
48. Wong Fillmore (1979) noted similar processes in the strategies Spanish-speaking children used to learn English upon their entry into English-language schools in California. She further noted that this was a first step in the development of English proficiency: once these routines are used properly, they then serve as a basis for analyzing their different linguistic components, which children can then begin to use productively.
49. Indeed, one consequence of Quebec's increasing monolingual nationalism is a concern among francophone Québécois over who among them will have access to national and international markets through the mastery of English, that is, over the ways in which the distribution of the knowledge of English creates inequalities among them.
50. As we noted in Heller and Barker (1988: 45):

> Kagan (1985) would term the technique used (...) the "coop-coop" approach. For him, the groups involved in a Jigsaw technique eventually end up in competition with each other, or else students are individually evaluated, while in the coop-coop approach they collaborate in some project at the level of the whole class.

Since our activities could be used in any of these ways even though we have favoured collaboration, and since they share elements of the same basic Jigsaw structure, we have chosen to retain the term "Jigsaw" here.

51. The description of the steps is my translation and adaptation of Heller et al. (1990), *Guide pédagogique*, pp. 12–13.
52. I would like to acknowledge here the collaboration of the following teachers in the initial development and trial phases of the work, as well as in later phases of adaptation and refinement: Gérard Boulay, Liliane Brown, Anne-Marie Caron-Réaume, Denise Drago, Gisèle Forest, Bernard Lachapelle, Céline Lacroix, Anne Leroy-Audy, Pierre Nadeau, Line Pelletier, Maryse Roussel, Arthur Roy, Jacques Samson and Christiane Turgeon (of the Toronto Board of Education, the North York Board of Education and the Metropolitan Separate School Board; some of the schools involved now form part of the *Conseil des écoles françaises de la communanté urbaine de Toronto* (CEFCUT)). I would also like to thank Suzanne Arsenault, Head of Curriculum, CEFCUT, for her advice concerning *Projet Histoire*.

    Unlike the other projects, *Projet Histoire* was developed following the two others, using the model which had emerged from the previous classroom trials. It was drawn up outside the classroom in collaboration with a teacher who was at the time on secondment to the Ministry of Education. The classroom trial did not take place until the fall of 1989.
53. The data presented here is drawn mainly from discussions in Heller – Barker 1988 and Heller 1989c.
54. The content of the skit revolved mainly around issues of power: that of the female principal as opposed to that of the male vice-principal, that of the parent as opposed to that of the school, and that of the parent as opposed to that of the child. It also took up the problem of violence in the schoolyard, and the school's responsibility to control or prevent that violence.
55. As with Group 1, and indeed most of the scripts, the content reveals preoccupations beyond the social and communicative content of the task as presented in the materials and by the teacher. While we have not developed the analysis of this facet of the students' work (except for cases which deal clearly with issues of language and culture), it is nonetheless important to note that it certainly provides a source of pedagogical opportunities which could be exploited in and of themselves.
56. This agency was disbanded as a result of budget cuts in 1992.

References

Arnopoulos, Sheila
    1982   *Hors du Québec, point de salut?*. Montreal: Libre Expression.
Aronson, Elliot
    1978   *The Jigsaw Classroom*. Beverly Hills: Sage.
Association canadienne-française de l'Ontario
    1985   *Les Franco-Ontariens tels qu'ils sont*. Ottawa: ACFO.
    1988   *L'éducation post-secondaire en Ontario français: grandes lignes d'une position de l'ACFO*. Toronto: ACFO.
    1989   *350 ans de présence francophone en Ontario*. Ottawa: ACFO.
Baillargeon, Mireille – Claire Benjamin
    1980   "Quelques scénarios concernant l'avenir linguistique de la région métropolitaine de Montréal", in: Michel Amyot (ed.), *La situation démolinguistique au Québec et la Charte de la langue française*. Québec: Conseil de la langue française, pp. 51–85.
Barth, Fredrik (ed.)
    1969   *Ethnic Groups and Boundaries*. Boston: Little, Brown.
Beniak, Edouard – Raymond Mougeon – Daniel Valois
    1985   *Contact des langues et changement linguistique: étude sociolinguistique du français parlé à Welland (Ontario)*. Québec: Centre international de recherche sur le bilinguisme.
Bereiter, Carl – Siegfried Engelmann
    1966   *Teaching Disadvantaged Children in the Pre-School*. Englewood Cliffs, NJ: Prentice-Hall.
Bernard, Roger
    1988   *De Québécois à Ontarois*. Hearst: Le Nordir.
Bernstein, Basil
    1975   *Class, Codes and Control*. London: Routledge and Kegan Paul.
Berthelot, Jocelyn
    1990   *Apprendre à vivre ensemble: immigration, société et éducation*. Québec: Centrale de l'enseignement du Québec.
Bibeau, Gilles
    1982   *L'éducation bilingue en Amerique du Nord*. Montreal: Guerin.
Bordeleau, Louis-Gabriel – Pierre Calvé – Lionel Desjarlais – Jean Séguin
    1988   *L'éducation française à l'heure de l'immersion*. Toronto: CEFO.
Bourdieu, Pierre
    1977a   "L'économie des échanges linguistiques", *Langue française* 34: 17–34.
    1977b   *Outline of a Theory of Practice*. Cambridge: Cambridge University Press.
    1982   *Ce que parler veut dire*. Paris: Fayard.

Bourdieu, Pierre – Jean-Claude Passeron
    1977   *La reproduction: éléments pour une théorie du système d'enseignement*. Paris: Minuit.

Bourhis, Richard
    1984   "Cross-cultural communication in Montreal: two field studies since Bill 101", *International Journal of the Sociology of Language* 46:33–47.

Bowles, Samuel – Herbert Gintis
    1976   *Schooling in Capitalist America*. New York: Basic Books.

Breton, Raymond
    1984   "The production and allocation of symbolic resources: an analysis of the linguistic and ethnocultural fields in Canada", *Canadian Review of Sociology and Anthropology* 21(2):123–144.
    1985   "L'intégration des francophones hors Québec dans des communautés de langue française", *Revue de l'Université d'Ottawa* 55(2):77–90.

Caldwell, Gary – Daniel Fournier
    1987   "The Quebec question: a matter of population", *Canadian Journal of Sociology* 12: 16–41.

Canadian Parents for French (CPF)
    1992   *The CPF Immersion Registry 1991/1992*. Ottawa: CPF.

Canale, Michael – Merrill Swain
    1980   "Theoretical bases of communicative approaches to second language teaching and testing", *Applied Linguistics* 1: 1–47.

Cardinal, Linda – Caroline Andrew – Laurette Lévy
    in press   *Actes du colloque du Réseau des chercheures féministes de l'Ontario français*. Ottawa: Presses de l'Université d'Ottawa.

Cardinal, Linda – Cécile Coderre
    1990   *Pour les femmes: éducation et autonomie*. Ottawa: Réseau action-éducation femmes.

Cardinal, Linda – Jean Lapointe
    1989   "La sociologie des francophones hors Québec: un parti-pris pour l'autonomie", *Canadian Ethnic Studies* 22(1): 47–66.

Carisse, Colette
    1966   "Accommodation conjugale et réseau social des mariages ethniques au Canada", *Revue française de sociologie* 7: 472–486.
    1969   "Orientations culturelles dans les mariages entre canadiens français et les canadiens anglais", *Sociologie et sociétés* 1: 39–52.

Carrier, Denis
    1985   "Langue d'enseignement et comportement universitaire des Franco-Ontariens", *Revue du Nouvel-Ontario* 7: 67–90.

Cartwright, Donald
    1982   "Spatial patterns in Franco-Ontarian communities", in: Raymond Breton – Pierre Savard (eds.), *The Quebec and Acadian Diaspora in North America*. Toronto: Multicultural History Society of Ontario, pp. 137–158.

1987 "Accommodation among the anglophone minority in Quebec to official language policy: a shift in traditional patterns of language contact", *Journal of Multilingual and Multicultural Development* 8(1,2): 187–212.

Castonguay, Claude
1979 "Exogamie et anglicisation chez les minorités canadiennes-françaises", *Canadian Journal of Sociology and Anthropology* 16: 21–31.

Cazabon, Benoît (ed.)
1987 "L'immersion et les Franco-Ontariens", *Revue du Nouvel-Ontario* 9: 9–160.

Chevalier, Gisèle
1990 "L'enseignement de la langue de la minorité à la majorité: l'immersion française au Canada", paper presented at the AILA World Congress, Thessaloniki, Greece.

Choquette, Robert
1977 *Langue et religion: histoire des conflits anglo-français en Ontario.* Ottawa: Les Éditions de l'Université d'Ottawa.
1987 *La foi gardienne de la langue en Ontario, 1900–1950.* Montreal: Bellarmin.

Churchill, Stacy – Normand Frenette – Saeed Quazi
1985 *Éducation et besoins des Franco-Ontariens: le diagnostic d'un système d'éducation.* Toronto: CEFO.

Clément, Richard – Yves Beauregard
1986 "Peur d'assimilation et confiance en soi: leur relation à l'alternance des codes et à la compétence communicative en langue seconde", *Canadian Journal of Behavioural Science* 18(2): 189–198.

Clift, Dominique – Sheila Arnopoulos
1979 *Le fait anglais au Québec.* Montreal: Libre Expression.

Collins, Randall
1989 "Femmes, stratification sociale et production de la culture", *Sociologie et sociétés* 21(2): 27–45.

Conseil de l'éducation franco-ontarienne
1989 *Plan directeur de l'éducation franco-ontarienne.* Toronto: CEFO.

Coulombe, Danielle
1985 "Doublement ou triplement minoritaires", *Revue de l'Université d'Ottawa* 55(2): 131–136.

Daigle, Jean
1982 "The Acadians: a people in search of a country", in: Raymond Breton – Pierre Savard (eds.), *The Quebec and Acadian Diaspora in North America.* Toronto: The Multicultural History Society of Ontario, pp. 1–10.

Dannequin, Claudine
1976 *Les enfants baillonés.* Paris: CEDIL.

Desjarlais, Lionel – Hervé Cyr – Gérald Brûlé – Vincent Gauthier
    1980   *L'enfant parlant peu ou pas français dans les écoles de langue française*. Toronto: Ontario Ministry of Education.

Edwards, Vivian
    1986   *Language in a Black Community*. Clevedon: Multilingual Matters.

Erickson, Frederick – Gerald Mohatt
    1982   "Cultural organization of participation structures in two classrooms of Indian students", in: George Spindler (ed.), *Doing the Ethnography of Schooling*. New York: Holt, Rinehart and Winston, pp. 132–175.

Fennario, David
    1980   *Balconville*. Vancouver, Los Angeles: Talonbooks.

François, Frédéric (ed.)
    1983   *J'cause français, non?*. Paris: La Découverte, Maspéro.

Frenette, Normand – Lise Gauthier
    1990   "Luttes idéologiques et cultures institutionnelles en éducation minoritaire: le cas de l'Ontario français", *Revue Éducation canadienne et internationale* 19(1): 16–31.

Fullan, Michael – Michael Connelly
    1987   *Teacher Education in Ontario: Current Practice and Options for the Future*. Toronto: Ontario Ministry of Education.

Gaffield, Chad
    1987   *Language, Schooling and Cultural Conflict*. Montreal, Kingston: McGill-Queen's University Press.

Gagnon, Robert
    1989   "Capital culturel et identité sociale: les fonctions sociales du discours sur l'encombrement des professions libérales au XIXe siècle", *Sociologie et sociétés* 21(2): 129–146.

Gal, Susan
    1989   "Language and political economy", *Annual Review of Anthropology* 18: 345–367.

Gardner, E.
    1986   "Unique features of a band-controlled school: Seabird Island Community School", *Canadian Journal of Native Education* 13(1): 15–33.

Genesee, Frederick
    1978   "Second-language learning and language attitudes", *Working Papers on Bilingualism* 16: 19–42.

Genesee, Frederick – Richard Bourhis
    1982   "The social psychological significance of code-switching in cross-cultural communication", *Journal of Language and Social Psychology* 1: 1–28.

Gibson, Margaret
    1987   "The school performance of immigrant minorities: a comparative view", in: Evelyn Jacob and Cathie Jordan (eds.), "Explaining the School Per-

formance of Minority Students", *Anthropology and Education Quarterly* 18(4): 262–275.

Giddens, Anthony
1984 *The Constitution of Society: Outline of the Theory of Structuration.* Berkeley: University of California Press.

Government of Canada
1967– *Report of the Royal Commission on Bilingualism and Biculturalism.*
1969 Ottawa: Queen's Printer.

Gouvernement du Québec
1972 *Rapport de la Commission d'enquête sur la situation de la langue française et sur les droits linguistiques au Québec.* Québec: Éditeur officiel.

Grillo, Ralph
1989 *Dominant Languages: Language and Hierarchy in Britain and France.* Cambridge: Cambridge University Press.

Handler, Richard
1988 *Nationalism and the Politics of Culture in Quebec.* Madison: University of Wisconsin Press.

Harley, Birgit
1984 "How good is their French?", *Language and Society* 12: 55–60.

Hart, Douglas – Sharon Lapkin – Merrill Swain
1988 *Early and Mid-Immersion Programmes: Linguistic Outcomes and Social Character.* Final report on Part 1 of the research commissioned by the Metropolitan Toronto Board. Toronto: MLC, OISE.
1990 *Prospects for Immersion Graduates: Bilingualism in the Private Sector.* Final report submitted to the Ontario Ministry of Education (OISE Transfer Grant). Toronto: MLC, OISE.

Heath, Shirley Brice
1983 *Ways With Words.* Cambridge: Cambridge University Press.

Heller, Monica
1982a *Language, ethnicity and politics in Quebec.* Unpublished Ph.D. thesis. University of California, Berkeley.
1982b "Negotiations of language choice in Montreal", in: John Gumperz (ed.), *Language and Social Identity.* Cambridge: Cambridge University Press, pp. 108–118.
1984 "Language and ethnic identity in a Toronto French-language school", *Canadian Ethnic Studies* 16(2): 1–14.
1985 "Language and ethnicity in the workplace", in: Nessa Wolfson and Joan Manes (eds.), *Language of Inequality.* Berlin: Mouton de Gruyter, pp. 75–90.
1987a "L'école de langue française à Toronto", *Revue du Nouvel-Ontario* 9: 71–92.

1987b　"The role of language in the formation of ethnic identity", in: Jean Phinney and Mary Jane Rotheram (eds.), *Childrens' Ethnic Socialization*. Newbury Park: Sage, pp. 180–200.

1988　(ed.), *Codeswitching: Anthropological and Sociolinguistic Perspectives*. Berlin: Mouton de Gruyter.

1989a　"Aspects sociolinguistiques de la francisation d'une entreprise privée", *Sociologie et sociétés* 21(2): 115–128.

1989b　"Speech economy and social selection in educational contexts: a Franco-Ontarian case study", *Discourse Processes* 12: 377–390.

1989c　"Communicative resources and local configurations: an exploration of language contact processes", *Multilingua* 8(4): 357–396.

1990　"French immersion in Canada: a model for Switzerland?", *Multilingua* 9(1): 67–86.

Heller, Monica – Graham Barker
1988　"Conversational activities and contexts for talk: learning activities for Franco-Ontarian minority schools", *Anthropology and Education Quarterly* 19(1): 20–47.

Heller, Monica – Graham Barker – Laurette Lévy – Françoise Pelletier
1990　*Projet "Coopération et découverte"*. Ottawa: Centre franco-ontarien de ressources pédagogiques.

Heller, Monica – Jean-Paul Bartholomot – Laurette Lévy – Luc Ostiguy
1982　*Le processus de francisation dans une entreprise montréalaise: une analyse sociolinguistique*. Québec: L'Éditeur officiel.

Hughes, Edward
1943　*French Canada in Transition: The Effects of Anglo-American Industrialization upon a French-Canadian Small Town*. Chicago: University of Chicago Press.

Irvine, Judith
1989　"When talk isn't cheap: language and political economy", *American Ethnologist* 16: 248–267.

Jackson, John
1988　*Community and Conflict: A Study of French-English Relations in Ontario*. Toronto: Canadian Scholars' Press Inc.

Jacob, Evelyn – Cathie Jordan (eds.)
1987　"Explaining the School Performance of Minority Students", *Anthropology and Education Quarterly* 18(4).

Joy, Richard
1972　*Languages in Conflict*. Toronto: McClelland and Stewart.

Juteau-Lee, Danielle
1980　"Français d'Amérique, Canadiens, Canadiens français, Franco-Ontariens, Ontarois: qui sommes-nous?", *Pluriel-Débat* 24: 21–42.

1982　"The Franco-Ontarian collectivity: material and symbolic dimensions of its minority status", in: Raymond Breton – Pierre Savard (eds.), *The*

Quebec and Acadian Diaspora in North America. Toronto: The Multicultural History Society of Ontario, pp. 167–182.

Kagan, Spencer
1985 *Cooperative Learning Resources for Teachers*. Riverside, CA: School of Education, University of California.

Keyfitz, Nathan
1960 "Some demographic aspects of French-English relations", in: Mason Wade (ed.), *Canadian Dualism: Studies of French-English Relations*. Toronto: University of Toronto Press, pp. 129–148.

Labov, William
1969 "The logic of non-standard English", in: James Alatis (ed.), *Georgetown Monographs on Languages and Linguistics* 22: 1–44.
1982 "Objectivity and commitment in linguistic science: the case of the Black English trial in Ann Arbor", *Language in Society* 11(2): 165–202.

Lachapelle, Réjean
1990 "La position du français s'améliore, la proportion de francophones décroît", *Language and Society* 32: 9–11.

Lachapelle, Réjean – Jacques Henripin
1980 *La situation démolinguistique au Canada*. Montreal: Institute for Research on Public Policy.

Lacroix, Robert – François Vaillancourt
1981 *Les revenus et la langue au Québec 1970-1978*. Québec: Conseil de la langue française.

Lambert, Wallace
1967 "A social psychology of bilingualism", *Journal of Social Issues* 23(2): 91–109.

Lambert, Wallace – R. Hodgson – Robert Gardner – S. Fillenbaum
1960 "Evaluative reactions to spoken language", *Journal of Abnormal and Social Psychology* 60: 44–51.

Lambert, Wallace – Richard Tucker
1972 *Bilingual Education of Children: The St. Lambert Experiment*. Rowley, Mass.: Newbury House.

Lapkin, Sharon – Merrill Swain – Valerie Argue
1983 *French Immersion: The Trial Balloon That Flew*. Toronto: OISE Press.

Lapkin, Sharon – Merrill Swain – Norman Rowen – Douglas Hart
1988 *Bilingual Job Vacancy Survey: An Exploratory Study*. Final report submitted to the SSHRCC Small-Scale Grants. Toronto: MLC, OISE.

Lapointe, Jean – R. Poulin – J.-Yvon Thériault
1987 *La minorité francophone de Welland et ses rapports avec les institutions*. Report submitted to the Office of the Commissioner of Official Languages (Government of Canada).

Lee, Danielle – Jean Lapointe
  1979   "The emergence of Franco-Ontarians: new identity, new boundaries", in: Jean Elliott (ed.), *Two Nations, Many Cultures: Ethnic Groups in Canada*. Toronto: Prentice Hall, pp. 173–186.

Lieberson, Stanley
  1965   "Bilingualism in Montreal: a demographic analysis", *American Journal of Sociology* 71: 10–25.
  1970   *Language and Ethnic Relations in Canada*. New York: Wiley and Sons.

Lightbown, Patsy
  1988   "Educational research and theory in language policy: ESL in Quebec schools", *TESL Canada Journal* 5(2): 27–32.

Lucier, P.
  1987   *Pluralisme dans l'éducation*. Québec: Ministère de l'Éducation du Québec.

Lyster, Roy
  1987   "Speaking immersion", *Canadian Modern Language Review* 44(2): 701–717.

MacLennan, Hugh
  1945   *Two Solitudes*. Toronto: Collins.

Marchildon, Daniel
  1990   "Dix ans après: la tension existe toujours à Penetang", *Enjeu: Éducation nationale* 1. Association de la presse francophone/Commission nationale des parents francophones.

Maxwell, Thomas
  1977   *The Invisible French: The French in Metropolitan Toronto*. Waterloo: Wilfrid Laurier University Press.

McNaught, Kenneth
  1969   *The Pelican History of Canada*. Harmondsworth: Penguin.

Moll, Luis – Stephen Diaz
  1987   "Change as the goal of educational research", in: Evelyn Jacob – Cathie Jordan (eds.), "Explaining the School Performance of Minority Students", *Anthropology and Education Quarterly* 18(4): 300–311.

Mougeon, Raymond
  1987   "Impact de l'essor de l'immersion sur l'éducation et le devenir des Franco-Ontariens", *Revue du Nouvel-Ontario* 9: 31–50.

Mougeon, Raymond – Edouard Beniak (eds.)
  1989   *Le français parlé hors Québec: un aperçu sociolinguistique*. Québec: les Presses de l'Université Laval.

Mougeon, Raymond – Michael Canale – Monique Bélanger – Monica Heller
  1984   *Programmes dans les écoles de langue française pour les élèves de compétence inégale en français*. Final report submitted to the Ontario Ministry of Education. Toronto: CREFO, OISE.

Mougeon, Raymond – Monica Heller
1986 "The social and historical context of minority French-language education in Ontario", *Journal of Multilingual and Multicultural Development* 7(2,3): 199–227.

Ogbu, John
1978 *Minority Education and Caste: The American System in Cross-Cultural Perspective*. New York: Academic Press.
1987 "Variability in minority school performance: a problem in search of an explanation", in: Evelyn Jacob and Cathie Jordan (eds.), "Explaining the School Performance of Minority Students", *Anthropology and Education Quarterly* 18(4): 312–334.

Olson, C. Paul
1983 "Inequality remade: the theory of French immersion in Northern Ontario", *Journal of Education* 165(1): 75–98.

Olson, C. Paul – George Burns
1983 "Politics, class and happenstance: French immersion in a Canadian context", *Interchange* 14(1): 1–16.

Ontario Ministry of Education
1987 *Programme-cadre français*. Toronto: Ministry of Education.

Ossenberg, Richard
1970 "The Conquest revisited: another look at Canadian dualism", in: W. Mann (ed.), *Social and Cultural Change in Canada* Vol. 1. Vancouver, Toronto, Montreal: Copp Clark, pp. 208–224.

Ouellet, Fernand
1966 *Histoire économique et sociale du Québec 1760–1851*. Montreal: Fides.
1972 *Éléments d'histoire du Bas-Canada*. Montreal: Hurtubise.

Pauls, S.
1984 "The case for band-controlled schools", *Canadian Journal of Native Education* 12(1): 31–37.

Philips, Susan
1983 *The Invisible Culture*. New York: Longman.

Poplack, Shana
1988 "Contrasting patterns of code switching in two communities", in: Monica Heller (ed.), *Codeswitching: Anthropological and Sociolinguistic Perspectives*. Berlin: Mouton de Gruyter, pp. 215–244.

Porter, John
1965 *The Vertical Mosaic: An Analysis of Social Class and Power*. Toronto: University of Toronto Press.

Regnier, R.
1987 "Survival schools and emancipatory education", *Canadian Journal of Native Education* 14(1): 42–53.

Richler, Mordechai
- 1959 *The Apprenticeship of Duddy Kravitz*. Harmondsworth: Penguin.

Saifullah Khan, Verity
- 1980 "The "mother tongue" of linguistic minorities in multicultural England", *Journal of Multilingual and Multicultural Development* 11: 71–88.

Shamai, Shmuel
- 1992 "Ethnicity and educational achievement: Canada 1941–1981", *Canadian Ethnic Studies* 24(1): 43–57.

Sharan, Shlomo – Yael Sharan
- 1976 *Small-Group Teaching*. Englewood Cliffs, NJ: Educational Technology Publications.

Skutnabb-Kangas, Tove
- 1981 "Guest worker or immigrant: different ways of producing an underclass", *Journal of Multilingual and Multicultural Development* 22: 89–115.

Swain, Merrill
- 1985 "Communicative competence: some roles of comprehensible input and comprehensible output in its development", in: Susan Gass – Carol Madden (eds.), *Input in Second Language Acquisition*. Rowley, Mass.: Newbury House, pp. 235–253.

Swain, Merrill – Sharon Lapkin
- 1981 *Evaluating Bilingual Education: A Canadian Case Study*. Clevedon, U.K.: Multilingual Matters.

Sylvestre, Paul-François
- 1980 *L'école de la résistance*. Sudbury: Prise de Parole.

Trudelle, Clément – Pierre Fortier
- 1987 *Toronto se raconte: la paroisse du Sacré-Coeur*. Toronto: Société d'histoire de Toronto.

Vaillancourt, François (ed.)
- 1985 *Économie et langue*. Québec: Conseil de la langue française.

Vallières, Gaetan
- 1982 "The Franco-Ontarian experience", in: Raymond Breton – Pierre Savard (eds.), *The Quebec and Acadian Diaspora in North America*, Toronto: The Multicultural History Society of Ontario, pp. 183–196.

Vogt, Lynn – Cathie Jordan – Roland Tharp
- 1987 "Explaining school failure, producing school success: two cases", in: Evelyn Jacob – Cathie Jordan (eds.), "Explaining the School Performance of Minority Students", *Anthropology and Education Quarterly* 18(4): 276–286.

Welch, David
- 1988 *The Social Construction of Franco-Ontarian Interests towards French-Language Schooling*. Unpublished Ph.D. thesis. University of Toronto.

Williams, Raymond
    1973   "Base and superstructure in Marxist cultural theory", *New Left Review* 87: 3–16.

Willis, Paul
    1977   *Learning to Labour*. Westmead: Saxon House.

Wolf, Eric
    1982   *Europe and the People Without History*. Berkeley, Los Angeles: University of California Press.

Wong Fillmore, Lily
    1979   "Individual differences in second language acquisition", in: Charles Fillmore et al. (eds.), *Individual Differences in Language Ability and Language Behavior*. NY: Academic Press, pp. 203–228.

Woolard, Kathryn
    1985   "Language variation and cultural hegemony: toward an integration of sociolinguistic and social theory", *American Ethnologist* 12(4): 738–748.
    1989   *Double Talk: Bilingualism and the Politics of Ethnicity in Catalonia*. Stanford: Stanford University Press.

Yuzdepski, Iris
    1983   "Indian control of Indian education", *Canadian Journal of Native Education* 11(1): 37–43.

List of Abbreviations

ACFEO: Association canadienne-française de l'éducation de l'Ontario. The first Franco-Ontarian lobbying group, established in Ottawa in 1910. In 1968 the ACFEO became the ACFO (see ACFO below).

ACFO: Association canadienne-française de l'Ontario. The major Franco-Ontarian lobbying group, with a head office in Ottawa and local chapters across the province. ACFO sets its priorities annually, and organizes at provincial, regional and municipal levels to accomplish goals linked to the development of the Franco-Ontarian community (such as the establishment of a local French-language radio station, the provision of health services in French, the establishment of a Franco-Ontarian university, etc.) (see ACFEO above).

ACSFO: Association des conseillères et des conseillers scolaires franco-ontariens. This association brings together school trustees elected to govern French-language schools across Ontario. Established in 1944, it represented both the Catholic and public sectors until a separate organization for Catholic schools was established in recent years (see AFOCEC below).

AEFO: Association des enseignantes et des enseignants franco-ontariens. This province-wide federation of Franco-Ontarian teachers was established in 1939 and has its headquarters in Ottawa. It is now part of the Ontario Teachers' Federation, an umbrella group for all Ontario teachers. AEFO is active not only with respect to contract negotiations and government lobbying, but more broadly with respect to teacher training and professional development.

AFOCEC: Association franco-ontarienne des conseillères et des conseillers d'éducation catholiques. Established in the late 1980s as a splinter group of the ACSFO (see above), this association brings together Franco-Ontarian Catholic school trustees.

AIFO: Association interculturelle franco-ontarienne de l'Ontario. Established in 1990 as a splinter group of the AMFO (see below), this association brings together francophone members of visible minorities. There are ideological differences between AMFO and AIFO: AMFO is concerned to ensure the representation of francophones from outside Canada in matters relevant to the whole francophone population, while AIFO is concerned to fight racism in the Franco-Ontarian community.

AMFO: Association multiculturelle franco-ontarienne. Established in 1987 as a splinter group of ACFO (see above), this association brings together francophones from outside Canada (see also AIFO above).

APE/API: Association Parents-Enseignants or Association Parents-Instituteurs. These are school-level parent-teacher associations, responsible for such things as the organization of after-school activities or outings, as well as for the discussion and planning of issues such as the curriculum, teaching materials, admissions criteria, etc. .

List of Abbreviations   243

APEC: Association for the Preservation of English in Canada. Established in the 1980s, this association carries on lobbying and publicity-generating activities designed to end or forestall the provision of French-language or bilingual services in areas with a majority anglophone population.

ASFO: Association des surintendantes et des surintendants franco-ontariens. This association brings together Franco-Ontarian school superintendants.

BNA Act: the British North America Act, passed in 1867 by the British Parliament and establishing Canada as an independent nation.

CAFO: Conseil des affaires franco-ontariennes. From 1974 to 1985 the CAFO, composed of members of the Franco-Ontarian community from all regions and diverse domains, advised the provincial government on francophone affairs. In 1985, as a result of the passage of the French-Language Services Act, the CAFO was disbanded and replaced with the Office des affaires francophones, an administrative unit within the civil service structure (see OAF below).

CCLF: Comité consultatif de langue française. From the late 1970s to 1986, while francophones could not directly control their educational establishments, all of which were housed in school boards frequently dominated by anglophones, they were able to sit on CCLFs composed of school trustees and francophone parents or other concerned members of the Franco-Ontarian community. These CCLFs advised the school board on matters relevant to the French-language schools within the board (see CELF below).

CEFO: Conseil de l'éducation franco-ontarienne. From 1980 to 1989 the CEFO advised the Ontario Ministry of Education and the Ontario Ministry of Colleges and Universities regarding matters relevant to Franco-Ontarian education. It was composed of the Assistant Deputy Minister for Franco-Ontarian education and representatives of Franco-Ontarian educational associations and institutions. In 1992 it was replaced by two councils, one advising the Ministry of Education and the other advising the Ministry of Colleges and Universities.

CEFCUT: Conseil des écoles françaises de la communauté urbaine de Toronto. One of two homogeneous French-language school boards established in 1989, the CEFCUT brought together all French-language public schools in the Toronto metropolitan area. The second was established in Ottawa (and including both Catholic and public schools); in 1992 a third opened in the eastern counties of Prescott-Russell (see CELF below).

CEGEP: Collège d'enseignement général et professionnel. During the 1960s, the Quebec government re-organized the education system in order to facilitate access to all levels of education. As part of this reform, CEGEPs were established to either prepare high school graduates for university studies or train them in specific technical or vocational domains.

CELF: Conseil d'éducation de langue française. As a result of court challenges and decisions, in 1986 the Ontario government made provisions for the francophone population to exercise direct control over its educational establishments. In addition to establishing homogeneous French-language boards in some areas (see CEFCUT above), it established CELFs consisting of trustees elected by francophones to govern French-language schools within mixed boards (see also CCLF above).

COFTM: Conseil des organismes francophones de Toronto métropolitain. Established in 1977, this organization brings together francophones and francophone associations in the greater Toronto area. It also provides some direct services, such as assistance to newly-arrived francophone immigrants.

DJ: Direction Jeunesse. This organization brings together mainly Franco-Ontarian university students, but also includes other francophones between the ages of 18 and 30. It acts as a lobbying group in addition to organizing other activities for its members.

FFHQ: Fédération des francophones hors Québec. Established in the 1970s with headquarters in Ottawa, this federation acts as a lobbying group (principally at the level of the Canadian federal government) on behalf of francophones outside Québec. In 1991 the FFHQ changed its name to the Fédération des communautés francophones et acadienne du Canada, on the grounds that the former name implied an exile from Québec which they did not feel applied to them, and in reaction to the Québec government's failure to support them.

OAF: Office des affaires francophones. This administrative unit within the structure of the Ontario provincial government was established in 1986 to help the minister responsible for francophone affairs, notably with respect to the implementation of the French-Language Services Act (see CAFO above).

SAPELR: Sault Association for the Promotion of English-Language Rights. A local association established in Sault Ste. Marie (Ontario) to lobby the municipal and provincial governments to withhold or suspend the provision of French-language services (see APEC above).

SULFO: Société des universitaires de langue française de l'Ontario. Established in 1990, this association brings together francophone university teachers both to lobby the provincial government on matters of concern to them and to provide a network among faculty members who are often isolated from francophone colleagues.

Subject Index

Abitibi-Temiscamingue 58
Acadia 37–39, 42, 46
achievement (school) 13–15, 87, 89, 109, 226
– and social stratification 14–17, 60, 141
– and cultural difference 15–17
Act of Union 43
admissions committees 73, 117, 124–125
– criteria 151–162, 213
agriculture 39, 42, 44–49
Alberta 32, 49, 67–68, 226
American War of Independence 42–43
animation culturelle 107
Annapolis Valley 38
anti-racist education 130, 228
applied linguistics 85, 229
assimilation 28f., 87f., 125f., 210–216
Association canadienne-française de l'Ontario (ACFO) 14, 69, 73, 77, 116, 120, 131, 138
Association des enseignantes et des enseignants franco-ontariens (AEFO) 69, 193
Association for the Preservation of English in Canada (APEC) 80, 83, 99
Association française des conseillers scolaires de l'Ontario (AFCSO) 69
Association interculturelle franco-ontarienne (AIFO) 138, 228
Association multiculturelle franco-ontarienne (AMFO) 131, 138, 228
Associations parents-enseignants (APE)/ Associations parents-instituteurs (API) 107, 109, 162, 177

Battle of the Plains of Abraham 39, 169, 229
bilingualism (*see also* code-switching, language policy)
– demography 2, 27–28, 32–33, 48–52, 86, 136, 182, 224–228
– social psychology 2–3
– community studies 3
– literacy studies 3
– brokers 11, 45, 53–56, 63, 96, 171–177
– Royal Commission on Bilingualism and Biculturalism 61, 91
– bilingual schools 70–71, 90, 113, 162
– puns/wordplay 167, 170, 203–206
Bill 8 (Ontario Law on French Language Services) 75, 81, 83, 212, 215, 222–223
Bill 75 (Ontario law on minority-language education) 74, 116
Bill 101 (Quebec Charter of the French Language) 30, 62, 64, 75, 82, 92, 127
Bill 178 (Quebec sign law) 64, 82
boards of education 69–74, 90, 107, 113–117, 138, 177, 228
British Columbia 49
British North America (BNA) Act 20, 33, 43–44

Canada
– Upper and Lower Canada 42
– Canada East and Canada West 43
– Dominion of Canada 43, 85
– Confederation 43–44
capital (linguistic, cultural, symbolic) 6f., 25–27, 56, 93–98, 102, 111, 150–155, 161, 171–177

Cartier, Jacques 37
Catholic Church 1, 6, 9, 19f., 35f., 68, 74, 95, 100, 112, 126
– struggles with State 58–59, 100
Champlain, Samuel de 37
Charter of Rights and Freedoms (Canada) 72–75, 115–117, 124, 129, 226, 228
class (social) 152–162
classes d'accueil 125
Cobal 46
code-switching 31, 167–175, 197–206, 215, 221
colonization
– of Ontario 19–20, 46–47, 91
– of North America 37–46
Comités consultatifs de langue française (CCLFs) 71, 74, 109, 113–115, 131
Commission des services en français 75
communicative language learning theory 85–86
community colleges 69, 71, 76, 107, 118–120
Conseil des affaires franco-ontariennes (CAFO) 72, 75, 106
Conseil de l'éducation franco-ontarienne (CEFO) 71, 75, 77, 89, 106, 120, 134
Conseil des organismes francophones du Toronto métropolitain (COFTM) 138
Conseils de l'éducation de langue française (CELFs) 116
Constitution Act 42
cooperative learning 29, 163–164, 182–209, 229–230
Cornwall 71
coureurs de bois 19, 38–39
cours de rattrapage 125
cours de refrancisation 125
crosswords v

data-collection techniques 139–140, 150–151, 163–165, 195, 229
Direction jeunesse 120
distinct society 66, 75, 101, 130

écoles mixtes 70, 71, 90, 113, 162
economic specialization
– ethnic 14, 18, 72–76
– gender 18
Education Act (Ontario) 106, 114
educational objectives 152, 155–162
educational rights 20, 27–28, 64, 67–78, 80–81, 106–135, 155–162, 225–226 (*see* language rights, language of instruction, governance)
English-only movement 79–85 (*see* language policy, APEC, SAPELR, Sault Ste. Marie)
ethnic identity 23–27, 60f., 89f., 108f., 174f., 211f.
– Canadiens 23
– Canadiens-français 23, 129
– Franco-Ontariens 24, 129, 213–214
– Ontarie/Ontarois 24, 66
– francogènes 26
ethnolinguistic stratification 13–15, 19–22, 25, 35, 39f., 72, 90f., 128, 141, 210, 213
exogamy (linguistic) 47, 140–141, 150–154, 226

Fédération des communautés francophones et acadienne du Canada (FCFAC) 66–67
Fédération des francophones hors Québec (FFHQ) 66–67, 226
First Nations (Native population) 9f., 38, 47, 60f., 84, 91f., 104, 210, 224–225
founding nations 20, 61, 85, 127
francogènes 26
Franco-Ontarian political mobilization 65–78, 94, 97, 103–105, 110, 132–134, 210–211, 213, 221–223, 227
Franco-Ontariens 24, 129, 213–214
French immersion 8–9, 23, 85–90, 96, 113, 122, 137, 150f., 170–173, 189–192, 221f.

Subject Index 247

French language
- ideologies and values 142–181, 184, 186, 195–206, 216–221
- quality 142–146, 149, 177, 217, 219
- *le bon français* 143, 146, 149, 219

French Revolution 43
fur trade 19, 37–39, 42–45, 58, 224

gender 18, 50, 94, 133–134, 172, 214
gestion 26, 111–112, 132
governance (educational) 26–28, 111–112, 132, 225–226 (*see gestion*, educational rights)
grain 57–58
Great Lakes 38–39, 42, 58

Haileybury 46
Halifax 39
hegemony 16, 24–25, 99, 104–105, 212
Heritage Language programs 9
history (French Canada) 19–23, 32–78
Hudson River 38, 58
Hudson's Bay 38

immigrants 1, 8–14, 20–27, 45–47, 55, 65–67, 74f., 84, 91f., 124f., 175, 187, 195, 211f.
industrialization 45, 47, 57–58
intercultural education 225, 228
intermarriage (linguistic) 47, 140–141, 150–154, 226
Iroquois Falls 74

James Bay 58

Kirkland Lake 46

language choice 145–146, 148, 163–175, 195–206, 214, 219
language ideologies and values 142–181, 174–176, 184, 186, 195–206, 216–221

language norms 142–149, 177, 183–186, 195–206, 215–222
language of instruction 9, 18, 27, 62f., 85f., 101, 106f., 156, 175f., 183, 226 (*see* language rights, educational rights)
language policy
- Canada 1, 5, 22, 33–34, 44, 53, 61, 72–75, 80, 84–85 (*see* Charter of Rights and Freedoms, bilingualism)
- Ontario 10, 67, 69–78, 80, 86, 91, 102, 112–122, 225–226 (*see* Bill 8, Regulation 17, Bill 75)
- Quebec 53, 62, 64, 75, 82, 101–102, 127, 225 (*see* Bill 101, Bill 178)
- municipal unilingualism (Ontario) 5, 9–10, 79–85 (*see* APEC, SAPELR, Sault Ste. Marie, Thunder Bay, Bill 8, English-only movement)
language rights 25–26, 44, 64, 67–85, 91–92, 106–135, 156, 162, 225–226 (*see* language of instruction, educational rights)
language teaching 85–90, 184–194
linguistic proficiency 26, 87–90, 109, 111, 122–133, 148–149, 152, 173, 183, 192–195, 201, 212–220, 226
linguistic repertoire 93, 185–186, 190, 192, 203, 206, 212–213
Loyalists 20, 39, 42
lumber industry 44, 46–47, 49, 57–58, 224

Manitoba 47
Marchand, Jacques 115–116, 227
metalinguistic awareness 196, 202–203
migration 19, 28, 32, 35–36, 39, 45–52, 63, 127, 136–141, 183, 211–212, 217–223
mining 46–47, 49, 57–58
Ministry of Colleges and Universities (Ontario) 106–107

Subject Index

Ministry of Education (Ontario) 106–107, 131–132, 141, 148–149, 216
mobilization (political)
- Franco-Ontarian 65–78, 94, 97, 103–105, 110, 132–134, 210–211, 213, 221–223, 227
- Québécois 57–65, 75, 94, 97, 100–105, 130
Montréal 21–22, 30, 32, 37, 42–43, 54, 57–58, 62–63, 86, 90, 127
multicultural education 131, 225, 228
multiculturalism 61, 84, 91–92, 111, 122–133, 225 (*see* language policy – Canada)

New Brunswick 68, 86, 97, 140
New England 45–46
non parlants 26–27, 111, 122–123 (*see* admissions)
North Bay 71
Northwest Territories 49
Nouvelle-France 9–21, 37–46

Office des Affaires francophones (OAF) 72, 75
Ontarie/Ontarois 24, 66
Ontario Institute for Studies in Education 4, 6
Orange Lodge 99
Ottawa 10, 22, 47, 59, 71, 76, 107, 117–119, 148, 228
Ottawa River 57

Parizeau, Jacques 17
Parti Québécois 17
Penetanguishene 113–116, 226
Porcupine 46
Prescott-Russell counties (Ontario) 42
private schools 9, 69–71, 138
public schools 9, 27, 68–71, 113, 117, 126, 138, 150, 218, 226–228

quality of French 142–146, 177, 217 (*see* language norms)
Quebec Act 42
Quebec City 37, 39, 57
Quiet Revolution (Quebec) 2, 21, 59–65

Regulation 17 (Ontario) 68–69
Rilke, Rainer Maria 224
Royal Commission on Bilingualism and Biculturalism 61, 91

St. Lambert 86
St. Lawrence River 37–38, 42, 57
Saskatchewan 49
Sault Ste. Marie 9, 26, 66, 74–75, 79–85, 95, 126, 162, 224, 226
Sault Ste. Marie Association for the Preservation of English Language Rights (SAPELR) 80
school programmes (*see* language of instruction)
- Heritage language programmes 9
- French immersion 8–9, 23, 85–90, 96, 113, 122, 137, 150, 154, 157, 170–173, 189–192, 221–227
school-research relations 206–209
schools
- public 9, 27, 68–71, 113, 117, 126, 138, 150, 218, 226–228
- separate 9–10, 27, 68–71, 74, 80, 113, 117, 126, 150, 218, 226–228
- private 9, 69–71, 138
seigneurs 38–39
Seven Years' War 39
Société des universitaires de langue française de l'Ontario (SULFO) 120
speech economy 93
state bureaucratization 59–60
structuration 17
Sturgeon Falls 162
Sudbury 10, 46, 71, 74–75, 83, 107, 118, 126, 148, 226
symbolic marketplace 6–7, 95–96, 175

teacher training 131, 164, 184–194, 207–208
teaching strategies 184–194
Thunder Bay 9, 11, 74–75, 126, 162, 224
Timmins 46, 71, 74–75, 126
Toronto francophone institutions and associations 137–139
Trans-Canada Railway 47
Treaty of Paris 39
Trudeau, Pierre Elliott 22, 59, 104

university system 48–121

Voltaire 224
voyageurs 19, 38–39, 44

Welland 21, 47, 70–71, 162
Windsor 116
World War II 47, 58

Yukon 49

Author Index

Anctil, P., 2
Andrew, C., 134
Arnopoulos, S., 5, 43, 57, 60–61, 70, 72, 225
Aronson, E., 187
Association canadienne-française de l'Ontario, 14, 72, 77, 121, 134

Baillargeon, M., 54
Barker, G., 185, 186, 229–230
Barth, F., 12, 53
Beauregard, Y., 3
Bélanger, M., 125, 227
Beniak, É., 3, 21, 47
Benjamin, C., 54
Bereiter, C., 13
Bernard, R., 14, 24, 47, 49, 52, 66, 72, 78, 128, 225–226
Bernstein, B., 13
Berthelot, J., 65, 91, 127, 130–131, 225
Bibeau, G., 90
Bordeleau, G., 89
Boulay, G., 186, 230
Bourdieu, P., 6, 7, 11, 13, 16, 61, 95, 150, 152, 174, 227
Bourhis, R., 3
Bowles, S., 13
Breton, R., 4, 61, 64, 98, 127
Brûlé, G., 89
Burns, G., 86, 226

Caldwell, G., 65
Calvé, P., 89
Canadian Parents For French (CPF), 86
Canale, M., 85, 125, 185, 227
Cardinal, L., 18, 133, 134
Carisse, C., 3

Carrier, D., 121
Cartwright, D., 2, 55
Castonguay, C., 2, 72
Cazabon, B., 89
Chevalier, G., 88
Choquette, R., 11, 14, 20–21, 45, 47, 53, 68–69, 112
Churchill, S., 70, 72, 89, 118, 121
Clément, R., 3
Clift, D., 43, 57, 60–61
Coderre, C., 18
Collins, R., 153–154
Connelly, M., 192, 207
Conseil de l'éducation franco-ontarienne (CEFO), 77
Coulombe, D., 18, 50, 134
Cyr, H., 89

Daigle, J., 37, 39
Dannequin, C., 13
Desjarlais, L., 89
Diaz, S., 16

Edwards, V., 13
Engelmann, S., 13
Erickson, F., 16

Fennario, D., 3
Fournier, D., 65
Frenette, N., 70, 72, 74, 89, 112–113, 118, 121
Fullan, M., 192, 207

Gaffield, C., 42, 45, 53
Gagnon, R., 43, 224
Gal, S., 4
Gardner, E., 61

Gauthier, L., 74, 112–113
Gauthier, V., 89
Genesee, F., 3, 87
Gibson, M., 14
Giddens, A., 17
Gintis, S., 13
Government of Canada, 14, 60
Gouvernement du Québec, 14, 60
Grillo, R., 13

Handler, R., 60–61, 64, 101, 129
Harley, B., 88
Hart, D., 86–87, 226–227
Heath, S. B., 16, 184
Heimbecker, C., 61
Heller, M., 4, 55, 58, 69, 72, 86–89, 124–126, 140, 163, 186, 227, 229–230
Henripin, J., 22, 33, 48, 225
Hughes, E., 3, 54

Irvine, J., 4

Jackson, J., 3, 6, 20, 24, 72
Jacob, E., 13
Jordan, C., 13, 16
Joy, R., 2
Juteau-Lee, D., 46, 66, 70, 72

Kagan, S., 187, 229
Keyfitz, N., 42

Labov, W., 13
Lachapelle, R., 22, 33, 48, 59, 225
Lacroix, R., 2, 14, 58, 60
Lambert, W., 3, 86
Lapkin, S., 86–87, 226–227
Lapointe, J., 21, 47, 66, 70, 109, 113, 133
Lévy, L., 134, 186, 230
Lieberson, S., 54–55, 225
Lightbown, P., 90

Lucier, P., 130
Lyster, R., 88

MacLennan, H., 3, 224
Marchildon, D., 114, 115, 227
Maxwell, T., 1, 47, 71, 136
McNaught, K., 43
Mohatt, G., 16
Moll, L., 16
Mougeon, R., 3, 21, 47, 69, 72, 89, 125–126, 227

Ogbu, J., 13–14, 16
Olson, P., 86, 226
Ontario Ministry of Education, 144
Ossenberg, R., 14, 39
Ouellet, F., 39, 42

Passeron, J.-C., 13, 174, 227
Pauls, S., 61
Pelletier, F., 186, 230
Philips, S., 16
Poplack, S., 3
Porter, J., 14
Potvin, K., 61
Poulin, R., 21, 47, 70, 109, 113

Quazi, S., 70, 72, 89, 118, 121

Regnier, R., 61
Richler, M., 3
Rowan, N., 86–87, 226–227

Saifullah Khan, V., 13
St-Pierre, F., 186
Sankoff, G., 3
Séguin, J., 89
Shamai, S., 14
Sharan, S., 187
Sharan, Y., 187
Skutnabb-Kangas, T., 13

Statistics Canada, 33, 48–52, 225
Swain, M., 85, 87–88, 226
Sylvestre, P., 70, 114

Tharp, R., 16
Thériault, J.-Y., 21, 47, 70, 109, 113
Tucker, R., 86

Vaillancourt, F., 2, 14, 58, 60
Vallières, G., 45, 66
Valois, D., 21, 47
Vogt, L., 16

Welch, D., 45, 53, 69, 72, 109, 112–113, 134
Williams, R., 17
Willis, P., 13, 17, 174
Wolf, E., 11, 37, 224
Wong Fillmore, L., 229
Woolard, K., 4, 17, 61

Yuzdepski, I, 61

Ministry of Education & Training
MET Library
13th Floor, Mowat Block, Queen's Park
Toronto   M7A 1L2